European Capital,
British Iron, and
an American Dream

Ohio History and Culture

A.&C. 5 W.R.R.

European Capital, British Iron, and an American Dream

The Story of the Atlantic & Great Western Railroad

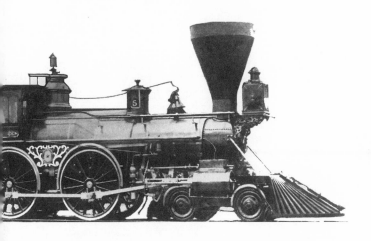

By William Reynolds

Edited by Peter K. Gifford and Robert D. Ilisevich

 The University of Akron Press

Manufactured in the United States of America

First edition 2002

05   04   03   02   5   4   3   2   1

LIBRARY OF CONGRESS CATALOGING-IN-PUBLICATION DATA
Reynolds, William, 1820–1911.

    European capital, British iron, and an American dream : the story of
    the Atlantic & Great Western Railroad / By William Reynolds ; edited by
    Peter K. Gifford and Robert D. Ilisevich.— 1st ed.

        p.   cm. —   (Series on Ohio history and culture)
        Includes bibliographical references and index.
       ISBN 1-884836-91-7 (cloth : alk. paper)
        1. Atlantic and Great Western Railway Company—History—Sources.
    2. Railroads—United States—History—Sources.   3. Reynolds, William,
    1820–1911.   I. Gifford, Peter K., 1955–
    II. Ilisevich, Robert D.   III. Title.   IV. Series.

    HE2791.A845R49 2002
    385'.0973'09034—dc21

                       2002006527

✿✿ Contents

✺ List of Illustrations

❧ Editors' Preface

The story of William Reynolds's memoir of the Atlantic & Great Western Railroad (A&GW RR) preserved by the Reynolds family and Allegheny College is such a fine example of serendipity that it deserves to be told. A good deal of credit for bringing the memoir to light has to be given to the late Dr. Russell J. Ferguson of the University of Pittsburgh. Some sixty years ago, while doing research on western Pennsylvania politics, Professor Ferguson uncovered the Reynolds railroad history among the papers and letters loaned to him by William's son, John Earle Reynolds of Meadville, Pennsylvania. Intrigued by the memoir's substantive contents, Ferguson immediately suggested that it be edited and published. In preparation, according to correspondence between Ferguson and Reynolds, Mrs. Ferguson typed a transcript of more than 270 pages.

An edited version of the memoir never reached a publisher, however. The Erie Railroad expressed an interest in underwriting the cost of publication, but then backed off when the company went into receivership. In 1940 Ferguson was editing the memoir for the University of Pittsburgh Press, but did not complete the manuscript. He then entered the U.S. Navy and deposited the memoir, the transcript, and the rest of the Reynolds papers with the Western Pennsylvania Historical Society for safekeeping. The railroad collection enabled Paul Felton in 1943 to write his dissertation on the A&GW RR; Edward Hungerford used Felton's work for his chapter on the A&GW RR in *Men of Erie, a Story of Human Effort*, published in 1946. Felton never published his dissertation. Apparently Ferguson did not finish his manuscript, or if he did, there is no knowledge of its whereabouts. He died in 1957.

After John Earle Reynolds's death in 1947, his widow asked Ferguson to return the papers, which he did. Unfortunately, upon arrival in Meadville the collection was broken up, with many of the papers being given to the Crawford County Historical Society and the remainder, including the memoir, the transcript, and papers relating to the A&GW RR, to Allegheny College. For fifty years, they remained in a college trunk, unorganized and unknown until they were recently rediscovered. At present, they are still unavailable to the general public.

The significance of the memoir is twofold. First, it gives us a better understanding of what went into the building of a nineteenth-century railroad, as told by a railroad president. Second, the full importance of the A&GW RR has yet to be evaluated in terms of general railroad history, the oil industry, and the American Civil War. Much of its fascinating history has been neglected by historians and publishers. The memoir helps fill the void.

From the beginning, the railroad faced almost insurmountable odds: financial stress, public apathy and hostility, pressure from competitors, and the war itself. Yet Reynolds, Marvin Kent, and their English partners, James McHenry, T. W. Kennard, and Sir Morton Peto, made the impossible happen. Rapid construction of the line during the war years shocked both believers and skeptics. Its completion brought immediate praise and benefits: supplying Union forces, providing low rates on freight, opening the oil region (with Cleveland eventually becoming a refining center), and establishing a direct line for Midwest cities to the port of New York.

Acknowledgments

While preparing this manuscript, a number of people extended to us assistance which we gratefully acknowledge. We received professional help and cooperation from the staff of the Erie Historical Society, the Historical Society of Western Pennsylvania, the Western Reserve Historical Society, and the Archives division of the Pennsylvania Historical and Museum Commission. A special thanks goes to the Pelletier Library staff of Allegheny College, including former director Connie Thorson, current director Cole Puvogel, Jane Westenfeld, and Donald Vrabel. In addition, Susan J. Beates, curator of the Drake Well Museum, Mark Roche of the Cochranton Heritage Society, and Laura Polo and Anne W. Stewart of the Crawford County Historical Society contributed to the endless search for maps and photographs.

The publishing of this manuscript was due to the encouragement and expert support provided by the staff of the University of Akron Press. We owe special thanks to Director Michael J. Carley, Copy Editor Nancy Basmajian, Production Coordinator Amy Petersen, Marketing Coordinator Jodi Arment, and the manuscript's reviewers for their criticisms and suggestions. An editorial staff could not have been more helpful.

Our deepest debt of gratitude is owed to the many individuals, including Larry Smith and Robert L. Gifford Jr., who took the time to read all or parts of the manuscript, and to Jennifer Gifford for help with the illustrations. Finally, we thank our wives and families for their enduring patience and loving encouragement.

❦ Railroad Abbreviations

Abbreviation	Railroad and Description
A&GW	Atlantic & Great Western *Later became part of the Erie RR*
A&GW in NY	Atlantic & Great Western in NY *Later combined into the A&GW RR*
A&GW of OH	Atlantic & Great Western of Ohio *Later combined into the A&GW RR*
A&GW of PA	Atlantic & Great Western of Pa. *Later combined into the A&GW RR*
B&O RR	Baltimore & Ohio *Early east-west trunk line from Baltimore to Wheeling, West Virginia*
B&SL RR	Buffalo & State Line Company *Later became part of the New York Central*
CH&D RR	Cincinnati, Hamilton & Dayton RR *Western connection for the A&GW*
C&M RR	Cleveland & Mahoning *Leased by the A&GW RR*
C&T RR	Cleveland & Toledo
CP&A RR	Cleveland, Painesville & Ashtabula
CZ&C RR	Cleveland, Zanesville & Cincinnati RR
Clinton Line	Clinton Line *Partially graded through Ohio, but few if any rails were ever laid*
E&NY City RR	Erie & New York City RR *Later became part of the A&GW*
E&NE RR	Erie & North East RR
Erie RR	Erie RR Company *The earliest trunk line, originally ran from Piermont, New York to Dunkirk, New York*

F&W RR — Franklin & Warren RR
*Marvin Kent's original railroad—
later became the A&GW of Ohio*

Meadville RR — Meadville RR Company
*First the Branch (of the P&E),
later the A&GW of Pa.*

NYC RR — New York Central RR
Major competitor with the A&GW and Erie

NY&E RR — New York & Erie RR
Later reorganized as the Erie RR

O&M RR — Ohio & Mississippi
*Western end of the six-foot gauge route
to St. Louis*

OC RR — Oil Creek RR
*Originally operated as part of the A&GW,
later taken over by the PRR*

PRR — Pennsylvania RR
*Major competitor of the A&GW,
especially for oil traffic*

P&E RR — Pittsburgh & Erie RR
*Parent road of the Branch, later Meadville RR,
which became the A&GW of PA*

S&E RR — Sunbury & Erie RR
*Renamed Philadelphia & Erie in 1861,
Later became part of the PRR*

Timeline of the Atlantic & Great Western Railroad, 1851-1864

March 10, 1851	Marvin Kent receives charter for the Franklin and Warren Railroad Company of Ohio
Sept. 1853	Franklin & Warren Railroad Company becomes the Atlantic & Great Western Railroad Company of Ohio
April 3, 1857	Pennsylvania legislature charters the Meadville Railroad Company to build a railroad from Meadville to Erie
July 13, 1857	Meadville Railroad Company is organized and William Reynolds is named president
July 23, 1857	The Pittsburg & Erie Railroad Company transfers its branching rights to the Meadville Railroad Company
April 15, 1858	Meadville Railroad Company becomes the Atlantic & Great Western Railroad Company of Pennsylvania
May 1859	Atlantic & Great Western Railroad Company in New York is chartered
Sept. 11, 1860	A&GW opens from Salamanca, New York, to Jamestown, New York
May 27, 1861	A&GW opens to Corry, Pennsylvania
Nov. 10, 1862	A&GW opens to Meadville, Pennsylvania
March 12, 1863	Central Board of directors, two from each company, is formed to operate the combined companies
Nov. 18, 1863	Railroad opens to Cleveland through the lease of the Cleveland & Mahoning Railroad

June 20, 1864   A&GW is connected to the Cincinnati, Hamilton & Dayton Railroad at Dayton, Ohio, to complete a broad gauge from New York City to St. Louis

Sept. 30, 1864   William Reynolds resigns as president of Pennsylvania and New York companies and central board; Marvin Kent resigns as president of Ohio company

❧ Introduction

❧ Introduction

"Americans," remarked Ralph Waldo Emerson, "take to this little contrivance, the railroad, as if it were the cradle in which they were born." What impressed the poet was the nineteenth-century craze for building railroads. In the decade before the Civil War, thousands of miles of track crisscrossed the country. Some tracks went from town to town; others seemed to go nowhere in particular.

Along the Atlantic Coast, from Boston to Savannah, merchants looked on the railroad as a godsend as they competed for the interior trade. Meanwhile, lines from midwestern cities reached eastward to meet trunk lines creeping along the Mohawk Valley and crossing the Alleghenies into the Ohio Valley. Linking East and West with a better transportation system than the canals, riverboats, and roads could ever provide became a common goal of businessmen and national leaders who called for a united economy.

The development and popularity of the American railroad paralleled the national quest for unity. Early in the nineteenth century many Americans believed the railroad to be the best hope of achieving this unity. This was a time when sectionalism prevailed and nationalists like Henry Clay and John Q. Adams looked to economic issues like internal improvements to bring the states closer together.

Railroad pioneers promised that the railroad could do

3

this. Historian James A. Ward writes that these men also argued that this technological marvel was in tune with the national character and actually would improve it. Creating popular images of the railroad and linking the industry to that character helped shape favorable public opinion.[1]

Yet the railroad did not impress everyone. Henry Thoreau referred to the locomotive as "that devilish Iron Horse." Andrew Jackson failed to see how the railroad was going to help the farmer. Other critics decried the railroad's destructive capabilities: forcing cities to engage in deadly competition, destroying the landscape and farmland, and driving other transportation systems into bankruptcy. Was this an early brand of populism emerging? Sarah H. Gordon looks at the social effects of the railroad and concludes, perhaps simplistically, that it helped destroy much of what was good in America, particularly the small town.[2]

Railroad mania was contagious, but technical hurdles existed. Just as Americans had turned to Europe for tips on turnpike and canal construction, they now took an interest in English railway experiments. Tramways started to evolve in England as early as the sixteenth century. Wooden planks eventually gave way to rails along which carts with flanged wheels were drawn by animals. Two centuries later, the use of steam ushered in a new era. The first locomotive aroused little enthusiasm, but English public opinion became more favorable in 1829 when George Stephenson won the top prize offered by the Liverpool & Manchester Railroad with his "Rocket."

The Americans also built tramways, yet it was the successful locomotive that interested them the most. In 1829 the Delaware & Hudson Canal Company imported from England the "Stourbridge Lion" and used it to transport coal between Carbondale and Honesdale, Pennsylvania. During the early days of rail transportation, the Americans used English locomotives, but later they preferred models developed by their own countrymen, such as Matthias Baldwin of Philadelphia, for their adaptability to American curves and grades.

Technological improvements of the railroad, accumulating incrementally, came close to stalling in the decades prior to the Civil War.

Early emphasis was on increasing distances, connecting cities, and reaching inland rather than on safety or comfort. The first train cars were wooden, light in construction, and dirty from all the dust and smoke. They rocked and bounced and provided little protection to the passengers. Flying cinders and the likelihood that the engine would explode always posed serious risks. Storms and extremes in temperature made a long journey unbearable.

Yet the locomotive symbolized awesome power, and this helped popularize it. The first locomotives proved to be too heavy not only for the wooden tracks but for the malleable wrought-iron rails that replaced them. Neither the wheels nor the tracks could bear a very heavy load. It was also obvious that massiveness and weight did not guarantee efficiency. And, despite all the power the engine generated, horses and mules still had to be used at first to pull cars up a steep grade. Going down a hill often proved to be a real adventure, for braking systems were inadequate, and brakes on passenger cars had to be applied by hand.

Time has made every technological innovation in transportation, from ships to planes, more efficient. So it was that railroad improvements eventually demanded the attention of both builder and public. The first important railroad periodical, the *American Railroad Journal,* founded by D. Kimball Minor in 1831, provided many technical and engineering articles that helped advance the new industry.

Equally significant in rail construction was the money problem. Investment was always a gamble with every transportation system. An early belief prevailed that backing a railroad in a densely populated area was always financially less chancy than supporting one along the frontier. There was a correlation, therefore, between an adequate investment return and the growth of the area through which the railroad must run. The opposing argument held that profits of a railway in a populated area with several competing lines were likely to be less than those of a single line in a sparsely settled area. Both camps had their share of believers but neither held the high ground whenever a financial crisis erupted.

After the War of 1812, the issue of internal improvements became an easy sell in America. Financing their construction, however, was another matter. In the first decade of the century the federal government had demonstrated its willingness to help by directly contributing to the construction of the National Road. The secretary of the treasury, Albert Gallatin, reported in 1808 on a system of roads and canals to overcome the barrier of the Appalachian Mountains. It was the first attempt to come up with a comprehensive plan of internal improvements, and several parts of his plan later received appropriations.

These occasional monies committed by the government often failed to match the ambitions of promoters. In addition, New England and the South opposed congressional subsidies to roads, while Presidents James Madison and James Monroe believed such legislative action to be unconstitutional. President Jackson's veto of the Maysville Road bill slowed the use of federal funds for internal improvements but did not bring an end to it. Regardless, with the idea of nationalizing the transportation system drawing less and less favor with the Jacksonians, the problem of financing internal improvements passed to the states.

The states accepted the challenge and became heavily involved. To the companies they granted charters with liberal provisions and tax benefits. Some states, including Maryland and Pennsylvania, granted bank charters on the condition that the banks subscribe millions of dollars to the capital stock of turnpike, canal, and railroad companies. They watched the railroad boom spread with remarkable speed throughout the eastern states. Albro Martin refers to the 1830s as the "demonstration decade" of the railroad age.[3] Countless mass meetings and petitions to legislatures called for more railroads. An article in Samuel Hazard's *The Register of Pennsylvania* (May 1831) describes this mania.

The states also reached out to European investors. Unfortunately, the financial crisis of 1837 and the depression that followed left some of the states and their banks embarrassingly insolvent. The value of American bonds and securities plummeted. American and European investors faced ruin. The reckless manner in which the states had borrowed here and abroad to fund improvements contributed to the '37 Panic. Some of the early railroads were still in the first stages of development when backers found themselves pressured to halt further construction.

Any time the money markets were disrupted, internal improvements either slowed or stopped. Yet the depression years did not see a total end to the building. Railroad mileage steadily increased. The financial crisis actually may have benefitted the railroads by throttling canal expansion.

Following the hard times, construction resumed, and several changes began to occur, the most important one being in railroad capitalization and ownership. The first lines were short and were built through local efforts and state funding. Pennsylvania, Michigan, South Carolina, and Georgia had financed their first railroads; other states had helped the rail companies either by lending money or by subscribing to their stock. Longer lines with branches followed, as did combinations and competition. These extended lines demanded more than local investment and states would or could provide. As costs accelerated, taxpayer approval wavered.

There was a shift from state-financed and locally subsidized roads to private companies backed by eastern money lenders. Angered by states that had repudiated their debts, and shaken by the instability of American money markets, European capitalists momentarily held back. In his annual message of December 1841, President John Tyler made reference to the states' indebtedness to Europeans for the sum of not less than $200 million. The states were responsible and must meet their obligations, he cautioned.

Without European investors, only the Northeast had enough wealthy entrepreneurs willing to put their money into a promising yet venturesome undertaking like the railroad. They viewed the railroad as a practical adjunct to the growing communities with their mills, factories, and mines, and one that someday might even prove to be very profitable. In addition, they assumed that, once the rails penetrated the Ohio and Mississippi Valleys, food supplies for the eastern worker would increase and markets for eastern manufacturers would expand. A lasting courtship between the East and West therefore seemed only logical and inevitable.

Venture capital in the East had earlier seized the first opportunity to open channels to the West. And it was the Erie Canal of New York that provided the ideal model of transportation. Opened in 1825 from the Hudson River to Lake Erie, the canal offered at the time the best approach to the Great Lakes from New England and eastern New York. Overnight it became the most heralded route to the West. By the mid-1830's many passengers reaching Buffalo by this waterway continued their westward journey on steamers. Farmers redirected a large part of their business, which used to flow through New Orleans, to the harbor of New York City.

Initially the public hysteria over the Erie Canal dampened the hopes of early railroad enthusiasts in New York. For a time the state prohibited railroads from hauling freight in competition with the canal and its branches. Public officials and even some railroad executives did not want to do anything to offend the powerful shipping interests. It was hard to deny either the popularity or success of this engineering marvel. Tolls during the first nine years amounted to $8.5 million—more than the initial cost of construction, $7 million. New York cities thrived and took on new life, while those in the Great Lakes region—Detroit, Cleveland, Buffalo, and Chicago—entered a period of growth and began to rival Cincinnati, St. Louis, and New Orleans as marketing centers.

Every transportation system has its competitors, and the Erie Canal, successful as it was, sooner or later had to meet its severest challenger, the railroad. Schenectady and Albany businessmen conceived a plan to connect their cities and to divert trade southward from the canal to Albany. In 1827 Erastus Corning chartered the successful Mohawk & Hudson RR that spanned the short distance between the two cities. It began to operate in 1831 when the "DeWitt Clinton" made its trial run. A number of other lines followed during the decade, including the Utica & Schenectady and the Syracuse & Utica. In 1853 Corning engineered the merger of more than a dozen short lines into a continuous route between Albany and Buffalo—the New York Central.

The railroad came early to eastern New York, specifically, to Long Island. The horse-driven Brooklyn & Jamaica was completed in 1834.

That same year the Long Island RR came into being. Its managers dreamed of not only traversing the entire length of Long Island, but also making their road a link in a through route up the seaboard from Charleston to Boston. It was one of the first railroads in the country to adopt the iron horse for its power. In 1837 the line was completed to Hicksville, and in 1844, to Greenport, where ferry connections transported passengers to the Connecticut shore.

New Yorkers had become too complacent with their highly touted canal. They received a shock in 1841 when the Western Railroad of Massachusetts cut across the Berkshires to Albany. There was also the Boston & Worcester. Threatened by a probable diversion of western traffic to Boston by these two lines, New York City politicians and investors scrambled for ways to maintain their city's coastal supremacy. An all-rail route from the Hudson to Lake Erie now became their goal. Time saved in using rail transportation became a strong selling point. The roadbeds were rough, the engines noisy, the smoke and cinders intolerable to poorly protected passengers, but speed compensated for these discomforts.

To accomplish this end of reaching out to the West, a railroad already existed. The New York legislature had authorized the New York & Erie Railroad in April 1832 with a capitalization of $10 million. The company elected Eleazar Lord as its first president and investors came slowly forward. Ground was finally broken in November 1835. Designed to satisfy the counties of the southern tier who envied the advantages the Erie Canal enjoyed, the company adopted the broad gauge (six feet) so that it would not have to share its traffic with roads of different gauges.

The completion of the NY&E RR in 1851 was widely regarded as a major achievement. For the formal opening of the line from Piermont on the Hudson to Dunkirk on Lake Erie (460 miles), President Millard Fillmore, a fellow New Yorker, attended the ceremonies, as did prominent statesman Daniel Webster. The new line was to play a major role in the future construction of the Atlantic & Great Western.

With the inception of the NY&E RR, residents of the Genesee Valley had hoped the line would run to Buffalo and not Dunkirk. After realizing that this was not about to happen, they reacted by planning branch lines southward to connect with it. From this planning came the Attica & Hornellsville RR, connecting Attica with the extension of the Tonawanda RR to form a through route into Buffalo. Another road was the Genesee Valley RR. Meanwhile, the NYC had built its direct route from Batavia to Buffalo.

The NY&E RR and the NYC became fierce rivals over the eastbound traffic at Buffalo. Homer Ramsdell became president of the former line and did his best to develop the company's administrative structure and facilities. He retired in 1857 in favor of Charles Moran, who quickly turned to Wall Street for help. Unable to resolve the company's problems, he withdrew two years later and the company went into receivership. Nathaniel Marsh came in first as receiver and then as president of the newly created Erie Railway Company, which came into existence in December 1861.

As early as the 1830s, residents in the northern parts of New York and in New England clamored to have a railroad connecting their regions to the West. Boston was just one city that desired this route to tap inland resources. Citizens of Montpelier, Vermont, proposed a rail from Lake Champlain across to Ogdensburg and by the Welland Canal to the upper Lakes. Progress was slow, however. Not until 1836 was the Lake Champlain & Ogdensburg RR incorporated with a capitalization of $800,000. Additional delays eventually forced the project to be dropped. What emerged in its place was the Northern Railroad, organized in 1846 at Ogdensburg and completed four years later. Though considered a first-class road, it found profits hard to come by.

One railroad that prospered from the beginning was the Watertown & Rome RR. Incorporated and organized in 1832, the road began by the side of the Utica & Syracuse track at Rome and finally reached Watertown in 1851. Extension of the line to Cape Vincent followed the next year. Like many of the lines in northern New York, the Watertown & Rome took a long time to build. Aside from the usual money headaches, builders had to contend with the harsh winters and the desolate nature of the region. Only the perseverance of a dedicated few kept the hopes of having a railroad alive.

Both New York and Pennsylvania stretched from the seaboard to the Ohio Valley and Great Lakes. Settlement of their western regions followed similar patterns. Both states, like the federal government after the formation of the Union, failed to develop a satisfactory policy of selling the public lands to actual settlers, and that failure led to a long period of nasty politics and unfettered speculation.

Land companies like the Holland Land Company (HLC) sprang up, financed by European and American capitalists. The HLC alone purchased about 900,000 acres in Pennsylvania and a greater amount in New York. Often the companies hired jobbers and unscrupulous agents who took advantage of unwary settlers. The Pennsylvania courts tolerated fictitious names on land warrants issued by the state to the companies. Thus, continuous nagging conflicts over land titles between the companies and actual settlers led to utter confusion. The land question became as important an issue in the western regions of the two states as the matter of establishing the first governments.

Still, development in these regions proceeded as though on schedule. The passion to drive westward proved to be stronger than the resisting forces of hostile tribes, crooked land agents, and an untamed environment. And the states had little choice but to assist the settlers by promoting internal improvements. One of their basic aims was to connect the East with the expanding frontier. Turnpikes and canals provided the practical means to do this.

The canal system in Pennsylvania was actually a combination of canal and railway. The thirty-seven-mile Portage RR crossed the Alleghenies from Hollidaysburg to Johnstown by means of ten inclined planes, five on the eastern and five on the western slopes of the mountain. Canal boats were raised or lowered on flat cars, at first using horsepower and later stationary steam engines and cable.

In time it became evident that Pennsylvania's canals had not solved the growing transportation problem any more than had turnpikes and the Conestoga wagon. The rage to build canals had eased after the '37 Panic, and the Commonwealth had pulled back from further investment. Public interest in the canal simply diminished as popularity of the railroad escalated. The major pressure for the railroad in the state grew out of the need to transport heavy freight faster than by means of anything that floated. Besides, railroads were cheaper to build and unlike canals, they were not restricted to low areas for access to water, nor did they freeze in the winter.

The railroad also came early to eastern Pennsylvania. Anthracite coal producers undertook some of the most successful railroads in the country. The anthracite region of Pennsylvania may justifiably be called the birthplace of American railroading. The emergence of the Philadelphia & Reading, the Delaware & Hudson, and the Lehigh Valley soon made canals reminders of the past. As mentioned, the first steam locomotive run on rails in America was the "Stourbridge Lion." In 1834 the "Iron Rail Road" from Philadelphia to Columbia on the Susquehanna near Lancaster was completed. Former state historian Sylvester K. Stevens referred to it as "the first railroad in the world built by a government."[4]

Inspired by the canal systems of New York and Pennsylvania, Maryland citizens had organized the Chesapeake & Ohio Canal Company, which broke ground on July 4, 1828. Its promoters believed their ditch would go from Washington over the mountains to the Ohio River and beyond. But the waterway never passed Cumberland, which lay at the base of the mountains.

In the previous year the Maryland legislature had incorporated the Baltimore & Ohio RR, again with the intention of reaching the West. As historian James Dilts points out, the Baltimore business community demonstrated courage in rejecting the prevailing canal craze and its technology and choosing a primitive form of rail transportation used in the mines to develop a long-distance carrier.[5] On a trial trip in 1830, Peter Cooper's tiny locomotive "Tom Thumb" made the thirteen miles from Baltimore to Ellicott's Mills in little over an hour, a feat that convinced skeptics that steam was better than the horse.

Profits for the B&O had been impressive in the beginning, but the economic slowdown following the '37 Panic reduced revenues. Officials had to borrow about $50,000 from local banks to keep their surveys and operations going. Once the money situation had improved, Baltimore businessmen pressed for the resumption of full construction.

The line continued westward until in 1853 it reached Wheeling on the Ohio River.

This achievement marked a significant chapter in the long history of the rivalry between Wheeling and Pittsburgh to become the "Gateway to the West." The first blow to Pittsburgh's commercial prestige had occurred when Congress decided to make Wheeling the point at which the National Road should cross the Ohio River. The net result had been a great boost for Wheeling. Pennsylvania's answer to the National Road was the incorporation of turnpike companies funded by private subscriptions and state subsidies. Soon turnpikes reached across the state, but it was not until the Pennsylvania Canal entered Pittsburgh in 1834 that citizens of that city felt they had finally met Wheeling's challenge.

Prior to the completion of the Pennsylvania Canal, the B&O had obtained from the Pennsylvania legislature a charter giving it fifteen years to extend its line to Pittsburgh. While the Pittsburgh business community became euphoric, Philadelphians panicked. They foresaw Baltimore siphoning off the commerce of the Ohio country to their disadvantage. Citizens of Pittsburgh just wanted a railroad; they dismissed Philadelphia's selfish concerns. Yet the B&O wavered in its selection of a western terminus; Pittsburgh, Wheeling, and Parkersburg were the three Ohio River contenders.

When the charter to the B&O lapsed, the legislature had to choose between renewing it or authorizing a new company, the Pennsylvania RR, to run its line across the state. In the end the legislature authorized both railroads but stipulated that if the PRR raised $3 million in stock subscriptions by a given date the Maryland company would lose its charter. Philadelphians worked hard to meet the deadline; even western Pennsylvania contributed. The money was raised and the B&O, rejected, then turned to Wheeling as its terminus. The Pennsylvania legislature had imposed so many discriminatory provisions favoring Philadelphia in the charter that the B&O did not want to accept it had it been offered. The PRR completed its line to Pittsburgh the year before the B&O reached Wheeling.

This rail run to Pittsburgh was a dramatic story in the connection between the eastern and western portions of the state. At first the Columbia and Portage Railroads had to be used to complete the great distance but two years later, thanks to spectacular engineering that carried the railroad across the mountains via the Horseshoe Curve west of Altoona, the PRR's own trains traversed the three hundred miles.

By the time the B&O and the Pennsylvania RR were reaching their western termini, two developments regarding the American West had become evident: slavery in the territories was becoming the dominant political issue, and changes in the nation's population and commercial patterns were bringing the West and East closer together. While the two sections of the country searched for common ground to halt the extension of slavery, they also looked for more ways to cooperate economically.

Although the West and the South remained marketing partners, a fundamental correction in that relationship was already forecast. The western farmer gladly would have continued to sell the bulk of his surpluses to southern customers, but the railroad had matured enough to challenge the steamboat, the river barge, and the canal that carried his produce southward. The new form of transportation was changing the commercial landscape as rapidly as slavery extension was reshaping the political one. Being weaned away from his traditional customer in the South, the farmer of the Ohio Valley now enjoyed the luxury of choosing markets in Boston, New York, and Philadelphia in addition to those of New Orleans and Memphis.

Fierce competition to acquire a rail connection developed among urban areas. In every section of the country, intercity rivalries highlighted the growing importance of rail transportation. Coastal cities became particularly watchful of each other as they pushed their lines westward. Boston, New York, Philadelphia, and Baltimore were the big players in the East, while Chicago, Pittsburgh, Cincinnati, and Wheeling, just to name a few, emerged as competitors in the Ohio country and beyond.

Despite problems of growth—housing, public health, and crime—the cities evolved as centers of commerce and manufacturing. A growing population and business community came to rely more and more upon an improved transportation system. The flowering of urban areas paralleled the rise of rail networks. Between 1790 and 1860 the country's population exploded from less than four million to more than thirty-one million. Reduced death rates and increased birth rates contributed to this growth, but so did immigration: almost one-eighth of the 1860 population was foreign born. Many settled in rural America, but larger numbers inflated the city masses. The largest concentrations remained in the big eastern seaports, with the river cities in the West next in rank.

The strenuous efforts of northeastern cities to benefit from the interior spurred the commercial centers of the Southeast into similar action. At first the merchants of Richmond, Charleston, and Savannah worried less about reaching the Mississippi Valley than about broadening their systems to stimulate the seaboard economy that had stagnated after the center of the cotton world moved westward. Their economic priorities were therefore more immediate and local. Yet this desire to extend internal improvements prompted railroad men to urge that lines go farther and farther inland. Their ambition helped launch the first southern railway projects.

Charleston took the lead in encouraging railway construction. In 1833 its business community and investors reveled over the completion of the South Carolina RR and Canal Company, which was then the longest railroad in the world (136 miles), from Charleston to Hamburg on the Savannah River. Goods destined to go downriver now could be diverted eastward. A year later these promoters financed the Georgia RR with two lines westward toward Athens and Atlanta. By the early 1840s hard times halted construction, however. Charleston's activities prompted merchants of Richmond to pressure the Virginia legislature to charter the Lynchburg & New River RR in the hope of reaching the Ohio Valley. Not to be outdone by her southern competitors, Savannah succeeded in having Georgia's lawmakers legislate the Central of Georgia RR and the Monroe RR to connect Macon with Atlanta. The city's merchants felt threatened by the rail from Charleston to Hamburg.

These early southern roads attracted the attention of farsighted businessmen of Cincinnati, Memphis, and Vicksburg. Why not try to connect with these lines, they asked, and open additional market possibilities? In 1835 Cincinnati seized the initiative by lobbying the legislatures of neighboring states to issue charters to the Louisville, Cincinnati & Charleston. Enthusiasm ran high.

A principal supporter of the plan was statesman Robert Y. Hayne of South Carolina, who was a promoter of the Charleston & Hamburg. He envisaged a golden opportunity to expand the cotton industry by developing rail connection with the Northwest. This connection he believed would assure an economic union between this section of the country and the South, a partnership allied against the Northeast. It was a bold yet interesting proposition, and one not without political implications. Unfortunately, sharp differences over the exact route of the new road caused friction among the participating states. Languishing interest in the project, Hayne's early death, and hard times put an end to perhaps the South's best chance to tie itself to the Northwest.

The plans of Memphis and Vicksburg proved no more fruitful. These cities lagged behind New Orleans in growth, and this fact alone, in their opinion, threatened their commercial future. A railroad to Charleston or Savannah they hoped might divert some of the Mississippi River traffic eastward and help expand the economy of the back country. South Carolina expressed special interest in the Memphis plan to run a line to Charleston. Because of its involvement with the Cincinnati group, however, South Carolina's promise of financial support dwindled. By 1839 only eight miles of the Memphis & LaGrange had been laid.

Merchants of Vicksburg, also interested in challenging the supremacy of New Orleans, began to plan a line from their city to Macon, where it would connect with the tracks of the Central of Georgia. But there was neither a leading political figure like Hayne to speak for the plan nor a group of investors large enough to back it. Instead, several local groups projected a few short lines, including the Montgomery RR between Montgomery, Alabama, and West Point, Georgia, although this also gave way to the economic depression of the late 1830s. The hope of a strong commercial relationship with southeastern cities for the moment vanished.

The failure of the river cities of the interior did not totally discourage the seaboard merchants. They already had ties with central Georgia and now looked to extend these farther inland. While Charleston investors backed the Georgia RR, those of Savannah financed the Macon & Western RR. The completion of the two lines prompted the state of Georgia to continue work on the Western & Atlantic RR which finally reached Chattanooga in 1849. By the following year Atlanta became the center of a growing network.

The few roads started in the South before the Panic of 1837 served as a beginning of the rail system that emerged during the financial recovery of the 1840s and 1850s. Still, a huge gap existed between what had been planned and what was constructed immediately before the Civil War. The miles of track laid in the South compared unfavorably with those of the Northeast and Northwest.

What little progress occurred lay in the increased east-west ties between the South Atlantic states and the lower Mississippi Valley, spurred by the advance of the cotton planter into new fertile lands of the Gulf states. Here, again, the staying power of slavery both politically and economically helped force the railroad into these states and away from the upper Mississippi Valley. With cotton prices rising, the commercial priorities for southerners seemed appropriate.

These developments strengthened the fear among some northerners and southerners that the South was rapidly becoming both nationalist and isolationist. They pointed to the business community and political arena to show how the institution of slavery managed to erect barriers that twisted "sectionalism" from a word suggesting regional differences and cultural diversity into one that smacked of disunion. If this mindset of separateness did indeed exist it made the railroad promoter both a participant and victim.

The failure of the South to provide itself with a unified system of lines resulted in part from an inability to agree upon the region to which the lines were to be directed. Southerners had a difficult time deciding whether they wanted a system that was regionally oriented, self-sufficient, and dependent upon their limited ports, or a north-south one that connected them to the northern emporia of Philadelphia, New York, and Boston. Business leaders divided on this important issue.

Critics point to a slave-based agricultural economy that kept the region and its individual states from having an outward strategy. Using Virginia as an example, John Majewski argues that the dearth of urban centers in the state militated against the creation of an urban-industrial economy linked to national markets by an integrated railroad network. Virginia and, for that matter, the south Atlantic seaboard, never developed a true centrality that could anchor a transportation system and accelerate industrial growth that could in turn lead to widespread commerce.[6]

In reality the numbers game played against the South. Notwithstanding the self-centered and self-righteous attitude southerners may have projected, the population increases in the North, along with superior capital investments and manufacturing, told the story. They made it much more difficult for the South to compete on an even field. Differences of all kinds were driving a deeper wedge between North and South. As they drifted apart, stronger bonds between the Northeast and Northwest resulted.

No less obvious than the way the two northern regions of the country came together commercially was their legislative alliance on national issues. They united on the tariff and denounced the southern attack on federally supported internal improvements. In this connection, one development stood out above all else. The emergence of the Republican Party as a purely northern party dedicated to the tariff and the nonextension of slavery meant further isolation of the South. The legislative measure that gave the party added leverage to unite the Old Northwest with the Northeast was the Homestead Bill. It evolved as an essential plank in the party's platform. When the idea of free land to settlers first surfaced in the mid-1840s, the West and Northeast showed interest while the South remained ambivalent. A decade later the northern states aligned themselves behind the bill; the South vigorously opposed it.

The states of the Old Northwest were never passive in their bonding with the Northeast. The initial success of the Erie Canal had stimulated interest throughout the region. Merchants looked to provide a continuous inland waterway from New York to the Ohio Valley by connecting the Ohio River with Lake Erie.

In 1825 the Ohio legislature authorized two canals: the Ohio & Erie, to extend from Portsmouth on the Ohio to Cleveland, and the Miami & Erie from Cincinnati to Toledo, following the course of the Miami and Maumee Rivers. By 1833 Ohio had more than four hundred miles of navigable canals; a dozen years later the total had doubled. The rapid growth of agriculture and industry plus a surge in population in the two decades prior to 1850 hinged upon the transportation opportunities opened by the canals. Admittedly no great volume of through traffic passed over these waters, but local traffic and transport of local goods for out-of-state markets rose steadily.

Neighboring states followed Ohio's lead. In 1832 Indiana started the Wabash & Erie Canal, which connected the Ohio River with Lake Erie. More than 450 miles in length, it was the longest canal thus far built in the country. Illinois constructed the Illinois & Michigan Canal between Lake Michigan and the Mississippi, from Chicago to LaSalle on the Illinois River. Wisconsin's efforts to join Green Bay with the Mississippi between the Fox and Wisconsin Rivers succeeded in 1856. In the previous year, a canal around St. Mary's Falls connected Lakes Huron and Superior. Begun by the state of Michigan, the project was later turned over to the United States government.

Both from a local and engineering standpoint, canals were a huge success; as a commercial link to the Northeast, however, they told a different story. By 1840 canal mileage in the country was estimated at 3,700. Yet in this year only one-seventh of the freight carried through the most famous New York canal system originated outside the state. In Ohio, canal business climaxed in the early 1850s. After this, receipts declined so rapidly that by 1856 for the first time they fell below expenditures. Railroad enthusiasts used these statistics to argue that, regardless of expectations of canal backers, the artificial waterways remained largely local in impact. For the long haul they were slow, expensive to build, and too limited in capability.

States had borrowed heavily (a good deal of the investment had come from England) to build the canals. After the Panic of 1837 nearly all of them wanted to get out from under the financial burden by selling these improvements to private companies. Some of them, including Pennsylvania, Indiana, and Michigan, repudiated their debts, causing considerable concern in European markets. Almost bankrupted by its canal investment, Pennsylvania sold a major part of its holdings in 1857 to the Pennsylvania RR.

Financial reverses and growing public jitters over use of tax dollars for internal improvements during lean years did not deter railroad proponents in the West. Admittedly, capital became more of a problem after European credit was temporarily cut off. If railroad construction were to persist, the money had to come from eastern backers. By the end of the 1840s, capitalists of Boston, New York, and Philadelphia expressed a willingness to make that commitment. They saw that not only was the South losing favor as a market for western produce, but that its shipments to the Ohio Valley were also declining.

In Ohio, life returned to some of the railroads that had been put on hold with the '37 Panic. Excited by the promise of new financial aid, promoters reorganized the Mad River & Lake Erie RR and by 1848 completed it between Springfield and Sandusky. Meanwhile, another north-south line, the Mansfield & Sandusky, reached Newark on the Ohio Canal. Fearful that Sandusky might become the state's most important port on Lake Erie, Cleveland businessmen proposed an all-rail route to Cincinnati. The plan was to attract the farm products of central Ohio northward. In 1847 they formed two companies—the Columbus & Xenia RR and the Cleveland, Columbus & Cincinnati RR. Three years later rail travel was possible from Cincinnati to either Sandusky or Cleveland.

Ohio built many, if not most, of its early important railroads in the 1850s. Others were planned and incorporated but never completed, for the mortality rate among infant companies remained high. The first lines represented a general plan to join the Ohio River with Lake Erie, but by the mid-1850s east-west lines became the rage.

The first railroads brought business to the Ohio River, which continued to carry local produce, passengers, and heavy freight. But rail lines soon appeared as competitors, rather than feeders, of river traffic. Passenger travel by water began to decline. Again, speed proved to be a factor in the switch from one mode of travel to another. The trip from Columbus to Cleveland by stage normally took the better part of two days; by rail it took about five hours. The Ohio & Mississippi, opened in 1855, cut the time to travel between Cincinnati and St. Louis in half. Still, many local merchants and farmers had to ship their goods by water. Compared with other parts of the state, the poorer sections of southern Ohio offered few prospects of profit for the railroads.

Talk of extending lines eastward across Ohio interested prospective investors in the East. Ohio promoters undertook to stretch the New York Central and Erie systems along the shore of Lake Erie. By 1853 the Erie & Northeast RR west of Buffalo, the Cleveland & Erie RR, and the Cleveland, Norwalk & Toledo RR were opened to traffic. Two other lines intended to bring the Pennsylvania RR into Ohio by constructing the Cleveland & Pittsburgh RR and the Pittsburgh, Ft. Wayne & Chicago RR. The latter reached Crestline on the Cleveland, Columbus & Cincinnati RR to complete the first rail route between Cincinnati and Pittsburgh.

Given the railroad mania, Cincinnati hoped to remain a pivotal commercial center in the Ohio Valley. In 1850 she was one of the largest cities in the country. Because of her favorable situation where drovers' trails and water transportation met, she had won acclaim as the "Porkopolis of the West," with some five dozen slaughtering houses. Preferring to be called the "Queen City," she enjoyed great preeminence as a river town. Yet there was no assurance she would become a railroad center.

Cincinnati faced several problems in terms of railroad design. One was a question of focus and direction. A few years before, she had been jubilant over a proposed rail connection with Charleston, South Carolina, but now she was thinking of running east-west lines and reaching out to make contact with the B&O. Alphonso Taft in 1850 urged a railroad scheme to connect Baltimore with Cincinnati, St. Louis, and eventually San Francisco. So while Cincinnati's planners looked to the East and West, Kentucky and Tennessee proceeded to push southward. The rivalry between Cincinnati and Louisville matched that of Pittsburgh and Wheeling. The building of the Louisville & Nashville RR, chartered in 1850, threatened to place the Kentucky city, and not Cincinnati, in direct communication with many of the South's principal cities. Another handicap for Cincinnati and other state planners was the Ohio Constitution of 1851. The Locofoco movement, the radical force that had demanded a constitutional convention, succeeded in writing its agenda into the new constitution. These radicals opposed banks and all types of corporations, including canal and railway companies. They capitalized upon the state's unfortunate experiences with internal improvements, which had placed a heavy burden on the treasury and naturally on the taxpayer. The radical movement in large part was a reaction to the system of unregulated companies operating with government subsidies.

The Constitution of 1851 limited the state debt and forbade the state from assisting private enterprises by loaning its credit or buying stock in any corporation. The prohibition also extended to local governments, making counties and municipalities unable to provide financial assistance to companies within their areas. This was a blow to numerous railroad projects like those of Taft. Thus, Ohio began to divest itself of investments in canals, railroads, and turnpikes. After 1851 railroad construction therefore had to depend on venture capital. Still, according to the federal census of 1860, some 2,300 miles of track were laid in Ohio in the previous decade, more than in any New England or Middle Atlantic state, but less than in Illinois.

Michigan likewise looked to private funding to help her become a part of the network of rails between the Northwest and Northeast. The Michigan Central RR and the Michigan Southern RR were operating reasonably well in 1845 when the state legislature, alarmed by future costs of completing the lines, decided to sell them. Boston and New York financiers, including John M. Forbes, came to the rescue and acquired both lines for $2.5 million. Rapid construction followed. Michigan Central's tracks ran across Indiana to the Illinois border and eventually made contact with Chicago. At the same time, the Michigan Southern moved steadily to LaPorte, Indiana, and from there to Chicago. From Detroit, lines stretched eastward along the northern shore of Lake Erie and southward toward Toledo.

As suggested, growing cities generated interest in rail construction. This was certainly the case with Indianapolis and Chicago. Both Indiana and Illinois had lagged behind their neighbors in laying track, but they made up ground in the decade before the Civil War. The influx of eastern capital helped prime the pump as promoters eagerly began to string a web of lines from the two midwestern cities. By 1855 at least a half dozen railroads radiated from them. Five years later rail transportation from both cities to the East Coast became possible. Before that time three of the railroads in Indiana were completed: the Bellefontaine & Indiana, the Indiana Central, and the Terre Haute & Richmond.

In Illinois as in other states, towns and counties assisted in railroad building. The Galena & Chicago Union RR moved westward while the Chicago, Alton & St. Louis RR started to lay tracks to St. Louis. More ambitious than the cross-state lines was a plan conceived in the town of Cairo to connect Chicago and Mobile, Alabama. With the help of Stephen A. Douglas, prominent senator from Illinois, Congress in 1850 granted to the state of Illinois over 2.5 million acres of public land lying in alternate sections along the projected route of the Illinois Central RR. This grant was turned over by the state to the railroad with the understanding that 7 percent of the company's gross earnings be reserved for the state. An eastern syndicate of investors the next year secured the right to build the Illinois Central from Cairo to Galena and Chicago.

What happened in Illinois occurred in a number of states. Before federal land grants and homestead legislation, the government had a hard time giving away some of the land. But the railroad changed all this. The demand for railroad transportation had become so great and the inability of the many states to underwrite construction so apparent that direct aid from the federal government was solicited.

The result: states in the West and South received significant land grants. The railroads then disposed of these lands to provide cash and to build communities along the route. These grants therefore promoted both railroad construction and settlement. Other states, including Ohio, Pennsylvania, and New York, were not so lucky as to be recipients of the federal government's benevolent policy of giving away the public domain to assist railroad building.

The Atlantic & Great Western RR was born during this period of growth, confusion, and financial uncertainty for the railroads. It became a component of the overall scheme to connect the fertile West and the eastern seaboard. Specifically it emerged from three separate lines in Ohio, Pennsylvania, and New York—the Franklin & Warren RR, the Branch or Meadville RR, and the Erie & New York City RR, respectively. It connected with the NY&E at Salamanca and eventually with the Cincinnati, Hamilton & Dayton RR (CH&D RR) at Dayton. At Cincinnati the CH&D connected with the Ohio & Mississippi RR, thus completing a broad-gauge line between the seaboard and the Mississippi River opposite St. Louis.

What lay in part behind the building of these individual lines was the abundance of natural resources in central Ohio, northwestern Pennsylvania, and southwestern New York. In Ohio it was the coal, limestone, and potter's clay; in Pennsylvania, coal, timber, limestone, and oil; and in New York, hardwoods—oak, chestnut, and hickory. In addition, each geographical region had its livestock and farm produce to market and growing cities that demanded increased commerce.

It was a time when railroad construction entered a new era. By 1850 hope that an orderly rail system was about to connect all parts of the country had kindled nationally. In a few years that hope was becoming reality. Both the B&O and the Pennsylvania RR reached the Ohio River, while the NY&E touched the Great Lakes at Dunkirk. Expansion became bolder everywhere. By the end of the decade, the rail system traversed thirty-one states, with mileage tripling in the ten-year span.

Investment strategy was also changing. Before 1850 only small portions of rail investments came from the money markets of Europe. Suddenly the discovery of gold in California in 1849 prompted the renewal of interest by European investors in America. They were also entreated by American promoters who realized that the states and cities had limited resources. The campaign to recruit European capital started to show results. By 1853 more than two hundred companies reported that more than $43 million of American railroad securities were held by foreigners.

Visionary New Yorkers deserve much of the credit for the future route of the A&GW. Governor DeWitt Clinton envisaged a passageway from the western terminus of the Erie Canal through southwestern New York, Pennsylvania, Ohio, Indiana, Illinois, and Missouri, thus creating a commercial link between the Mississippi River and the Atlantic seaboard. William C. Redfield had a similar dream to connect by railway the canals and waters of New York, Pennsylvania, and the Northwest with the Mississippi Valley.

To build a railroad as suggested by Clinton and Redfield required addressing a variety of problems. Obviously the money question loomed as the biggest, but there was also the anticipated opposition to a new railroad by companies that had already been chartered to lay track.

A typical situation existed in eastern Ohio, where a number of rail companies competed. Construction of early railroads in Ohio was primarily a local venture with little profitability. When eastern trunk lines touched the Ohio River in the early 1850s, their officials looked for western connections. They found the Ohio lines incomplete and deficient in capital. The Ohio River presented another problem to any east-west link, for no railroad crossed the river until a bridge was completed at Steubenville during the Civil War. Shipping interests at Pittsburgh and Wheeling opposed any bridging of the Ohio.

By furnishing capital and managerial help, the eastern lines persisted in their influence. The Pennsylvania RR came to control the Pittsburgh, Ft. Wayne & Chicago RR, which ran the breadth of Ohio, while the Marietta & Cincinnati RR served the B&O. Before 1850 Cleveland hoped to become a major rail center on Lake Erie. Earlier she had worried that Sandusky might emerge as the principal port city on the Lake. Now she wanted to reach the seaboard. Tying herself to an eastern trunk line might not be that simple, she discovered. She therefore looked southward to Cincinnati with possible eastward links and to neighboring Pennsylvania to help her in her quest.

In addition to the Cleveland, Columbus & Cincinnati RR, the Ohio legislature chartered a number of railroads with Cleveland as their focus. It incorporated the Cleveland & Mahoning RR in 1848 to construct and operate a road from some point in Cleveland to some point in or near Warren, Ohio. The company had the option to continue into Pennsylvania to any destination approved by the legislature of that state. The Cleveland & Ashtabula RR was to run from Cleveland along the shore of Lake Erie to the Pennsylvania state line. Then there was the Clinton RR that was also to begin at Cleveland and make a connection at the Pennsylvania border near Kinsman, Ohio.

When its promoters projected the Cleveland & Pittsburgh RR in 1847, large subscriptions came from the citizens of Franklin (now Kent, Ohio), who hoped that the line would run through their town. But it never happened. Some of the company's officials and directors lived in Ravenna, a rival town. As expected, they rejected the request of Franklin citizens.

Marvin Kent of Franklin refused to abandon the idea of seeing his small village connected to a railroad. Moreover, he looked beyond having a local road to one that was to become part of an interstate line. Born in 1816, the son of Zenas and Pamelia Kent, Marvin enjoyed a good education which he later used to help manage his father's mercantile business. Other interests held by the Kents included a flour mill and tannery. In 1850 Marvin Kent also became associated with a window-glass factory. As a respected businessman he complained about the high cost of transporting goods by wagon. He wanted a railroad.

When the directors of the Cleveland & Pittsburgh refused even to run a spur of only three miles to Franklin, Kent had his attorney, J. W. Tyler, draw up a plan for an east-west road from Franklin east to the Pennsylvania line and west to Akron. State Senator Milton Sutliff then introduced legislation containing Kent's plan under the title "Coal Hill Road." The camouflage was clearly designed to prevent backers of established railroads from blocking the bill's passage. The strategy worked. In March 1851 the bill was adopted and the name was eventually changed to the "Franklin and Warren."

In order to obtain the charter of the new company, Kent had to sub-

Marvin Kent in his later years. Kent was a banker, merchant, prime mover in the A&GW, and president of the A&GW of Ohio. *(Reynolds Collection, Allegheny College)*

scribe for the full amount of stock required by law for the incorporation. Furthermore, he had to indemnify some of the first board members for payment of one share subscribed by each to render them eligible for election.

In June 1851 formal organization of the Franklin & Warren took place. Marvin Kent became president, and except for a few years he remained president until September 1864. Other pioneers associated with the railroad's beginnings included Thomas Earl and Zenas Kent of Portage County, and F. Kinsman and J. W. Tyler of Trumbull County.

The directors of the new railroad pointed to the liberal provisions of their charter. They could run the line from Franklin to any point within the state and connect with any other road. Any gauge might be used. Directors had the power to combine with any other railroad and to issue bonds secured by mortgages on the company's property. Capital stock authorized was $2 million. Most important, the franchise under the charter was special and could not be disturbed; no individual responsibility existed.

The company's officers and directors estimated that nearly $1 million of stock subscriptions had to be raised to justify the sale of first-mortgage bonds at par, to pay for the right of way, and to prepare the route between Dayton and the Pennsylvania border. An all-out effort netted about $900,000. This sum satisfied the directors, who proceeded to authorize the start of construction. Henry Doolittle of Dayton received the contract for grading and preparing the roadbed along the entire route in Ohio. On July 4, 1853, Kent turned the first spadeful of dirt for his railroad. The first section of the future A&GW was under way.

As the grading for the F&W RR progressed, further subscriptions raised the total collected to over $1 million. This was indeed encouraging and, for the moment, everything looked promising. Then a sudden drop in the money market and a serious drought across Ohio occurred. When railroad securities declined in value and many investors stopped payment on their subscriptions, work on the roadbed came to an abrupt end.

In western New York, investors who had profited with the Erie Canal believed they might do even better with the railroad. It was not uncommon in any of the states for canal promoters to become early boosters for the railroad. Hardly anyone believed that the railroad would attempt to parallel adequate waterways, such as the canals provided. Its usefulness was in its potential to run over elevations and high plateaus to shorten the distances the waterways had to traverse.

New Yorkers saw that the rapid development of the Great Lakes region and the scattering of railroads throughout the Old Northwest called for linkage through their state. Civic-spirited citizens met in Jamestown, New York, to address this need. They proposed to build a railroad from the mouth of Little Valley Creek (later Salamanca), a point on the NY&E, to Erie, Pennsylvania. The group completed a survey and obtained a charter. Monies were sufficient to commence construction, but serious financial difficulties prevented continued progress as they had in Ohio.

Thus, two legs of the future A&GW were in place, but the final connection—the Pennsylvania link—was anything but automatic. In late 1851 Judge Kinsman of Kinsman, Ohio, and others interested in Ohio's railroads met with John Reynolds and a few citizens of Meadville, Pennsylvania, to search for a way to secure a connection in Pennsylvania. The Meadville group expressed interest in a possible railroad from Jamestown, New York, to Meadville, Warren, Ravenna, and Akron. To attain this goal Judge Gaylord Church went to Harrisburg to apply for a charter, but after weeks of unsuccessful efforts, he returned home. Opposition from Erie, Philadelphia, and Pittsburgh proved to be too much for any new railroad venture in the northwestern region of the state. Pennsylvania legislators did not want to endorse a railroad that intended to connect with another road at the state's border unless the transportation systems already in place benefited from such a plan.

The failure of Judge Church to secure a charter was a setback, not a defeat. Because the direct approach with the legislature had not worked, the Meadville promoters decided upon an end-run action. In the summer of 1852 the Pittsburgh & Erie offered to cooperate with the Meadville parties in building a connecting line between New York and Ohio under the "branching" privileges of its charter. A large gathering of those interested in the proposal met in Cleveland. Representatives included Marvin Kent, Judge Kinsman, and Jacob Perkins of Ohio; Judge B. Chamberlain, president of the Erie & New York City; William Gibson of the Pittsburgh & Erie; and Darwin Finney and William Reynolds of Meadville.

More meetings followed. The NY&E also expressed an interest, but financial difficulties prevented the company from making any real commitment. The Meadville group then turned to the Pittsburgh & Erie and accepted that company's offer to use its branching option. In early 1853, at a meeting in New York City, the Meadville Branch interests, along with promoters from Franklin, Ohio, and Jamestown, New York, decided to build the connecting line from Little Valley Creek to Dayton. Thus, the final leg of the future A&GW—the Pennsylvania division—was to be built under the charter of the Pittsburgh and Erie.

A problem that these railroad men faced was that of gauge. Variations in gauge, commonplace in a number of states, frustrated those promoters who sought networking based on a standard gauge. Early railroads were primarily a means for local traffic, so there was little cry for uniformity. With the development of trunk lines, owners and users of these lines demanded regional adoption of the standard gauge.

Still, some communities like Erie did not want physical connection between two lines that allowed uninterrupted passage. Instead they preferred transshipments from one line to the other. A break in passage was considered good for local businesses and labor. In Erie, peanut vendors protested that they would not be able to sell their wares to passengers while they changed cars. The issue led to violence that lasted for several years, a struggle that was mockingly called the "Peanut War."[7]

A unique feature of the A&GW was its six-foot (broad) gauge. By the mid-1850s two broad-gauge railroads, the Ohio & Mississippi and the NY&E, lay at opposite ends of a proposed line to link the two. Marvin Kent's dream of a through route from St. Louis to New York City "without break of gauge" depended upon an outlet through Pennsylvania. His dream was echoed by others. The *New York Herald* editorialized in 1864 that this A&GW would in time become part of the "grand highway" connecting New York City and San Francisco. Kent's A&GW of Ohio, along with the Pittsburgh & Erie and the Erie & NY City agreed to cooperate to build such a railroad using the broad gauge.

The agreement to build the A&GW displeased the Pennsylvania RR which, sensing increased competition from newer lines with the six-foot gauge, like the Delaware, Lackawanna & Western RR, had used its influence with the legislature to bar future lines from adopting the broad gauge.

Now that everything seemed to be in place, the directors of the Meadville Branch looked to raise the necessary capital. Arousing public interest in the railroad and securing a county subscription were the logical first steps. The commissioners of Crawford County (in which Meadville is located) recommended a subscription of $200,000 on the condition that it first meet public approval. In August 1853, after a campaign addressed the question "Railroad or no Railroad," an overwhelming number of voters approved the subscription (3,236 to 173).

The next day groundbreaking ceremonies took place in Meadville and the commissioners authorized the subscription. Formal acceptance by the Pittsburg & Erie RR followed.

A growing number of opponents to the Branch and general financial stress made subscription payees slow in meeting their obligations. Using legal means to collect from the subscribers might be counterproductive, railroad men argued, for it might turn still more of the public against the railroad. Many residents remembered their bad experiences with the public-supported canal system. Meadville promoters William Reynolds and John Dick therefore used personal funds to meet payroll and construction costs. Reynolds appealed to the NY&E for financial assistance. The company expressed a cautious willingness to help but only after the Branch people enlisted sufficient local support.

The lack of capital initially slowed progress all along the line of the future A&GW. Yet the three separate divisions had established a legitimate beginning by raising some local funding to begin grading operations. The three partners determined to fight the odds against them until their dream of a continuous line from Western New York to Dayton was realized—an event that was truly significant in the commercial connection between the Northwest and Northeast.

In the vast literature on railroads in America, the most vivid and fascinating sources are the diaries, letters, and memoirs of men like Marvin Kent and William Reynolds. They describe in detail and not without emotion how difficult it was to build a railroad—any railroad—in the nineteenth century. Aside from the technological and engineering problems, and they were many, there were those of raising capital, securing the right-of-way, finding qualified labor, and fending off competitors and negative opinion. In the case of the A&GW, the dependency on foreign monies and materials, the exigencies created by the Civil War, and the unlimited opportunities of the oil boom represented the most serious problems. In his history Reynolds alludes to all these obstacles and shows how they were overcome by a small group of dedicated pioneers.

Born in 1820, Reynolds grew up in Meadville, the son of John Reynolds, who had come with his father in 1797 to nearby Cherry

Township, Venango County. They had emigrated from England where, as Dissenters, they had suffered much persecution and property destruction during the Birmingham riots. John later removed to Meadville, taught school and surveyed for the Holland Land Company. In time he studied law, but that profession paled in comparison to the adventures of land speculating. He became more enchanted with business pursuits than the steady humdrum of the courtroom. He acknowledged that "the practice of law held no charm for me." In 1814 he married the rich widow of Dr. Thomas Kennedy, the former Jane Ellicott, daughter of Andrew Ellicott, prominent surveyor and former Surveyor-General under George Washington. They had two daughters and two sons, of whom William was the youngest.

At the time of William's birth, Meadville was a slow-growing town of 666 residents. Yet it was already the cultural oasis in the vast wilderness of northwestern Pennsylvania. It boasted of having the earliest college (Allegheny College, founded in 1815) and the first newspaper (*Crawford Weekly Messenger*, first issued in 1805) in the region. There were also private libraries, a school system, and a number of churches in place. Being the county seat, Meadville served surrounding townships of nearly 10,000 citizens. Its first court initially had jurisdiction over the newly created counties of Erie, Mercer, and Venango, in addition to Crawford. Finally, the regional office of the Holland Land Company was located in the town. Whatever the reason, Meadville's institutional development attracted a number of intellectually inclined and civic-minded pioneers determined to succeed despite harsh frontier conditions.

Historically the town and its location had always been important. Founded by David Mead in 1788, the settlement occupied a strategic position on the north-south axis connecting the Great Lakes region with the Ohio Valley. Because of this, the area had been in contention between the English and the French decades prior to Mead's arrival. It had also been a potential war zone between the Seneca and the hostile tribes of the Northwest. Later, the area served as a conduit for thousands of transients on their way to Ohio and the lands beyond. Early daybooks and business ledgers reveal the extent of this east-west traffic of families in search of good, cheap lands.

As one who speculated in land, John Reynolds experienced the ups and downs of an unstable market. The land issue dominated all other issues in the early settlement of northwestern Pennsylvania. The struggle between the land companies and the actual settlers, so viciously fought in the courts and legislature, divided the community into rival factions and political parties. As John Reynolds wrote, "So embittered was the strife that social parties were always of one political creed."[8] Whoever supported the land companies and their warrantees generally favored the Federalists, while those who sided against the companies tended to lean toward the Jeffersonians or Democratic-Republicans. Persistent disputes over land titles created a bonanza for lawyers and permanent scars on the community.

Even as a youngster, William Reynolds saw how the land issue had polarized his neighbors. He knew that his family belonged to the affluent class that accepted the duties and responsibilities of privilege. Many distinguished citizens—jurists, lawyers, teachers, ministers, and political leaders—visited the Reynolds home. He enjoyed listening to them. One frequent visitor was Henry Baldwin, who had been appointed associate justice of the United States Supreme Court by Andrew Jackson. Baldwin was married to William's aunt, Sally Ellicott Baldwin. Years later William was to handle Aunt Baldwin's estate and to purchase from her the Meadville retirement home built by Baldwin before his death. The home still stands as a museum.

Another group that fascinated William, though it is doubtful that he socialized with any of them, were the teamsters, stagecoach drivers, and boatmen who manned the canal barges and the packet boats for carrying passengers. Not only did these men bring provisions and strangers into town, but they also provided excitement and news from elsewhere. William was likely one of many starry-eyed youngsters who ran after the stage or followed a barge as it meandered through Meadville on the Feeder Canal. Transportation was especially intriguing to Reynolds's community, for it was the only means of communication with the outside world. He was fortunate to experience all the major advances in transportation from the stagecoach to the automobile and airplane.

In 1837 William graduated from Allegheny College. Four years later he was admitted to the bar and at the time of his death in 1911 he was the oldest living member of the bar in the county. But the prospects of practicing law in his hometown did not look promising. There was an abundance of lawyers, a situation caused in part by several decades of litigation over land titles. He therefore decided to make an eastward journey in hope of finding employment.

Reynolds's diary of 1841 reflects the uninhibited impressions of a twenty-one-year-old. He first visited the big cities of the East—Boston, Philadelphia, New York, Baltimore, and Washington—and then travelled westward through Virginia and continued on until he reached Cincinnati. His reports of scenic wonders, national monuments, and the cities and their people highlight the work. Except for his descriptions of beauty in nature and young women, his writing is generally devoid of feeling. His observations are therefore too often uncritical, casual, and blasé. With respect to slaves, for example, he simply writes that "they appear to be very happy . . . and enjoy a great deal of liberty." Equally bland is his reporting of meetings with some of the country's leading citizens. On June 11 he writes, "This morning I called on the President [John Tyler]. . . . He is a very plain affable man in his manner and agreeable in his conversation."[9] How many twenty-one-year-olds would report with such detachment a meeting with the president of the United States?

In 1845 Reynolds married Julia Thorp of New York City. Two years later, with daughter Frances Louise, they moved into the mansion built by Baldwin. Here three other children were born: Julia, Henry William, and John Earle. Special thanks is due John Earle for safeguarding his father's papers and making them available to posterity.

Reynolds began adulthood when railroad fever reached the western counties of Pennsylvania. Encouraging rumors about the rails coming to Meadville were being heard by 1841 when Reynolds took the "cars" from Chambersburg to Harrisburg. By then many of Meadville's rabid canal supporters were agitating for the railroad to come through their town. The troublesome land issue was receding; economic challenges were taking its place.

While Meadville remained essentially a small town in a rural setting,

William Reynolds, author and president of the A&GW of PA, A&GW in NY. Photo by Disderi & Co., Paris, probably taken during his 1861 European trip. *(Reynolds Collection, Allegheny College)*

its economic development still demanded attention. More businesses and small factories were starting, and farming was becoming more specialized. By 1850 the population had climbed to nearly 2,600. The neighboring townships and counties, so dependent upon Meadville's resources, continued to grow as well. Netting these communities together with a strong transportation system that would reach beyond northwestern Pennsylvania was foremost in the minds of Reynolds and other railroad enthusiasts. Turnpikes, canals, and river transit were no longer sufficient. It was at this time Reynolds's involvement with the railroad began, as does his history of the A&GW.

Most likely he wrote his memoir during the last decade of the nineteenth century, nearly forty years after the events it describes. The accuracy of some of his statements might therefore be questioned were it not for his lavish use of excerpts from financial statements, diary entries, and hundreds of letters. In addition, there are the public documents and newspaper articles. The abundance of primary sources provides a solid base of credibility. Every direct quote in his memoir went through a painstaking check by the editors against the original source. Admittedly, the result is a manuscript heavy with quotations. The editors feel, however, that the record of events embellished with the exact words of the participants adds vitality to the reading.

Even though Reynolds was a moderately accomplished writer, his memoir is plagued by inconsistencies, most of which are of style rather than substance. Without sacrificing the integrity of the memoir the editors took the liberty of correcting many of these stylistic inconsistencies. Passages were rearranged to achieve a chronology of events and dates checked against those in the original documents. The memoir was then organized into chapters, each prefaced by a capsule of events. Improper grammar and punctuation were not corrected unless clarity was at stake. First names were eliminated wherever possible. And because so many names are included, the editors added an appendix with biographical sketches of those persons central to the story and about whom some information was available. Obviously not everyone cited in the text could be identified beyond a cursory remark or two. In these cases, the identification is given in an endnote.

One of the memoir's holds upon the reader's attention is its ability to convey a sense of urgency of the moment, as railroad men struggled against time to raise capital, meet payroll, and fend off challenges from every direction. Reynolds is a keen observer who faithfully records what he saw and what it meant to him. He has neither the eye of a poet nor the imagination of a novelist, but he demonstrates a talent for description. He writes as a lawyer-businessman, and not as a historian. Although he tells his story of the A&GW against a backdrop of financial panics, the Civil War, the oil boom, and national expansion, he often fails to connect his history to the bigger picture. This is unfortunate: because he wrote his memoir a generation after major happenings had occurred, hindsight should have enabled him to be more analytical. Instead, he provides what he considered to be a personal history of events he had helped shape, and he is thorough in doing it.

Most written works follow a theme of some kind. If there is a theme in Reynolds's memoir it is that perseverance and honesty usually pay off. Despite all the obstacles he faced, he remained steadfast in accomplishing his goal, namely, to build a railroad. People working together can often antagonize each other, and this proved to be the case with Reynolds. Yet his best reporting comes when he writes about those he worked with. He did not hesitate to find fault with others. When he disapproves of someone's behavior, he conveys his impression with conviction and little remorse. If he appears to be ruthless in judging some, he does it with the best interests of the railroad at heart.

Reynolds takes special delight in assailing his English colleagues, James McHenry and Thomas Kennard. The former was responsible for selling railroad securities abroad and delivering to America the iron for construction. Kennard was a brilliant engineer sent to America to offer his expertise and oversee the interests of European investors. None could deny that all three men were indispensable in completing the A&GW, yet Reynolds finds it easier to criticize McHenry and Kennard than to applaud their efforts. He had an ally in Marvin Kent of Ohio who, like Reynolds, distrusted the inflationary and over-capitalization schemes of their English colleagues.

The essence of the differences among these men had to do with power. While Reynolds and Kent searched for ways to improve management and develop lines of fiscal responsibility, McHenry and Kennard sought to broaden their authority. Since each division of the A&GW operated independently of the other two, European investors were able to increase control over management with relative ease. They simply reminded their American critics that nearly all of the money and materials for the railroad came from Europe.

Positions on boards of directors sometimes went to Europeans without the usual procedure of formal election. Agents, and not trustees, slowly acquired responsibility over money and materials. As a result, overlapping functions and lack of accountability led to mutual distrust and persistent bickering. With an election of board members approaching, Reynolds and Kent resigned as presidents of their respective boards on September 30, 1864. They feared that the new board, dominated by McHenry, would be willing to juggle the accounts still further and to cover up unsupported claims against the American companies.

Without diminishing the significant roles played by McHenry and Kennard, it was the crucial leadership of Kent and Reynolds that assured the completion of the railroad. Their presidencies of the three branches of the A&GW provided both the continuity and stability a new railroad needed. Kent and Reynolds faced similar problems and both took credit for succeeding with what many from the beginning had believed to be an impossible task. None of the four would step down from the pedestal he had erected for himself, however. In face of such egomania it is amazing that the railroad was built at all, especially during the Civil War. In the following pages the reader can relive the experiences of one of the four, William Reynolds.

European Capital,
British Iron, and an
American Dream

The Story of the Atlantic & Great
Western Railroad

❧ Author's Preface

The full history of the Atlantic & Great Western Railroad[1] (A&GW RR) has never been written. As one of the few survivors of those actively interested in the enterprise, I write this history to perpetuate the memory of those citizens who were prominent in the completion of the first railway connection between the Atlantic Seaboard and the Mississippi River.

As a large part of the negotiations and correspondence were conducted through me, I, for convenience, write the history as a narrative of my personal official relations with the enterprise—with acknowledgement of the full degree of labor shared by the Directors, to whom equally with myself is due the credit of success. Of those more especially prominent in the A&GW of Pennsylvania was Darwin A. Finney, through whose persevering efforts as a member of Legislature the charter was obtained. Gaylord Church was connected with the enterprise from its inception to completion, ever ready to bear his full share of the burden and responsibility. As attorney for the companies his judgment was ever sound, and at most critical times, his advice reliable. James J. Shryock devoted to the years of construction persevering effort, evincing keen sagacity in all business detail. John Dick was, from the first, a constant and reliable advisor and aid. The A&GW in New York is greatly indebted to the assistance of William

Hall, Augustus F. Allen and Selden R. Marvin, residents of Jamestown. The A&GW of Ohio attained success chiefly through the unremitting efforts of Marvin Kent, its president, to whom is due the credit of being the father of the enterprise in that state.

Notwithstanding the gigantic railway enterprises which have signalized in more recent years, it is safe to say that not one of them has been brought to completion in the face of such great difficulties, as the Atlantic and Great Western. During the early years, from 1854 to 1857, after the failure of the first contractors, the "Branch"[2] was embarrassed by the persistent hostility of the railway interests of eastern and western Pennsylvania, and by the general business depression. When the charter of the "Meadville Railroad" was secured (April 1857), the repudiation of the Crawford County subscription and the application of the commissioners in June 1857, was most disastrous, as credit of this subscription had in great measure been the basis of our foreign negotiations. Then came the fearful panic of 1857–8, with the ruin of hundreds of houses regarded as the strongest in the land, the suspension of specie payments, and universal distrust. The panic extending to Europe involved commercial and manufacturing houses in bankruptcy, and forced many banks to close their doors. The greater part of American securities were held abroad, and depreciated in value or became worthless. The financial negotiations, which had been partially successful, were abandoned, to await improvement in times.

Hardly had work been resumed, when the nation was plunged into the fearful disasters of the Civil War, amid which, with business prostrated, finances deranged, gold at enormous premium, labor scarce, wages exorbitant, and the very permanence of our government doubted by foreign nations on whom we were dependent for the negotiation of our railway securities—in the face of all these formidable obstacles, the enterprise was crowned with success.

Wm. Reynolds

❧ 1. "Railroad or No Railroad," 1851-1857

*In the decade prior to the Civil War, railroad mania contin-
ued to grip the nation. A number of lines had already been constructed or projected in western New York and northeastern
Ohio, but the cities of Philadelphia, Erie, and Pittsburgh
guarded against railway connection between the two states
through northwestern Pennsylvania. In 1851, William
Reynolds of Meadville, Pennsylvania, and railroad leaders
from Ohio planned to support such a connection. Reynolds
helped organize a branch of the Pittsburgh & Erie Railroad.
The branch was later called the Meadville Railroad Company.
When the state Supreme Court allowed Crawford County to re-
pudiate its bonds and the Panic of 1857 threatened the future of
the railroad, Reynolds and Marvin Kent of the Atlantic &
Great Western RR of Ohio decided to appeal to European investors. To this end contractors A. C. Morton and Henry
Doolittle were sent to England to begin negotiations. Upon
their return, Morton demanded a new contract, which
Reynolds refused to grant.*

Railroad Mania 1851

The close of the year 1851 witnessed a very general interest
in railway extension. Few long lines were as yet constructed by
single companies. The Erie RR Company,[1] after many years of

effort and discouragement, had connected the Hudson at Piermont with Lake Erie at Dunkirk, May 18, 1851. This was the longest line then built. The connection between Albany and Buffalo had been completed by several distinct corporations. The Buffalo & State Line Company (B&SL RR) had built to the Pennsylvania state line, there connecting with the Erie & North East Railroad (E&NE RR) of six-feet-gauge, January 10, 1852. The Pennsylvania Railroad (PRR), extending westward from Philadelphia to Pittsburg [*sic*], offered the only connection from the seaboard to the west, south of the state of New York.

Other lines of railway had been projected in Ohio for connection with the lines already constructed to the seaboard, but were barred from progress by the narrow and selfish policy of Pennsylvania, whose legislature was controlled by the influence of Philadelphia, Pittsburg, and Erie. Philadelphia persistently opposed every railway enterprise which should open a connection with the rival city of New York, unless tributary to her. Pittsburg opposed all connections through northwestern Pennsylvania; and Erie wished all lines to terminate at her harbor. The united interests of Philadelphia and Erie had projected the Sunbury & Erie Railroad (S&E RR), not then built, with valuable water front, [and] the Pittsburg & Erie Railroad (P&E RR) from Pittsburg to the Erie harbor. Also the Erie & New York City Railroad (E&NY City RR) had been organized for a direct connection with the Erie Railroad. With these four lines concentrating at her harbor, she [Erie] foresaw great commercial prosperity if western outlet through Pennsylvania could be prevented. Actuated by these motives, each of these cities sent men of ability to Harrisburg, whose important duty was to vigilantly guard against railway connection between New York and Ohio.

In northeastern Ohio three railway enterprises had been organized with a view to an eastern connection through Pennsylvania; the Cleveland, [Painesville] & Ashtabula (CP&A RR) to the State line, the Clinton Line from Cleveland to the Pennsylvania line near Kinsman, and the Franklin & Warren (F&W RR, later A&GW of Ohio) from Dayton to the state line near Orangeville. The [first] of these railroads was already constructed to the state line, and under a covert power inadvertently granted to the Franklin Canal Company, arrangements were be-

Judge Gaylord Church, director and legal advisor to the A&GW.
(Crawford County Historical Society Collection)

ing made to extend to Erie. Near the close of the year 1851, Judge [Marvin] Kinsman, of Kinsman, and other gentlemen interested in the Ohio railways, visited Meadville, and at the office of John Reynolds,[2] met with a number of our citizens, including John Dick, David Dick, and Judge Gaylord Church, to advise as to the practicability of securing a railway connection through this state.

As it was improbable that any direct legislation could be obtained, it was determined to secure the end by covert powers to be granted, the object concealed. (This by no means commendable character of legislative enactment had become common and was characterized by the name "snake.")[3] Church was sent to Harrisburg to secure some legislation which would meet the emergency. It was decided [to make] a direct application for a railroad charter, as supplement to the charter of the Meadville, Allegheny & Broken-straw Plank Road Co. and obtain authority for that company to lay iron rails on their road, ostensibly as a tram-way. Church, after efforts of many weeks, was unable to secure any satisfactory legislation, and returned home in April 1852.

The P&E RR Company had been chartered in 1845, and was empowered to build lateral roads or branches in any county and *adjoining counties* through which the main line should pass. The company had done little work and had not been able to secure stock subscriptions, although in 1846 they were authorized to receive subscriptions from the counties through which the road should be located. In the summer of 1852 an overture was made by this company to some of our Meadville citizens to join interests and build the connecting line between Ohio and New York under the branch powers of their charter, which was ample for the purpose. On October 8, 1852, a meeting of interested parties was held at the American Hotel in Cleveland.[4]

Judge [B.] Chamberlain [E&NY City RR] was appointed chairman, and after deliberation it was determined to appoint a committee to meet with the Erie Railroad Company at New York and enlist their interest.

In accordance with this resolution Prof. H. N. Day, of the Clinton Road, E. Sankey, Henry Doolittle of F&W RR, Church and Wm. Reynolds met the directors and Benjamin Loder, president of the Erie RR Co., on October 26-28 at which time all proposed plans were discussed and the interest of the Erie RR Company aroused. The Erie RR Company agreed at their own expense to make a preliminary survey in Pennsylvania to ascertain the character of the route. The survey was placed under the charge of Thomas Hazzard, who had located the line of the E&NY City RR. On December 28, the Ohio & New York committee with Church and Reynolds representing Pennsylvania line, again met [with] the Erie RR Company. Nothing definite was accomplished, the financial difficulties of that company rendering it impossible to extend more than good wishes.

County Subscription 1853

In the summer of 1853 it was determined to make an effort to build the Branch road and secure in addition to the private stock subscription, county subscriptions on both the main line and Branch, each specially applicable to the several lines. A portion of the line west of Meadville was located, and some right of way obtained, and parties found willing [to] contract for the work, upon a reasonable basis. These were the Howard Brothers,[5] who offered to take the entire work, five-eighths stock and balance in cash and county bonds. Application was made to the commissioners of Crawford County [Penn.] for a subscription. On August 14, Commissioners James L. Henry, J. D. McIntire, and Nicholas Snyder, and the Grand Jury of Crawford County recommended, subject to an expression of public opinion, a subscription of $200,000.

On the following day thousands of posters were distributed throughout the county, asking a vote of approval or disapproval of the subscription on the 18th, and returns to be made to the commissioners on the 19th. These posters were headed "Railroad or No Railroad," and were signed by the commissioners. Every district in the county voted with the exception of three. Resulting vote in favor of subscription, 3,235; against, 173.

Aug. 22. Under authority of the supplement to the P&E RR charter April 21, 1846, the subscription was made by the commissioners. Bonds payable at twenty years in City of New York. On the same day the commissioners appointed Joseph McArthur, Samuel B. Long, Alexander Power, and Wm. Reynolds, Directors for the county.

Before the execution of the contract, the ceremony of breaking ground is thus noted in the *Crawford Democrat* [August 23, 1853.]

Commencement of Work.

At one o'clock on Saturday the Pittsburg & Erie RR broke ground amid the roaring of artillery and the soul stirring music of the Meadville Band. At one o'clock the procession was formed on the Diamond. John McFarland was Marshall of the day, and Horace Cullum and Major Samuel Torbet Assistant Marshall. The order of procession to the ground selected on the bank of French Creek south of the borough (just south of gas works) was:

> Directors of the company,
> Engineers
> Meadville Sax horn Band
> Early Settlers in carriages
> Laborers with shovels preceded by foreman
> Contractor
> Plough drawn by four yoke of oxen
> Citizens

In the absence of the president Hon. G. Church announced the order of exercises, after an address giving the history of the enterprise and its future bright prospect.

Mr. David Compton, one of the oldest settlers, broke ground with a shovel.

The first furrow was run by Mr. Taylor Randolph, his brother Edward Randolph driving the team of four yoke of oxen. These brothers were among the earliest settlers, and the latter is said to have driven the first team in Crawford county.

This done, a large number of employes [*sic*] went to work, in a short time prepared a portion of the ground for the rails.

Aug. 25. The contract for construction was made with the Howard Brothers payable five-eighths in stock, $150,000 county bonds.

Aug. 26. The county subscription was presented at a meeting of the P&E RR Company at New Castle. A resolution of the board was passed setting apart from the first moneys received a sum to meet the interest on the county bonds as expended. The supervision of the branch was given to Church, Wm. Gibson, and Reynolds. On Sept. 21, the P&E RR Co. by resolution pledged the "Faith credit and property of the company for the payment of the interest on the county bonds." James R. Dick was appointed "Disbursing Agent" for the Branch and instructed to call in the first installment of $2.50 per share. On October 17, Howard Bros. were awarded first estimate.[6]

From the beginning of the enterprise a constant and determined opposition and inveterate hostility was manifested by some of the citizens, which greatly impeded the efforts of the company, and caused distrust of the project, thus preventing subscriptions and the prompt payment on the subscription already made. Much courage and perseverance was required to contend against those efforts, and at the same time work for the enterprise. Owing to the distrust so industriously disseminated at the very commencement, the company was embarrassed for means to meet expenses. To collect by legal process would create ill feeling and extend prejudice. It was hoped the opposition would be allayed by the prosecution of the work and money to meet present emergencies was advanced by Church, Reynolds, and John Dick.

In the latter part of December 1853, owing to our financial difficulties, I went to New York to enlist the Erie RR Company and secure aid from them.[7] Homer Ramsdell, president of the company, seconded me in my efforts with the board, and took great interest in the project. Yet I was unable to accomplish anything financially, as the company (Erie) and its friends had exhausted their means on their own road. Yet Ramsdell gave me the written assurance of $150,000 from [his] company when we could show a reliable subscription and means within that sum for completion.

J. C. Chessbrough had been appointed Engineer and surveyed the several lines east of Meadville. The desire was to locate through the eastern part of the county to the Brokenstraw and Warren counties to the New York state line. The Mill Run route from Meadville was found impracticable. A line was explored up Woodcock through the townships of Richmond, Athens, Rome, and Sparta, but found objectionable on account of grade and heavy work and the line was forced into the valley of the French Creek. After the preliminary surveys east of Meadville were completed, Chessbrough resigned, and the greater part of the engineer corps was discharged. The work of Howards was principally west of French Creek and reduced to meet financial ability of the company.

In December, the Branch was under charge of a committee, and the offer was made to me of the charge of the work as superintendent, with a salary of $1,200. But owing to the responsibility of the position, on account of the opposition and hostility encountered at every movement, and our embarrassed finances, I declined the offer, although I accepted at a later date.

A Bad Start 1854

On March 3, the P&E RR Company met at Meadville and appointed an executive committee.[8] Reynolds was appointed Superintendent of Branch at a salary of $1,500, and John A. Waugh Superintendent of Main Line. Church and Garvin of Mercer were added to the executive committee. Hazzard was appointed engineer of [the] Branch. I again visited the Erie RR Company to secure aid of $200,000, but without success.

Our efforts to obtain stock subscriptions were not relaxed, and on May 10 Wm. Hope, agent of the Branch, reported subscription of 4,882 shares. This included the county subscription, leaving individual stock subscription at $44,100. The Erie RR Company's Ramsdell advised, owing to the stringency of the times, patience and caution: "Agitation now and preparation to act by and by." On improvement of times the company would contribute the last $200,000, and if desired, operate the road until the company could furnish its own rolling stock.[9]

Church and I went to New York in May, and spent some time in an effort to secure subscriptions among the merchants. We called on Horace Greeley of the *New York Tribune,* who offered his columns for such publications as we might wish to make. We met several of the merchants and Ramsdell at the Irving House, and presented the claims of the road. The impression made was favorable, but the closeness of the market and the opposition we encountered at home, prevented our securing the advantages so promising.

In Ohio the F&W RR had a force of a thousand men for part of the summer, and much work was done on the Clinton Line. The subscription to the Branch was raised, exclusive of the county, to $70,000. But the efforts of its enemies were persistent. Early in August a meeting was called at Conneautville by Meadville opponents, at which the project was denounced and an appeal [made] to the public fear of the loss of the county bonds. On August 14, a meeting was called for the same purpose at Meadville. The [Court] House was crowded. I addressed the meeting at length, and answered all the charges which had been made, and the meeting by an overwhelming majority sustained the company in all its course.

The disagreement with the [Howards] culminated in the cessation of work and the abandonment of the contract in November and the discharge of the Engineer corps in December.[10]

The Meadville Branch 1855

On July 12, a meeting of various interests was held at Erie to arrange the railway difficulties, which had existed for a long time, preventing railway connection through the city. Legislation had been obtained authorizing a subscription by the Buffalo & State Line RR to other roads entering Erie, in consideration of which a connection was legalized with the Cleveland Painesville & Ashtabula RR without break of gauge. It was proposed that the B&SL RR and Erie & Northeast RR should subscribe $400,000 towards the constructing of the P&E RR by way of Meadville and Waterford, and thus secure right of connection west to Cleveland through Erie, without break of gauge. The E&NE RR had before this time agreed by a vote of 1,645 to 28 to accept the compromise, but Erie citizens would not yield. Wm. Kelley[11] was opposed to any such settlement on the part of the city.

James Thompson and others addressed the meeting, generally advocating the settlement. I also spoke on behalf of the P&E RR line and on immediate settlement and completion of P&E RR by Waterford, thus giving direct route from Meadville to Erie, and a connection west, and urged a subscription by the city of $300,000 and $200,000 by the county. The committee[12] reported resolutions in favor of the city and county subscriptions. All these efforts proved of no avail.

In the fall of 1855 most of the railway enterprises in the country were in an embarrassed condition, and the companies in this part did not escape. The Clinton Line made great efforts with partial success to increase their subscriptions. The F&W RR operated with a much diminished force. The E&NY City RR suspended work, but increased their subscriptions to that extent that they determined to prosecute the work the following summer.

I spent some time during the summer along the line of the Meadville Branch and addressed many meetings to excite some interest among others, at Waterford, Union [Mills],[13] and Columbus.[14] The Warren [Pennsylvania] papers, after adopting the French Creek route, were very active in their opposition to the Branch. In addition to other discouraging circumstances there was much conflict of opinion between members of the board on Main Line and Branch, and great inefficiency on the part of the president.

A meeting of the stockholders was called to meet at the office of the company in the Betts Block, Meadville, December 10, to consider the interests of the road.[15] A very strong and decided preamble and resolutions were adopted, and a demand made on the president that an election be held for directors, not later than Jan. 10. A committee was appointed to secure signatures for a legal call on the president for holding such election, which call was signed by the residents of Meadville and the county commissioners.

The president [Ramsdell] in his report of January 3, 1856 says, "So small an amount has been paid on the individual subscription on the Meadville Branch as to render it impossible for the board to meet their engagements. Several hundred dollars are due for the engineering, and the interest on a large portion of the Crawford County bonds which have been paid out by the company remains unpaid. The subscribers to this stock refuse to pay their instalments [*sic*] unless the work was progressing, consequently the contractors Merriman and Cullum were ordered to commence work, which they did; but this does not appear to stimulate the stockholders, and the only course left is to compel payment, which must be done to a sufficient extent at least to enable the company to meet its engagements. Unless a better spirit is manifested along this line, there can be but little accomplished."

Such was the very discouraging condition of the Branch at the close of 1855. The efforts made by some of our own citizens to thwart the enterprise naturally had the effect to render our subscribers distrustful of success and fearful of loss. The western part of the county, influenced by the Conneautville press, was in bitter opposition to the further payment out of the county subscription. Warren and Erie counties were hostile to the Branch, and the Pittsburg and Philadelphia papers used their efforts to discredit and prostrate the Branch road. As a result, many of its early friends became discouraged and lukewarm, and were disposed to abandon all further effort.

It did indeed appear hopeless to attempt to raise money or secure influence sufficient to build the road in the face of such adverse circumstances. A very few, however, did not lose hope, and determined to continue their exertions. These comprised John Dick, Shryock, Cullum, Finney, myself, and very few others. We had not only to encounter the opposition and ridicule but the abuse of many prominent citizens.

Six Feet from New York to St. Louis 1856

The year 1856 opened under very discouraging prospects for the Branch. Company in debt, stock subscribers unwilling to pay their installments under the uncertainty of the future, a general feeling of apprehension as to the liability of the county for the bonds already issued, all work suspended, and the engineer corps disbanded. And more dispiriting than all, the persistent efforts at home as well as abroad to frustrate every effort for building a connecting road from the Erie RR except by the Lake Shore route.

For a time all effort was paralyzed. The spring and summer passed without progress of any importance on the Branch. Yet some work was prosecuted on the E&NY City RR and on the F&W RR. The latter road was absolutely dependent on an outlet through Pennsylvania by some connection. The report of this company (name now changed to Atlantic & Great Western of Ohio) for 1855 by Marvin Kent, president, shows assets of all kinds $1,937,789, liabilities $77,294, and general expenditures $866,939. Cash expenditure $395,006.[16]

On October 28, I received a letter from A. C. Morton, suggesting a meeting of those interested in extending from the Erie RR across Penna. & Ohio to take place at Meadville on November 11. This met with approval and again roused our despondent company to action. The meeting convened at Rupps Hotel.[17] A full report was made and unanimously adopted, and a committee of three appointed "to prepare a mutual agreement to be executed by the representatives of the companies present, for a concentration of effort and such united action as may be best calculated to secure an early combination and completion of the extended line reported upon by the committee."[18]

This agreement provided for a uniform gauge of six feet; for immediate surveys and locations so as to form connections at the state lines, and for every arrangement for a combined action and a complete united railway from New York to St. Louis, or for such distance as the three roads should control. A committee was to be appointed by the board of each company to meet in New York in November.[19]

On account of the necessary absence of the president and many directors of the Erie RR, the date of meeting was deferred to December 10. At that date I went to New York and on the part of the P&E RR with Thomas J. Power, Ward, Chamberlain of the E&NY City RR, and Doolittle and Morton met Ramsdell and Erie RR directors. Several interviews were held with the Erie RR board. Nothing definite in securing aid from that company was effected, but a committee was appointed to examine and report the proper action to be taken in furtherance of the enterprise.

Doolittle and Morton remained to confer with the committee of the Erie RR board. On the 23rd they wrote me of the favorable impression [of] the company, and urged my return as the authorized agent of the company, stating "with such effort by yourself here for the space of two or three weeks I believe material aid can be obtained from that corporation, and now is the time to follow up the good impression made. . . . Power was here yesterday and expressed himself in most decided terms that no man connected with your company could manage this business but yourself, and I am quite convinced of the truth of this and that your services are indispensable for success in this matter."

Discouragement and Panic 1857

My business did not permit my compliance at that time, but after earnest solicitation from Doolittle and Morton, I went to New York and

met Ramsdell and the Erie RR board on January 29. My effort was to
secure a subscription of $200,000 by that company applicable to the
Branch. Ramsdell seconded my efforts and several days were spent in
interviews with members of the board and at board meetings, and it
was at last agreed to meet at the St. Nicholas Hotel, and by formal action of the Erie RR board, make a subscription of $300,000 to con-
struction of the Branch.

I was however doomed to disappointment. Letters received from
Europe by the Erie RR Company that afternoon changed their views.
Ramsdell then suggested that possibly means might be devised by
which they could give us material aid in the way of credit in our foreign
negotiations, even if they could not, owing to their financial embarrassment give us money, and expressed his willingness to give a bonus for a
term of years on the mutual interchange of business.

The Meadville Railroad Company

Acting on this suggestion, a contract for a bonus was matured on
February 5, formally sanctioned by the Erie RR Company, agreeing to
pay a bonus of ten per cent on the gross receipts of passengers and
freight to and from the Branch road for five years, and a bonus of five
per cent for an additional five years.[20] Conflicting interests between the
P&E Main Line and Branch made it desirable that the Branch should,
if possible, secure independent charter. Through the efforts of our senator, Finney, on April 3, the "Meadville Railroad bill" passed the senate, authorizing a road from Meadville to Erie and with the right of extension to cover connection desired between New York and Ohio. This
act of incorporation became law May 20.[21] On July 13, the company was
organized by the election of Reynolds, president, John Dick, Church,
Finney, Shryock, Merriman, James E., and John McFarland, O. Hast-
ings, A. W. Mumford, James R. Dick, L. D. Williams, directors. Harper
Mitchell secretary, and James R. Dick treasurer.

County Repudiates Subscription

It is proper here to introduce an important episode in the history of this enterprise, viz: The Crawford County repudiation of its subscription. Three days after the passage of the act of incorporation of the Meadville RR Co., and the signature of the Governor, the commissioners of Crawford County, David Nelson, Joseph McArthur, and John McNamara, at the instance of certain citizens who had been most active in opposition to the railroad enterprise, secretly through S. N. Pettis, Atty., made application to the Supreme Court [of Pennsylvania] for an injunction to restrain the corporation from negotiating any bonds in the hands of the corporation or its officers.[22]

On July 14, the *Crawford Journal* published the application for the injunction and sustained the act of the Commissioners. I published in the *Journal* a history of the county subscription and deprecated the action as unwise and likely to result in loss to the county in costs, and very prejudicial to the interests of the projected enterprise of so great importance to the county.

This communication not only brought out a rejoinder from the *Journal,* but a most violent and abusive attack personally from the commissioners, who by a series of like abusive publication assailed not only the enterprise but me personally as the leading spirit of the same, and the one responsible for the county subscription and all the loss which might accrue to the county by the subscription. These were not discontinued or mitigated in vituperation during the pendency of the injunction proceedings.[23]

I, through the papers, endeavored to prevent injury to the railway project by their misrepresentations of the acts of the company in the past, which in so far as the Branch interests were concerned were in all respects straight forward and upright. To the personal attacks I did not descend to notice. So great, however, was the effect of the acts of the commissioners and their coadjutors upon those who had been friends of the enterprise, that they seemed to fear the responsibility of sustaining the proceedings of the company, and I was left to bear the brunt of the battle without an ally. Not a publication except mine was made in defense of the Branch direction, and not one to defend me from the false statements. The final result was as I predicted in my first article. The county had to pay the $30,000 [plus] interest and costs and fees amounting to near $6,000; and by the efforts of the commissioners and their allies were near defeating the railway. Such is a brief account of the county repudiation at a time when we most needed union, confidence, and strength at home to second our efforts.

After the bonus contract with the Erie RR Company, Morton, clothed with power by the A&GW RR of Ohio visited England, returning in May. In June he entered into negotiations with the P&E RR for a contract for construction of the Branch. On June 8 Morton wrote to me from New York relative to his visit abroad and the importance of an early organization of the company and transfer of the rights of the P&E RR, in order that he might on his return to Europe, be able to represent a united railway interest of the three states. On July 23, at a meeting of the P&E RR Co., when no representatives of the Branch interest were present, "the president laid before the board a certain contract with Morton for the construction of the lateral road by way of Meadville, [which] was unanimously approved."

At the first meeting of the Branch of the Meadville RR Co. on July 25, the terms of the purchase and transfer from and by the P&E RR Co. were presented and discussed. Connected with these was the contract of Morton. [Two days later] the terms of transfer were completed and ratified, and the contract with Morton accepted. I was notified by J. C. Calhoun, secretary of E&NY City RR, that R. T. Bailey [Morton's brother-in-law] on the part of Morton had negotiated with that company a contract for construction [of] that road to our connection at the state line.

Subscription books were opened for the new Meadville RR Co. The first installment of ten per cent was payable only when the engineer of the company should certify that fifty per cent of the earth work between Meadville and the New York state line was done. So greatly had confidence of the public been impaired by the acts of the commissioners and the misrepresentations of the opponents of the road, that this form of subscription was adopted.

Reaching Out to Europe

Morton and Doolittle went to Europe for negotiations. On August 31, Bailey wrote me from New York, stating that the bonds of the company would be needed by Morton for delivery on his negotiations on October 27. The Meadville board had authorized the president to prepare bonds and execute the proper mortgage for security of the same. Also, it appointed Morton "Agent" with power to negotiate sale of bonds for cash or iron, to employ agents and secure influence of persons in Europe or elsewhere, and to pay commissions not exceeding five per cent of bonds sold. These commissions [were] not to increase the aggregate amount of Morton's contract. To expedite, I had gone to New York and had in consultation with Bailey, Morton's representative, arranged for the engraving necessary for the bonds.

I spent from August 3–13, September 7–12 and September 29–October 15 in New York having the bonds engraved and signed by the trustees. The bonds were all executed, but owing to delay in Morton and Doolittle's negotiations, were not sent forward to Europe, but were deposited with Henry V. Poor, one of the trustees. This arrangement, as will be seen, was the source of untold vexation and trouble.

From Morton's letters in October it appears that negotiations were at this time pending with Gomperts of London, for money and iron on the securities of the company; but owing to the illness of Gomperts, [negotiations] had for a time been suspended. During the interval a financial crisis had commenced in this country likely to discourage foreign investment in securities on railway enterprises. Morton: "There are reasons for hope yet. . . . The parties who propose are retiring capitalists and contractors who have an abundance of means and are not easily discouraged. . . . They are thoroughly acquainted with the merits of the project, and have become much interested. . . . They say they will carry the matter through without fail."

It must be remembered that a disastrous panic overspread the country.[24] The Illinois Central RR and Erie RR became insolvent. All the banks suspended specie payments, and many of the most prominent merchants became bankrupt, spreading fear and distrust everywhere.

Yet, on October 30, Morton writes that he is happy to give the information that he had finally arranged matters on the other side. He and Doolittle would leave on the *Vanderbilt*, and on arrival he and Doolittle would visit Meadville and report.

Nov. 30. Morton from New York: "Having closed all my negotiations in England for sufficient means, with what is expected from the people along the line, to complete your road. I need hardly say that some modifications in my present contract with your company will be required to adapt the whole to my arrangements in England. I will submit the matter for the consideration of your board trusting that such action will be taken by you as will leave no room to doubt the completion of your road at an early period."

From private and confidential information, I was led to distrust the accuracy of Morton's statements of the successful results of his negotiations, as also his trustworthy character in carrying out his contracts in good faith, and was therefore prepared to examine with great caution whatever he might propose. On December 28, Morton came to Meadville, and a meeting of the board was called at my office on Water Street.[25] Morton made a very indefinite statement with regard to his agency in Europe, after which he presented a draft of a contract to Morton and Bailey for construction of the road. The terms were widely at variance with that made with the P&E RR Co. A long discussion ensued and various modifications were suggested, but with obstinate demand on the part of Morton. He also required of the board a guaranty of $3,000 per mile of subscription, in addition to the subscription.

Reynolds, Merriman, and Cullum were appointed a committee to confer with Morton in regard to a basis of a contract, which could be submitted to the board. In the evening I reported the only basis to which Morton and Bailey would consent, and the following resolution was passed: "That we deem it inexpedient in a matter of such importance to act without mature reflection, therefore the matter of contract is referred to a committee of three, Reynolds, Church, and Merriman, to carefully revise and report to next meeting." Morton and Bailey returned to New York much disappointed at the refusal of the company to accede without delay to their demand. On December 30, Doolittle served a notice on the company, claiming an interest in Morton's P&E contract, and protesting against any new contract without recognition of such interest, and objecting to giving Bailey any interest in the same.

Before closing the narrative of 1857, I should state that a change had been made in the presidency of the Erie RR, Charles Moran (a Banker) having been appointed president, instead of Ramsdell. The bonus contract negotiated by me on February 7, was for the benefit of the P&E Branch, and not available to the Meadville RR without recognition by the Erie RR Co. Not doubting that the Erie RR Company would ratify it without objection, I went to New York, and on August 10, called on Moran only to meet with a most decided refusal to recognize it in any manner. "Our directors who voted for such a contract were knaves or fools" was his remark. I induced him, however, to convene his board and permit me to present the question. The board were favorable to our enterprise, but in their financial disasters were unable to do anything objectionable to Moran, who represented so large a foreign credit. After several meetings, Moran seemed to view our project with more favor, and consented to a modification of the agreement of February to give a bonus of five per cent for five years on all business passing from the Meadville road over the Erie RR, being about one-sixth part in value to the Meadville road of the February contract, counting it on the basis of the business for the first five years; but taking into consideration the increased traffic of the additional five years of the old contract, the difference was much greater. Yet this last contract paid $400,000 to the A&GW RR Co. of Penna.

Thus the year 1857 terminated with a most discouraging outlook for the Meadville RR: A suit by the county to cancel their subscription, a disastrous financial crisis, a serious disagreement with the contractor.

Reynolds broke off negotiations with Morton and awarded the contract for construction of the road to Henry Doolittle and W. S. Streator. The Meadville RR, now know as the "Atlantic & Great Western RR of Pennsylvania," made bonds and stock available in England for cash and iron. James McHenry of London and Don José de Salamanca of Spain became principal fund-raisers. McHenry sent a reputable engineer, Thomas Kennard, to examine and report on the progress of the new line in America. Kennard proved to be a vital force in promoting the interests of the railroad; later he came to superintend its construction. A dispute with Christopher Ward of New York in 1859 led to the formation of the "Atlantic & Great Western RR in NY." With this organization, all the administrative groundwork for the A&GW RR was complete for a continuous line from New York City to St. Louis, using the six-foot gauge.

The Atlantic & Great Western RR of Pennsylvania 1858

After submitting to the counsel of the company, Church, for his written opinion regarding the rights of Doolittle under the powers granted by the company to him and Morton, and the claims he might have under and by virtue of agreements between himself and Morton, I decided to draw a contract fair in its terms recognizing the rights of Doolittle and offer it to

Morton for acceptance. In case of refusal, [I would] next offer it to Doolittle and some other responsible contractor.

I prepared such contract and informed Morton of the unsurmountable objections on the part of the company to the terms proposed by him: the indefinite terms leading to misunderstanding and controversy, the assumption by the company of obligations beyond their ability to perform, leaving them in default in case of controversy and the right of transfer of the contract without the consent of the company. His answer being unsatisfactory, I went on February 6 to New York and spent two weeks. Morton evidently thought that the company would in the end be obliged to accept his terms, and was indisposed to make conces-

Map of the Pennsylvania section of the A&GW. *(Reynolds Collection, Allegheny College)*

W. S. Streator, one of
the contractors for the
A&GW. Photo by Chas.
K. Bill's Photographic
Gallery, Broadway, New
York. *(Reynolds Collection,
Allegheny College)*

sions. I offered to him the contract I had drawn. He refused to sign it. I
then asked if he would carry out the terms of the contract made with
the P&E. This he declined to do. I offered the same contract to Doolittle and W. S. Streator who acceded to the terms and the same was executed, *subject* to the approval of the board. On February 28, the contract was submitted to and formally approved by the company. I
notified Morton of the termination of all negotiations with him and of
the making of the new contract.

Samuel T. Hallett states that the prospects [in Europe] are of a most
encouraging character: "The capitalists want the *whole* of the bonds of
all the companies. Will pay for them as fast as they can get them; and
will take all within 60 or 90 days. Were you here now with bonds, bills,
and powers, you could have all the money and warrants from the

strongest men in Europe." Moran, president of the Erie RR, then in Europe, wrote encouragingly of the prospects of the Meadville RR. It now became necessary that the company should send their bonds to trustees in London to be ready for the negotiations under the very rose colored advice from England.

These bonds had been executed and deposited with Henry V. Poor of New York, one of the trustees, a man supposed to be honorable in reputation and of good standing in the business community. On February 20, I wrote to Wm. Thorp, then residing in NY, requesting him to take the bonds from Poor and forward them to John Dick, treasurer. Our surprise as well as embarrassment was great when informed of his refusal to surrender them [due to] the present relations of the company with Morton. The contractors desired the bonds in London and we were powerless. It was soon evident that Poor and Morton were in league to force the company to terms, and were determined to use their power without scruple. I was equally resolved to make no concession but to stand upon what was right. I visited New York, talked with Poor without success. Church also talked with him, and was disposed to throw much blame on me for the contract with Doolittle on account of legal questions although I had acted on his written opinion of the legal points. Many of the directors became alarmed under the serious complication, but were yet willing to leave the settlement in my hands.

The imbroglio with Poor was by this denouement rendered more perplexing. On March 17, Church had written to me advising to *conciliate* Poor, and Poor, of same date, wrote me that Church coincided in his views. Upon consultation with Flagg the co-trustee, and then the Comptroller of the City, he sustained my position and wrote to Poor, but without effect. On April 9, I called on Poor and notified him that I should next day commence legal proceedings against him. He capitulated and next day surrendered the bonds to Flagg. On the same day I received a letter from Church advising a *compromise* with Poor. And on the April 10 another letter expressing his gratification that Poor had surrendered, and stating that he was not entitled to [any] compensation.

So ended this serious obstruction to our plan. Poor resigned his trust, and his name was erased by an ink line from the bonds. On April

15, by a supplement to the charter of the Meadville RR Co., the name was changed to "The Atlantic & Great Western RR Co. of Pennsylvania." In consequence of this legislation, it became necessary to engrave the new bonds and cancel the Meadville RR bonds. Owing to the blindness of Flagg, the company authorized Maria Flagg, his daughter, to sign for her father.

Sale of Bonds in Europe

The Penna. and Ohio companies appointed Ward, Doolittle, and Reynolds, with full power to negotiate in Europe for sale of bonds, purchase of iron, and all that they might deem necessary for the interest of the companies. On May 8, 1150 bonds, and $75,000 of shares were delivered to Ward and Doolittle, who sailed on that day for Europe. Hallett writes that he anxiously awaits their arrival. On news of arrival of Ward and Doolittle at Bremen, Hallett, Thomas W. Kennard, George F. Train, James A. McHenry, and [Nathaniel Beverley] Tucker[1] at once started to meet them in Paris.

July 20. Doolittle from London: "New and strong parties have joined Hallett and the arrangements are about perfected for all the rails, and an amount of money to enable me speedily to complete the road. . . . An engineer from here is to go out and report." Hallett writes to McDowell that Leon Lillo & Co., bankers to the Queen of Spain, subscribe £200,000 and the Kennards will take the balance.

Aug. 6. Advices of success rendered it prudent to place engineers in the field. Joseph Hill was appointed Engineer and John B. Taylor Assistant Engineer. I also organized a party under Isaac Doane[2] and instructed Hill to urge forward the location east of Meadville. Advices from Europe state that Ward and Doolittle are busy shipping the iron, and will be home in a few weeks. New York papers of September 3, announce the successful negotiation of the A&GW RR for $3,000,000.

Sept. 4. Doolittle returned from Europe and wrote me from New York, "The contracts for the 31,000 tons of rails and balance of money we want were signed before I left England. Ward sails this eve and brings with him an installment of £10,000 7⁄10 for your part of road.

Same amount to be advanced monthly, and shipment of rails to commence this month. A smaller installment was paid on execution of contracts. Engineers should be upon the line."

Sept. 11. Streator wishes the line to be in readiness as soon as possible, as work will be commenced as soon as Ward returns.

Sept. 14. Ward from London: "I found our negotiations in such a shape that it took not only weeks but months to get at the bottom of them so as to give you anything reliable. I found I could not believe any thing I heard, and not more than half what I saw. All the plans which Hallett wrote so glowingly about, which we conned over together in New York proved delusory, and many of them were only talk for the sake of talking. . . . There has been no moment up to within a fortnight that I could assure you of anything defined or settled. . . . Doolittle finally signed ten days since a contract with James McHenry, of Liverpool, and received £3,000 as the first payment or forfeit money. But McHenry depended upon the results of some arrangements with a Banking House in Paris of which the celebrated Spanish banker and railway king Salamanca was a partner. He (McHenry) was satisfied with the agreement of the Paris manager but I knew that the Paris manager had reserved in writing a right to withdraw from the subscription if Salamanca disapproved. . . . I returned from Paris on Saturday and after seeing him and after a week's anxious labor to secure him with us. This being now done, I write you, that with proper care and with economy and good management on the part of all concerned, I feel sure we shall be able to go through with our road. . . . I look upon the matter now if we succeed your stock will be better even than your bonds. . . . Your County Commissioners need not be afraid that the county subscription if carried out will ever be anything but a source of profit to the county. It is probable I may bring with me a gentleman (an engineer) whose favorable report . . . I deem important to smooth our way in the arrangement, which will be in progress here. . . . I believe I have finally conciliated Poor and thus far we have checkmated Morton."

The *New York Times* of September 15 published an attack on the enterprise and refused to publish a reply by Doolittle. Morton and Poor

James A. McHenry, British finan-
cier and promoter of the A&GW
enterprise. Photo by Disderi &
Co., Paris, probably taken during
Reynolds's 1861 European trip.
(Reynolds Collection, Allegheny College)

were supposed to have been the instigators of the article. McHenry
states that 1,000 tons of iron will be shipped on the 10th from the Ebbw
Vale[3] works, and 1,000 more in two weeks.

Sept. 15. Joseph Hill accepted the position of Engineer, and [select-
ed] September 20 for his commencement of duty.

Oct. 25. The Supreme Court of Pa. made a decree in the Crawford
County bond repudiation case annulling the balance of unissued
bonds $170,000, but in no way questioning any acts of the company in
so far as the P&E Branch was concerned. The decision rested exclusively on the fraudulent transfer of the original stockholders to irre-
sponsible parties, long previous to the Branch negotiations. These
county bonds had in all our European negotiations been represented as
part of our reliable assets, and the county subscription referred to as evidence of the public confidence in the result of the enterprise. It can be

readily imagined that this decree at this moment caused great chagrin and apprehension among the friends of the enterprise, and most grave fears for the result on our foreign arrangements.

Ward, Kennard (engineer sent over to examine and report on the road), and Train, arrived in New York, and the day after their arrival read in the New York papers the notice of the decree.

Nov. 4. Ward from New York: "I received this morning the discouraging and disastrous intelligence which I here append (notice of Supreme Court of Pa. decree). The subscribers to the loan in Europe counted upon this subscription's being available in completing the work; and such was always the information I received. If your County Commissioners will not renew this in some form, secure it how they please—or make it applicable to the iron rails, making sure that it will be applied to a finished line, or any way they deem best, I say, if I cannot be supported by Crawford County to at least this extent, I cannot answer for the consequences. Heaven knows my situation has been anxious and arduous enough and if engagements are kept on this side of the water, I will answer for completion of the road. If not, I have done my duty faithfully and must rest content with that conclusion. . . . I have not and shall at present not let [Kennard] know of the decision of the Supreme Court, hoping it can be remedied soon.

"Kennard is here to go over the line. Having arranged with Morton to take the E&NY City line in, we shall take that first in course, and hope to reach Jamestown on Monday next, the 8th. I hope to meet there at least yourself and some members of your board."

Nov. 8. In the evening Ward, Kennard, and Train arrived [at Jamestown] under charge of Hill, who had met them at Bucktooth.[4] The exploration had been under many disadvantages not only of weather, but bad roads, resulting in capsizing the carriage, fortunately without injury to anyone. Train was severe in denunciation of Hallett. Kennard did not at first create a favorable impression. He was thoroughly John Bull and probably not in the best humor after his ride. Next day Kennard and party under guidance of Hill, continued along the line, and we returned home.

Ward, Kennard, and Train reached Meadville. A public meeting was called at the Court House for the following evening. The room was packed, and was addressed by Ward, who gave an account of the prospects of the road if aided by the hearty cooperation of the citizens and county. Kennard had in the morning gone with some of our sportsmen to Conneaut Lake to shoot ducks, and found the sport so fascinating that he left late and did not reach Meadville until in the evening, and was at once driven to the meeting at the Court House. His entrance was greeted with cheers, and was called on for a speech. No refusal would be taken, and in his long boots and hunting jacket he mounted the platform but was for a time unable to say a word; the cheers redoubled, and he at last managed to make a short speech and was followed by Train, who made up for the embarrassment of Kennard and kept the house in a roar for an hour. The meeting was enthusiastic, and passed resolutions looking to serious work in securing subscriptions and right of way.

The enthusiasm of the friends of the road was met with equal bitterness by the enemies of the road. The commissioners had appointed directors in the P&E RR, some of those known to be active and hostile and at this time took steps to recover from John Dick the few bonds which were left in his hands as hypothecation for loans made for the road. Their plans were frustrated as the bonds had already been placed in other hands before service of the notice.

The progress of Ward, Kennard, and Train over the line aroused enthusiasm. Train wrote from Ravenna, "Energetic meeting at Greenville. . . . To have an energetic board of directors and to have you at their head there is no such word as fail." From Cincinnati, November 28, "The winter of our discontent has been made glorious summer by our reception along the line. Guns firing, music playing, speech making, public meetings. Kennard is hard at work on report. It will be a strong paper. . . . Two more cargoes of iron left Liverpool. . . . People begin to see that this great enterprise is a national work; other roads branches, this the trunk; other ribs, this the backbone."

The E&NY City as originally located to Erie, left a gap of ten miles from where the A&GW crossed the state line to connect near Ashville, NY. On December 1 Ward visited Jamestown, and without consultation with the A&GW interests, drew up the papers for organization of a railroad company for this connecting link, making the directorship such as to give him the control of the line. This act of Ward greatly impaired the confidence of those in interest in the A&GW, and was regarded as an attempt for selfish interests to own individually a link in the chain, and led eventually to the location of a new line and organization of the A&GW Co. in NY and dissolution of relations with him.

Dec. 10. Train: "The opposition is dead. All now are friendly. . . . I agree with Kennard and see no reason why we should not open to Akron two hundred miles by September next."

The following is from a letter of mine, dated December 16. "Reached New York Tuesday. Found Kennard and Train here, and spent the evening at the New York Hotel with them and their wives. Mrs. Kennard is a very pretty and agreeable lady. Mrs. Train is not pretty but is pleasant in manner. Kennard is much pleased with his visit west and expresses himself almost enthusiastically on the subject. He is very busy obtaining statistics for his report, and will go over the Pennsylvania RR to Pittsburg and over the Baltimore & Ohio RR. Poor and Morton yet need watching. I am very glad I came on that account, as I have already righted some very unsatisfactory matters. Unless Morton accedes to our terms, we will throw him out of the whole arrangement. (E&NY City)"

Dec. 24. Church and I were authorized to arrange with the S&E RR for a connection to Erie. This was to make a connection in compliance with the provisions of the charter of the Meadville RR Co. On December 18, McHenry wrote Doolittle, "Have just returned from Paris. Our friends are much gratified by the reports of Kennard and Train, and seem to consider the difficulties surmounted. Have just finished shipment 122 tons of rails. We shall push ahead with great energy, having broken down all calumnies, all opposition."

Dec. 30. Church and I again went to meet Kennard in New York, and I remained until January 8. Kennard was busily engaged writing his report at the New York Hotel where we spent much of our time meeting on one occasion at dinner Beverly Tucker who in some way is interested with McHenry, but in what manner I am ignorant. Mrs. Kennard was a valuable assistant to her husband in preparing the report, copying and correcting. She wrote well and rapidly, and impressed me as a clear headed lady.

It may be here stated that in the end the [financial status of the enterprise] was delusory. The conditional subscription was never paid. A large part of the right-of-way was forfeited by alterations of location, and was in most cases paid for at high prices, as well as the fencing on the line. The Erie Co. subscription to the P&E was never transferred to the A&GW or paid to the P&E. Mercer County or Erie County never paid a dollar of individual subscription. Thus after seven years of effort this year terminated with an aggregate result of work done at a cost of $45,983; the loss of the county subscription; and with a *paper* subscription on the line from which little was ever realized. But with much encouragement and bright hopes for the future.

The Atlantic & Great Western RR of New York 1859

Jan. 2. Kennard arrived last evening from Phila. Kennard has read his report to me. It is all we could desire; is very strong in its commendations and is substantiated with facts. He has submitted it to me for examination and suggestions. It will be copied tomorrow, and we will have a copy, not however, to be made public until it shall be printed in England. The work will commence early in March and will [be] forced along as fast as money end labor can do it. . . . I see nothing in future to impede our progress.

Kennard left immediately after the preparation of his report, for London. I remained with Church until the 7th, investigating and preparing the Morton case for court. Merrill of New York was engaged by Church to attend to the details of the suit. Flagg, our trustee under the mortgage, at this time had an operation performed for cataract, which proved unsuccessful, and the company by resolution authorized his daughter to sign for him.

Jan. 21. Kennard published his report in London. McHenry wrote that it gave great satisfaction. During the interim, before commencing work, it was decided to reduce expense by the discharge of most of the engineer corps until needed.

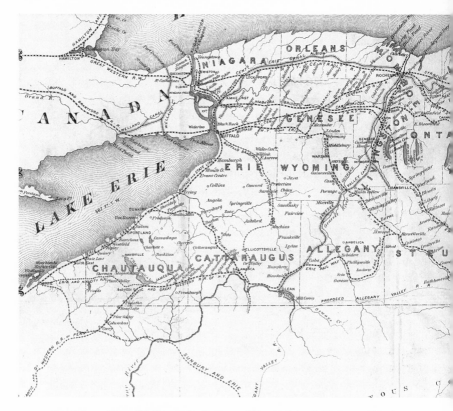

Detail from *Map of Railroads in the State of New York*, by S. H. Sweet, Weed, Parsons & Co., 1863. *(Reynolds Collection, Allegheny College)*

General Ward's Ten Mile Road

Early in February, McHenry wrote that Salamanca had placed all his bonds in Madrid, and they were arranging to bring out the remaining 1,200,000 in London. That he had secured the guarantee of Prescott, Grote & Co. London, of the payment of the coupons. Wishes work to be commenced at once, and is anxious about the E&NY City road now in Morton's control. Morton, holding a contract with that company, felt that he had the key to the position, as our anticipated connection with the Erie RR was by that road. He was disposed to use his supposed power to exact terms with Doolittle and McHenry to compensate him for the loss of the Penna. contract. Ward who had secured a charter for the ten miles between the Penna. line and the E&NY City road was also desirous that arrangements should be made with Morton for the interest of his "toll gate."

McHenry, under his contract with Doolittle, found that he possessed no adequate power to carry out such negotiations as were necessary to deliver the bonds or receive the money and iron on their sale, and through his attorney, John Fallon, of Philadelphia (the attorney of Duke Rianzares and Queen Christina), made application to the companies for the proper powers. It was also deemed prudent that legislative sanction should be secured for the various transfers from the P&E RR and other acts under the mortgage of the Meadville title changed to A&GW of Pa. Such a supplement was passed March 10.

March 22. Arrived at Phil₂ ᵗ ᵗⁿhia and [met] with Doolittle, Church, and Dick. Called on Fallon and consulted with regard to the proposed Power of Attorney to McHenry, and the modifications from the one heretofore sent over, and deemed insufficient. We have not yet placed them in proper shape, but will be able to arrange satisfactorily to all tomorrow.

With Church met several of the directors of the S&E RR with Moorhead, president, at their office, and discussed the proposed contract for connection over their road to Erie to fulfill the terms of the A&GW charter. They appeared favorably disposed for a business connection—but the greater number of those present expressed dissent to giving the right to lay a third rail from Union [Mills] to Columbus, or to use their right of way for our track. At least, without a large money consideration in hand.

March 29. This afternoon Thallon received a telegram from Halifax stating that Kennard would come out by the *Persia* to close the arrangements for the road and wishing the different parties to meet him here. This news was unexpected and we cannot divine the object of the unlooked for visit. The *Persia* will be due tomorrow.

March 31. Met Church, Ward, Kennard, and Thallon and heard the object of Kennard's sudden return. It seems that the European interests desire a greater concentration of action and interest between the several

Robert Thallon, McHenry's agent in New York who handled importing rails and money from England. Photo by Disderi & Co., Paris, probably taken during Reynolds's 1861 European trip. *(Reynolds Collection, Allegheny College)*

companies, and propose some plans for this object; most of these are unobjectionable and will be agreed to. We have telegraphed Fallon to meet us tomorrow. Made answer to Morton's suit.

April 1. Met Kennard, Church, Thallon, and Fallon and discussed the proposed contract of a mutual guaranty between the several companies. Ward at former meeting and since insists on the recognition of his ten mile road charter as part of the line and the guaranty of its bonds.

April 2. Church [and his wife] left this morning. He informed me that Ward manifested great dissatisfaction at a meeting between himself and Thallon, on account of the disinclination to recognize his road in the proposed mutual guaranty, and to come to some terms with Morton. Doolittle, Church and I arranged to meet at Jamestown on Monday and a full conference with the E&NY City Company, relative to their wishes and their power under the contract with Morton to join in the proposed mutual guaranty. I saw Kennard and obtained from him letters to be used at Jamestown. Doolittle and I went to the Erie RR cars at 5 P.M. but were met on the ferry boat by General Ward, James Ward (his brother), and Thallon. The General was greatly excited and insisted that we should remain in the city, that he had propositions from Morton and Hallett for full adjustment of all questions.

April 3. Washington Hotel. Have been surprised agreeably with the comfort and neatness of this Hotel where we have taken our quarters so unexpectedly. Our dining room overlooks the Battery Park and the table is served by young tidy waitresses. Thallon came over in the morning. Ward and Doolittle were on very hostile terms, giving little promise of amicable arrangement.

April 4. Ward this morning was very reserved on all questions. He agreed to meet me at Thallon's office but failed to meet his appointment. Later I met Kennard and Thallon. We are all satisfied that nothing can be effected with Ward and Morton and Co. who now virtually control the connection over the E&NY City road. It was determined that we shall organize a new company for all the part of the line in the state of New York from the Erie RR to the State Line and thus cut loose from all the embarrassments which have hampered us with our connection with the E&NY City and Ward's roads.

Contract of Mutual Guaranty

April 7. During the board meeting in Meadville, the contract of mutual guaranty as agreed upon at New York was submitted and approved by the company. Three copies were made and executed by me as president of the A&GW of PA and were sent by Joseph Hill to be presented for ratification by the Ohio board.

April 11. Drove to Erie where I met Hill with the contracts of mutual guaranty executed by the Ohio company, and forwarded a copy to Kennard to take to London. This contract was modified in some particulars at the request of Kennard who was dissatisfied that his name had not been inserted as engineer in chief, etc. The altered copy was executed as of April 20, and sent to London. Kennard sailed April 13 for England.

I had in March written to Henry Baker, President of E&NY City RR Co., explaining our relations with Morton from which I extract: "We will do all in our power to carry out our first plans (with the E&NY City) but of course will not place our interests in any measure under the control of Morton. I perfectly understand Morton's foreign arrangements to carry forward the work, but I do not know how far he will have the control of your road by virtue of his contract for construction. In other words, while he has the right to operate your road to January 1863, has he not the exclusive control? If so, you can readily see that such control could be used to our prejudice."

April 22. Instructions were given to Hill to survey an entirely new line in the state of New York independent of the E&NY City road, and suspend all further negotiations with that company until we should ascertain the feasibility of the new route.

McHenry, Salamanca, and European Capital

Our advices from London stated that Salamanca had successfully placed his loan of $1,000,000 in Madrid—Wiggins & Co. . . . Salamanca is worth his millions and could alone build the road with his own funds, yet you see he has got bankers at Barcelona, Cadiz, and Madrid. . . . Leon Lillo, Paris, have similar facilities, backed up by *Royal* funds. In London we have President of Bank of England. Heywood, Kennard & Co. A bonafide two years guarantee of the coupons from Prescott, Grote & Co., Barnard & Co. Liverpool, and our iron bought of two of the leading iron makers of England, etc. Such were the rose colored pictures sent from London. A great part were the pictures of the *imagination*. Possible events were represented as certainties.[5]

March and April were busy months. All the necessary powers of attorney and careful instructions were forwarded to McHenry and to Meron and Goddard, the trustees in London. Meron was an attaché of our Legation, Goddard at the head of the Rock Insurance Co. A contract of mutual guaranty had been made between the A&GW companies. Legislation confirming the acts and powers of the Penna. company had been obtained, and all negotiations in Europe seemed to be successful.

Our company in Pennsylvania however, had been very guarded in their letters of attorney to McHenry, and very specific in instructions to the trustees. The power of attorney was drawn by Church and the instructions by me.[6]

The following instructions to McHenry were sent with the letter of attorney [on] March 26th:

1. To obtain and receive from Meron and Goddard, trustees, at such time or times as may be convenient for the exercise of his powers under the letter of atty., certificates of capital stock and bonds of the A&GW RR Co. of Pa. giving said trustees duplicate receipts therefor, and report of the numbers and denominations of the bonds so received and also the stock certificates.

2. All iron received on the sale or negotiation of the bonds or stock of the company, or purchased for the use of the same shall be shipped and consigned to "Wm. Reynolds Trustee of the Atlantic & Great Western RR Companies of Penna. and New York," and the bills of lading shall be sent to "Wm. Reynolds care of Robert Thallon, N.Y."

3. All coupons past due at the time of negotiation or sale shall be cut off, cancelled, and returned to "Wm. Reynolds, President of the Company."

4. The bonds shall be so negotiated that they shall net the company not less than seventy-five cents on the dollar on the shipment of iron, or payment of the money in the City of New York.

5. The attorney to arrange with some person or banker in New York on whom the companies may draw at three days sight for all sums necessary under the stipulations of the contract, and to this end furnish said person or banker with letters of credit from some responsible banking house in London.

6. Said attorney before the fifteenth day of each month to make a full

report of all the bonds and stock remaining in his hands or issued during the preceding month, together with a statement of the amount of money subject to the order of the company for the ensuing thirty days.

The instructions to Meron and Goddard were equally precise and explicit. The manner in which they were obeyed will appear hereafter.

April 27. Thorp accepted the Secretaryship at a salary of $1,500 per year.

The surveys in New York through Busti and Frewsburg were pushed forward with energy by Hill and proved a practicable route if no satisfactory arrangements could be consummated with the E&NY City Co.

May 7. All papers for organization of the New York company were prepared ready for execution, as soon as the surveys should be completed.

May 21. The Atlantic & Great Western RR Co. in New York was fully organized, with same persons as president and directors as in the Penna. company. Triplicates of the papers executed by the Penna. and Ohio companies, power of attorney, contract of mutual guaranty, appointment of trustees in Europe, etc. were adopted and executed by the new company and sent to Europe. Ward was left out. Thallon was yet desirous that amicable adjustment should be made to retain the influence and friendship of Ward. Extracts of my reply to him will explain our positions:

"So far as the New York company is concerned, in their disagreements with [Ward], have had no influence on my course. . . . I was at first favorable to the adoption of the charter taken by [Ward] and its extension to Little Valley. This on mature reflection I was satisfied would not extricate us from the difficulty with the Little Valley road.

"1st that because its location rendered it necessary to either adopt the E&NY City road or build alongside of it, which would have rendered a compromise more difficult than heretofore.

"2nd and of most importance that the controlling power in Ward's company was in the hands of the Directors of the E&NY City RR who would have consented to no arrangements detrimental to their own interests in their road.

"3rd I was satisfied that after our road should be finished over their road, an effort would be made to open communication with the Erie City to Jamestown.

"4th That our line should be untrammelled as to location, and leave us free for the adoption of the best and shortest line."

The soundness of my second objection has been proven by the statements of the Jamestown parties themselves, and the efforts of Morton and Co. at Erie. This was also the opinion of Kennard, and we decided to act upon it. I spoke to Ward. He said it might perhaps be a good arrangement, but wished *it to be understood that he was to be considered entirely out of it and unconnected with the new company.* Giving the reason that his connection might be considered a breach of faith by the Jamestown people on account of his prior arrangements with them. I appreciated the motive and did not urge the matter. My action was not influenced by any misunderstanding between Ward and Doolittle, but by Ward's statements to me.

By the organization of the A&GW RR Co. in New York, all corporate powers were perfected for a continuous line from the Erie RR to Dayton, Ohio. The contract for construction of the Penna. division had been awarded to Doolittle and Streator on what was at that time a good contract for the company. The contractors were to furnish all materials, iron rail 56 lbs. per yard, spikes, frogs, and switch irons. Sixteen first class locomotives of from twenty to twenty-eight tons weight. Seventeen first class passenger cars, four second class passenger cars, four baggage and mail cars, seventy first class box freight cars, seventy platform and cattle cars, sixty gravel cars, also to expend $50,000 upon water tanks, station houses, woodsheds. The company was to pay therefor $33,000 per mile of main track and $28,000 per mile for side track. The company was to furnish right of way, quarry privileges, and surveys, roadways etc.[7]

The County subscription had been decreed invalid. Our individual subscriptions, owing to the discredit cast on the enterprise, were far short of anticipations and upon conditions. Our 1st mortgage was but $2,500,000, and outside of construction contract the company had to provide for engineering, right of way, and incidental expenses. It was evident that our means were far short of what was necessary for the work. Indeed, we had nothing beyond the bonds and stock of the company on which to rely to any extent. All this was fully explained to the contractors, who decided to undertake the work with all its risks—trusting to future negotiations and increase of subscriptions under more prosperous times in the financial world.

It was arranged between Doolittle and McHenry that the latter should at his own cost negotiate the bonds of the company for the contractors, and furnish 31,000 tons of rails and cash. He, McHenry, was to receive as compensation a certain proportion of the bonds at 75 cents and stock at par. It was agreed between Kennard, Doolittle, and Streator and the A&GW RR Company in New York, that Doolittle and Streator should build the New York division for the same rate as paid by the Penna. company per mile, with the proportion of equipment and expenditure for tanks, stations, &c.[8]

During June and July the surveys in New York were vigorously prosecuted and a considerable part of the line located through Busti. Right of way agents were kept busily at work and the line located from the New York line to Union [Mills].

The Austro-Sardinian War however, paralyzed all negotiations for a time in Europe, and the news during May and June was not encouraging but McHenry wrote June 25th: "I have been in Paris some days. I sent Salamanca copies of Reynolds' letters relative to organization of the New York company and made requisition for £50,000. This ends all uncertainty and enables us to proceed. . . . But until now I did not feel that we were in a position for action. . . . Kennard makes a determined fight for delay. . . . He has also been urging me to make terms with Irvin and Hallett, which under no circumstances can be admitted."

July 8. General Dick, Church, and I were elected into the Ohio Board of Directors.

July 12. McHenry was at Paris with Salamanca. July 29th McHenry and Kennard were with Salamanca at Paris and McHenry writes that Kennard is removing his family to Dieppe preparatory to leaving to U.S.: "Had a most agreeable interview with Salamanca. Kennard and

Train present. I receive £50,000 of Salamanca in 1, 2, & 3 months and propose to complete to Union Mills forthwith."

Before the above letters were received I had written letters July 12 and 21, and also to Kennard asking explicit and definite information, as to progress and their intentions as to the work. I stated: "The entire line is now perfect in its organization. The New York portion, reduced in distance as I before stated, is ready for the contractors to begin work. It can be finished very rapidly there being no heavy work to delay; although it is highly important that all bridge foundations should be laid before fall rains. The right of way is in great measure secured. The Penna. portion east of Meadville is all ready for the [work], and also west of Meadville with the exception of a few sections, where it is expected to make considerable improvement. The failure to meet public expectation excited by the promises made by Kennard and Train of early commencement of work has shaken the faith of many in our ultimate success."[9]

The Directors of the E&NY City RR Co. were naturally much alarmed with the prospect of a road being built parallel with their line and becoming a rival interest and the citizens of Jamestown were equally so at the certainty of their town being left some miles from a railway of such importance. Overtures were made to our company for arrangements which should include their road and utilize the work already done. The complication of that company with Morton's construction contract seemed to preclude all adjustment until that difficulty could be removed.

Sept. 10. Thallon writes [that] Hallett says if McHenry will pay certain commissions his creditors will buy $120,000 of bonds at 75 and pay cash as soon as the work shall be begun, as they are all banks and strong men and influential. I think it would be worth $200,000 to $300,000 to us. Doolittle and myself have strongly recommended it be done.

Sept. 27. McHenry: "Kennard pays a farewell visit tomorrow to his wife at Boulogne and will be accompanied by his father to America. This will give us great force, as his father is a member of Parliament, etc. etc."

Nov. 3. Church met Irvin who had powers from McHenry in the Hallett negotiation. This arrangement was entirely outside of the company, and Church was acting as counsel for McHenry. The negotiation was long and tedious, and in the end resulted in little of actual benefit to the railway, but was nevertheless one of the important episodes in the history of the A&GW RR and consequently deserves notice. Church wrote me [that] the bonds to be subscribed for are to be the Penna. and Ohio in proportion to length of each road. . . . Subscription bonds by creditors $220,000; Hallett to procure sale for $120,000 Ohio 2nd mortgage at 75 per cent, thus making $340,000.

Dec. 1. Left with General Dick and Church to attend meeting of Ohio board at Cleveland. Day very stormy with rain and wind. The roads almost impassable, with deep mud. Arrived at Weddell House, Cleveland. In the evening met with the board of directors and Doolittle. The important question was on the report of Ward, and a question as to certain bonds yet held by him as trustee. A committee was appointed to report the facts.

Dec. 2. Business occupied the entire day, the board not adjourning until late in the afternoon. We left Cleveland at 9:00 P.M. but did not reach Girard until 1:30 A.M.; very stormy, with snow and sleet.

Dec. 3. Left Girard at 8:00 A.M., weather very cold and stormy: The deep mud was frozen almost but not quite enough to bear the weight of the horses, who constantly broke through the frozen crust. We reached Crossingville in the afternoon completely chilled, and arrived home late in the evening after one of the most uncomfortable rides in my remembrance.

The E&NY City Co. again made overtures for an arrangement to occupy their line of road, and I sent J. B. Taylor, our assistant engineer in state of New York, to Jamestown to examine the engineering notes and profiles in their office and report to me. This he did in the middle of the month. Morton still was in the way, but the E&NY City Co. thought he could be disposed of in some manner by their company.

A letter written by Kennard to Hallett, dated December 6, was at this time published in the New York papers, stating that "With the sale of the bonds already made sufficient funds are provided to complete the road to Akron, Ohio."

Dec. 14. Anticipating from advices Kennard's arrival at New York, I left in sleigh for Waterford, there to join excursion party from Erie to Warren to celebrate the opening of the S&E RR. We remained at Cook's in [Waterford] over night, and on the morning of the 15th joined the party, chiefly citizens of Erie. We arrived at Warren and were made the guests of Thos. Struthers. A dinner was provided in Johnson Hall for four hundred guests, and the dinner and speeches lasted until 9 in the evening. We afterwards attended the ball given by the citizens, who deserved much credit for the completeness of their arrangements for the pleasure of the occasion.

Dec. 16. I left Warren and arrived in New York on the 17th (5th Ave. Hotel). Ramsdell called in the evening. Kennard had arrived [the previous week] and on the next morning I called to see him, but did not succeed in seeing him until the next day. He stated that including the iron he had at call £50,000.

Dec. 20. Received telegram from Hill stating he would be here tonight. Kennard sent for me to meet him at the New York Hotel, and seemed much worried with regard to the money paid Ward and Doolittle by McHenry and not accounted for by them.

Dec. 21. With Hill called to see Kennard, and from there to Thallon's. In the afternoon met Ward and Kennard at New York Hotel, and afterwards commenced preparation of the contract with Doolittle and Streator for the New York Division, which, with the assistance of Church, was completed satisfactorily to all parties the next day.

Ward having gone to New York, and there being a majority of the executive committee of the Penna. company they demanded of Ward a settlement of his bond accounts with the company. He refused to treat with them in the matter, but stated that he had no claim against the Penna. company whatever. Ward held $9,000 of Penna. bonds unaccounted for, independent of $1,000 he had given Chevelin Wicoff for his services.

The close of 1859, the eighth year from the first railway efforts, was marked by no actual construction for the year. The early part of the year was rendered useless to us by the conflict with Ward and Morton's control of the contract of the E&NY City road, and the eventual necessity of organizing a new company. The Austro-Sardinian War next paralyzed financial efforts abroad. A misunderstanding between McHenry and Kennard seems to have caused distrust and further delay. Change of arrangements between McHenry and Leon Lillo and Salamanca postponed the consummation yet further, while the attempt to raise means through Hallett's creditors diverted efforts from more reliable methods.

While these causes of delay were appreciated by those passing the information, the public were naturally disappointed in results so different from what had been [expected], and became skeptical with regard to any statement as to the prospects of the future. This distrust of the success of the project was fostered by the industrious efforts of the opponents of the road, so that at the very time when we were prepared to commence our work, no enthusiasm could be aroused when so important for prestige abroad.

What was also unfortunate for the company was that, relying on the rose colored promises made on the first visit of Kennard, Train, Ward, and Doolittle, the Penna. company had (to give confidence) limited their subscriptions to the condition of a certain amount of work to be completed in two years from that date. This subscription was approaching its limit and no work yet commenced and in the face of such facts the company could not add to their subscriptions.

❧ 3. Building the Road, 1860

Problems increased for Reynolds and the company. McHenry complained that he was not furnished with an adequate supply of securities. Reynolds responded by accusing McHenry's agents of illegal disbursement of proceeds from the sale of bonds; he feared that lack of control and accountability might result in disaster. It was the beginning of an endless confrontation between the two men. Reynolds also had to ward off overtures of the Erie RR to operate the A&GW RR. In addition to nagging financial stress, U.S. Customs seized a quantity of iron rails imported from England for improper invoicing. Despite these difficulties, the line was opened to Jamestown, New York, in August 1860.

Bonds, Rails, and Spikes

Jan 2. Thallon advises me of the receipt of another £4,000, making £8,000 within the fortnight; with instructions, "You will use these in case only that Reynolds has agreed to the Erie Contract." The Erie RR Co. as represented by English interests, were desirous at this early day to secure the operating of our line. As will be seen hereafter, they made a determined effort for a lease when the line was opened to Jamestown, and my positive refusal to sign the lease was the cause of much hostility to me by English Erie RR directors.

Church, for McHenry, went to New York where he was engaged in the Hallett and creditors negotiation from January 12 to 31, when he wrote me, "The subscription is completed at last and some $12,000 over." Kennard sends his certificate to Salamanca. He also drew a draft for £5,000.

Jan. 4. McHenry: "Everything wears a very bright appearance now. All difficulties, and they have been very serious owing to early mismanagement, have been surmounted. . . . I am preparing the Paris market for the New York bonds."

Jan. 20. Hallett subscription to date $165,000. 2,000 tons of iron arrived. Work can commence week after next.

A meeting was held in Warren early in the month, and resolutions passed asking for survey and location of our line through Warren county.

Jan. 31. Doolittle and Streator have ordered their cars on for the commencement of work. [Doolittle] to be at Cleveland first of week.

Purchase of the Erie & New York City RR

During the last week of January a delegation from Jamestown representing the E&NY City road visited Meadville with overtures for the occupation of their line.[1] They proposed that they would rid themselves of Morton and his contract, and would transfer their road to the A&GW Co. on their own terms. It was of course impossible to make definite propositions on either side until the E&NY City Co. should be relieved from the Morton contract. The large amount of work done and the right of way secured rendered the arrangement desirable if it could be consummated on fair terms.

Feb. 15. Left at noon with Doolittle, Streator, and General Dick and reached Waterford in time for the cars at 5:00 P.M. and arrived at Columbus at 6:30, where we met Kennard and Hill and Sexton, our right of way and subscription agent.

Feb. 16. Spent the day on the line arranging for right of way etc. In the evening Allen, Hall, Shaw, and Williams, of the E&NY City company arrived, and the evening was spent in the discussion of the

Jamestown route. I had instructed Hill to examine their line and office notes and make report. This report he made to me on the 18th, and strongly advised that arrangements for one securing their road should be consummated. The amount of expenditure on the road $261,000, and estimated to complete $133,000.

Feb. 22. From Diary. Wednesday I left home at noon in buggy with my horses. Day warm and clear, and snow almost gone. Roads muddy. Took plank road to Cambridge, Johnstown to Union [Mills]. One of the horses having lost a shoe, left my team to be sent to Columbus in the morning, and took the cars, where I met Judge Miles, and arrived at Columbus where I met Streator, Sexton, and Engineer Taylor, and corps.

Feb. 23. After breakfast, Hall, Baker, Chamberlain, and Shaw called and spent the morning in explanation of the condition of their road. I afterwards consulted with [S. E.] Marvin and Bennett on the legal points involved in the transfer of the road, and the necessity of legislation. After a full consultation it was decided to apply for the requisite legislation. In the afternoon with Baker and Marvin, walked over the line in the town, and afterwards Marvin drove me to Dexterville. The work I saw appears to be well done. In the evening I drew a bill to be presented to the legislature for the authority of transfer and purchase of the E&NY City road.

The E&NY City Co. agree to send a committee and close everything with Morton. This with the legislation will leave the way open for adoption of that line. The legislation authorizing the transfer of the E&NY City RR passed.

First Dispute with McHenry

March 14. I wrote in full to McHenry calling his attention to the irregularities which at this early stage had caused embarrassment by the failure to strictly adhere to the instructions of the company, stating that all the negotiations were based on the contracts of Doolittle and Streator. That Ward and Reynolds were the duly appointed trustees. That by Ward's resignation, Reynolds was the sole trustee. That all funds and rails obtained for shares or bonds of the company, and all moneys arising from negotiations was to be subject to the direction of the trustee. All bills or deposits made for remission to U.S. should be made payable to order of trustee and shipped in the name of the trustees to the Port of the City of New York.

That all funds and iron sent to New York should be subject to the orders of the president, drawn upon the certificate of the engineer. All iron consigned to "Wm. Reynolds, Trustee of the A&GW RR of Pa.," and bills of lading sent to "Wm. Reynolds, care of R. Thallon, N.Y.," [as defined in the instructions sent with the power of attorney.]

"You will notice (what appeared to have been entirely overlooked) that this trust forms the basis upon which the negotiations for the Penna. [company] have been conducted. It is one of the most important parts of the financial machinery of the company and all the details have been most carefully prepared to harmonize with it after full and mature consideration of all parties in interest. The interested European parties having been represented by Fallon. This feature cannot be overlooked now or the arrangements changed without endangering the success our plans. No legal power exists to make the disposition of one dollar of the funds of the Penna. company except through its agency. And any unauthorized changes will involve a personal responsibility . . . I shall not incur.

"It follows, 1st. All money, iron, or material obtained by you for the Penna. company must be placed to the credit of the company.

2nd. That therefore all moneys, letters of credit, and iron must be remitted to me as trustee of the company.

3rd. Every other disposition of the property of the company under the existing contractual powers is illegal.

"You see the working result of change by the position we now occupy. Your report shows an expenditure of Penna. company bonds of $160,000. Yet the books of the company do not show that they have received one ton of iron or one dollar of money. . . . I have received no official notice of the money or iron to our credit."

The above condensed extracts show the evils I attempted to avert at this early period.

March 20. Cold and snow. We walked to the work near [Columbus] and then drove to Pine Valley and saw Baker regarding right of way. Left Columbus [for] New York [and found] Doolittle very ill.

March 26. Advices from Europe £5,000 paid but some mistake with bankers, who will not pay until further advices which will delay until 17th—a disagreeable dilemma.

March 27. Prospects no brighter. In the morning with Church made statement of bonds and coupons prepared for Hallett negotiation. Called on [Henry A.] Kent[2] relative to an office in his store for the New York company.

March 28. The *Washington* in, but no further news. Things look very blue. We determined to raise $2,000 on the Hallett securities.

March 29. Another steamer, but no news. Drew from Bank of Commerce and Cont. Bank and paid note of Doolittle at Winslow and Lannier of $1,000.

March 30. Saw Doolittle today and found him better, but yet quite ill. The E&NY City Company have arranged all their business with Morton and the road is now open for purchase.

April 5. [Returned to Meadville.] Church, General Dick, and Reynolds, Committee of A&GW in NY met the Committee of the E&NY City Co. and spent a great part of the day in propositions and counter propositions, without definite result. Have given them our ultimatum to consider until tomorrow, when our efforts will terminate.

April 6. We again met the Committee of the E&NY City Company this morning, and arrived [at] a satisfactory arrangement and signed the preliminary contract for submission to the stockholders of the companies. Also executed the mortgage of the A&GW in NY for $1,250,000.

April 10. [With] my horses and buggy left home with Streator via Plank road and Marvin's Mills.[3] The day was rainy and the water in the creek very high. Roads very bad. Left Waterford at 5 in cars. The road from Columbus station was very deep and we left in a pouring rain. At one place the mud covered the axletrees and both singletrees were broken, leaving us helpless in the sea of mud until relieved by a passing wagon from our awkward [predicament].

During the evening transacted business of the engineers corps with

Hill, and talked with Waldron relative to the adoption of his patent chair[4] on the road.

April 11. Heavy rain last night and snow this morning. Paid Hill $1,000, also engineering account in full to April, $304.70, and to Sexton to arrange damage claims, $116.50. Made contract with H. D. Frances for fencing. Gave instructions to Hill and a notice to the contractors as to the quality of ties being delivered.

April 16. Left [Meadville] with General Dick, Church, Shryock, and Prof. Williams in the stage. A severe thunder storm in the night made the roads very muddy. The Ohio board met this evening and decided to remove the 1100 tons of iron now in New York to Cleveland.

April 17. At a meeting of the A&GW RR in NY the president reported the execution of a mortgage of $1,250,000 in pursuance of instructions of May 21, 1859, substituting Samuel Marsh, Esq., of New York as trustee in place of J. S. Huber, who declined to accept, dated May 25, 1859.

Also submitted for approval the contract with the E&NY City Company and the construction contract with Doolittle and Streator in pursuance of authority of May 1859.

I again was obliged to call attention of the agents of McHenry to the illegal disbursement of the proceeds of the company bonds. The last £5,000 having been appropriated and disbursed by Thallon and Kennard without vouchers from the proper officers of the company.

April 26. Doolittle, on account of failing health, sails for Cuba, giving a power of attorney to A. T. Purdon of Cincinnati to act for him. Purdon was a narrow minded man, and gave much trouble by constant and unwarranted interference.

The Work Progresses

As mentioned before, our Penna. subscriptions were on condition of completion of grading to Meadville within two years. This limit was approaching and as it was evident that the condition was not within the reach of possibility, an effort was made to renew the subscription, but met with little success. Some who had faith in the work being carried forward by European capital withheld any further personal [commitment]. Others were influenced by reports industriously circulated that the connection would be made from Union [Mills] to Erie, and the line would not be extended further west. Great dissatisfaction was caused in the vicinity of Cambridge by the abandonment of some large tie contracts, this giving color to the reports mentioned. It was determined for a time to make no further effort to extend the subscription.

The £5,000 [from McHenry] were received on the 31st.[5]

May 1. After breakfast saw several parties relative to fencing and walked through Pine Valley. The work is mostly done except what is left for abutments.

May 2. After breakfast went to the RR office and saw Hill, who was about to start for Bucktooth; obtained a list of the land holders from [J. C.] Calhoun.[6] Marvin and Hall called and with them we went to see Allen who is confined to the house. Phelps is here with teams en route for Bucktooth.

May 3. After breakfast Church and I went on the line. Afterwards saw Dr. Brown, Crowley, and Sheldon about depot grounds. Passed engineer Coolman laying out bridge foundations at Hatch. Met Hill and Streator, [who] wishes me to arrange with Erie RR Company for locomotive and cars for construction. Walked around "Meeting House" Hill and Jamison Hill. [Saw that] over one hundred hands are at work and making good progress. A large number are engaged in cutting ties. After dining at Boardman's, Phelps sent us in a wagon to Great Valley where we took the cars to New York. I am well satisfied with our purchase from the Jamestown company. All the work has been done in a substantial manner. There is not much heavy work remaining except along the Allegheny River and at Kennedyville. We were well received along the line and found all willing and anxious to assist the work. The contrast was very great between the feeling of the citizens in this state and of those in Penna., where every obstacle is placed in the way of progress.

May 4. We arrived at the 5th Avenue Hotel. After dinner we called at Robertson and Seibert's to urge speed in engraving the New York bonds.

May 5. After breakfast we called on Marsh with the deed of [trust] of the New York division for his signature as trustee. Then to the engravers of the bonds and from there to Thallon's where we met Kennard. Letters from Europe satisfactory except in remittance of money which is promised for next week.

From Thallon's we went to Kent and Lowber on Broad Street to arrange an office for the New York company. Then to the Erie RR office and saw [Superintendent] Minot who promised to send a locomotive and grampers car[7] to Bucktooth.

May 9. With Church met Kennard at Thallon's and with them went to S. L. M. Barlow[8] to consult him on some legal points. Drew check in favor of Erie RR Co. for Streator for freight on iron chairs etc. In the afternoon met Marsh and Minot at Erie RR office about freight bills and rent of engine, and with Church and Kennard left New York.

May 10. Breakfast at Hornellsville. The conductor stopped at the junction and we obtained a wagon at Boardman's and rode to Jamison Hill around which we walked in deep mud and with a pouring rain. Much work has been done since we were here and another week will finish to Meeting House Hill. We were here overtaken by King with a carriage from Little Valley. We dined at Randolph and arrived at Jamestown at 7 o'clock. We had a heavy rain all afternoon.

May 11. Settled estimate of Doolittle and Streator by draft for $6,000 and note paid by Church from Hallett negotiation, $1,000. Met Marvin, Allen, and Hall. Kennard and Hill went to Pine Valley and Church drew form of resolution for the E&NY City Co. confirmatory of the sale. Total estimate $13,460.57. We took the stage for Warren Pennsylvania and from there home.

On the 8th of May I found it necessary to again write to Ward to insist on the immediate return of $5,000 of bonds yet in his hands. On the same day Thallon received a draft from McHenry of £5,000. To McHenry I wrote: "We are in much perplexity in our company for want of the information relative to the disposition of our bonds desired in my letter of last of March. . . . May I again call your attention to the contents of the letter. The books of the company do not show as they should, the business transactions relative to the sale or negotiations of the bonds."

At this time (May 5th) McHenry: "I met Goddard . . . and taken into consideration your letter of March 24th with a view to regularly furnishing you the desired information in due form. . . . I have made very extensive arrangements on the Continent for such advances of money as makes me feel confident that we can now proceed to a conclusion without any hesitation beyond what Providence dictates." On May 19th McHenry again: "I am sure you will pardon my delay in replying categorically to yours of March 24th knowing how much I am occupied and how unsettled I have been. . . . However Meron, Goddard, and I have all your views in consideration for the purpose of giving them effect in best possible way, and hope soon to reply to you at length. . . . I shall complete rails this month sufficient to reach to Union Mills, say 7,000 tons but I'm awkwardly placed in absence of New York bonds which I hope will soon be removed by this arrival."

I also wrote another letter to Ward insisting on the immediate return of the $5,000 of bonds in his hands, and also asking the nature of the services rendered by "Chevelin" Wicoff in consideration of the $1,000 bond transferred to him. This information was never given, although the $5,000 were eventually delivered to the company.

May 24. Left in Linesville stage [then] for Mayville. Mrs. Allen was a passenger, rendering the trip a pleasant one. The evening was beautiful for the sail over lake [Chautauqua] in a rather antiquated specimen of steamboat. Arrived at Jamestown House where I spent the evening with Hill and Thatcher, contractor for the Cassadaga Bridge.

May 25. Visited the office and examined accounts with Calhoun. Walked to see the bridge masonry, met Streator and had conversation about my notice to him regarding ties and grading. Arrived at Great Valley. Thirty carloads of iron are at Bucktooth but no chairs.

May 26. Met Allen and Thorp on the cars. Breakfasted at Port Jervis and arrived in the City at 10:30.

May 30. Met Kennard and Waldron at Barlow's office and arranged for the use of his [Waldron's] chair for ten miles of road.

June 1. Wrote to McHenry explaining the delay in execution of the New York company's bonds from the delay in the location owing to the negotiations of the E&NY City Co. and the necessity of this for the making of the mortgage, and again called attention to my letter of March 24th and the failure to supply the report asked.

June 6. In the morning prepared right of way papers at office, and, with Church, drove to Kennedyville and Randolph for dinner, and walked over the line from Ewing's to Marsh and to Steamburg.[9] Saw many parties in relation to fencing, and returned to Randolph in the evening, where we met Crowley, Spencer, and others in relation to depot grounds.

June 12. To Thallon: "We are busy in the preparation of the necessary papers for McHenry. . . . The bonds have not yet come from New York. . . . I went to Jamestown on Tuesday expecting according to appointment with Kennard and was much disappointed by his absence. . . . The doctor [Streator] was obliged to borrow $6,000 to meet his Penna. payments of Saturday and I had to advance for the immediate necessities of the Engineer dept. This was annoying. . . . I also telegraphed for $2,000 for Pa. Co. but not one word in return. Next week, the payment to E&NY City RR falls due . . . Will you please see that a draft for the amount is at once forwarded to Allen who has given his own paper payable in New York for the E&NY City Company."

June 19. With Allen called on Kennard relative to the payment of the E&NY City Co. of $6,266.25. There are no funds on hand but a remittance is expected on next steamer. Kennard signed a draft for the amount which I take with me. Allen writes to Todd to protect his notes in case of failure of remittance. Kennard also signed draft on Continental Bank for $294. Left Jamestown with Church, General Dick, and Cullum with Church's horses. The work has made much progress. The water has been turned into the new channel at Kennedyville. Dined at Randolph where we were joined by Hill and Kennard. We took Hill and Kennard in our wagon and drove to Coldspring expecting to find the locomotive, but it had gone to Bucktooth for spikes. We were obliged to leave Hill and Kennard and drove to Great Valley just in time for the cars. General Dick drove the horses back.

June 20. We arrived in [New York] City. Church went direct to Merrill's office and I to Thallon's where I learned to my great satisfaction of the arrival of £8,000, and telegraphed the fact to Allen. I sent McHenry the Power of Attorney for New York company with very definite instructions and a plain letter in which I said: "You will notice that your powers are very definite and distinct with regard to the disposition of all iron, money, or other property received on negotiation of company bonds. . . . They require that the relation between you as their agent and attorney, and the company, should be immediate and direct. They can recognize no other agents than those appointed by themselves. . . . By close adherence to definite rules all interests will be perfectly protected without possibility of wrong or injury to any party or interest, while a departure from the same will result in confusion if not in serious disaster." Merrill dined with us and in the evening we accompanied him to the Atheneum Club.

McHenry: "Your views and explanations are very satisfactory and clear. . . . I sent to Thallon today bills of lading which completes 7,000 tons rail, which will take you to Union Mills. I am quite ready to proceed soon as you desire me. . . . I find I cannot make the [account] in your form exactly, though this information amount to the same thing. . . . I think we have decided on a form of which will be intelligible. . . . I shall endeavor to send [by] *Persia* a statement of Penna. bonds received in London and of my withdrawals. . . . I hope you will have a cheering celebration of your entrance into Jamestown to be followed by a similar demonstration at Union Mills."

June 21. Found very satisfactory letters from McHenry at Thallon's. Called on Marsh to inform him about the bonds being ready for his signature, and went to the Erie RR offices and paid $2,500.00 on account. Wrote McHenry statement of condition of New York company organized in May of 1859.[10]

June 22. Went to Warren and gave Todd a draft for $6,625.25 to meet the payment to the E&NY City Co. then to 45 John St. and found the bonds signed by Secy. Went to Thallon's, where I met Crooks, who wants money (on iron purchase of McHenry). Am fearful the £8,000 will be absorbed long before the next installment arrives.

June 23. Wrote to Secretary of State for certified copy of charter of the New York company. Grey, Waldron, and Tindel were here yesterday and went to Philadelphia to superintend the manufacture of the "Waldron Chair." Telegram received from Bucktooth "Out of spikes" but letter from Phila. giving shipment of 120 kegs. Telegraphed to Bucktooth for engine to meet us on Monday.

Extract from one of my letters from Jamestown, 25th: "Having telegraphed for the train to wait we had the pleasure of a ride over some dozen miles of the Atlantic & Great Western Railroad. The work is now progressing finely, and all along the line it really looks like business. It is almost the first time I have really felt that we were making a road; but it is now among the fixed facts, and no longer to be classed among the 'theories of a few crazy people.' Kennard has instructed the contractors to place a large force on the line west of Jamestown and McHenry writes to Kennard to prepare for active prosecution of the work to Meadville as soon as possible."

June 26. Streator returned last evening, also [Marvin] Kent, and the large corps of bridge builders with Thatcher the contractor. Calhoun copied the deed of trust which was placed in P.O. by Church for Marsh. After dinner Church and I drove to Poland Center;[11] saw Crosby and Liddell relative to fencing and right of way claims, and to the Cassadaga crossing.

June 27. Sent Calhoun to Cleveland and Buffalo to examine and study the various methods of accounts in the railroad offices. With Allen, Hall, Baker, Kent, Shaw, Church, and Hill examined ground for location of depot and after dinner with Church, Allen, and Williams rode over the western part of the line.

July 4. Kennard from Jamestown: "I am in the greatest fix about your check, as there are no funds at disposal to meet it after paying duties on rails, freight, chairs, etc. I had only $10,000 left, and when I arrived found an absolute call for this money, also for $1,200 for the engineers. I hope next week we shall be in funds."

July 5. Left with Church and J. M. Dick via Conneautville. Shryock met us at the depot. Dined at Erie. Dusty ride to Westfield and

Mayville. Passed Kennard between the two last places. Examined estimates and right of way papers [at Jamestown]. After, with Allen and Church drove to Ashville calling on many on the line.

July 7. After Breakfast left with Shryock, Streator, J.M. Dick, and Purdon. Church remained to look after right of way, etc. We had a delightful sail over the lake until near Mayville, when we were overtaken by a violent storm which continued until we reached Westfield. Arrived home by the Conneautville express.

I sent to the trustees in London $300,000 of the New York bonds with letter of instructions. "These bonds are sent to you to be held in trust for the purposes indicated in the letter of attorney, and instructions to James McHenry Esq. a copy of which and of the instructions is herewith enclosed to you. . . . In all cases you will take duplicate receipts setting forth the numbers and denomination of the bonds delivered and transmit one of the receipts to Wm. Reynolds, President of the Atlantic & Great Western R.R. Co. in New York directing the same to Meadville, state of Penna., U.S."

July 9. Church, after passing over the line east of Jamestown, went to New York to attend to business connected with the Hallett negotiation, which after all the time and trouble [threatened] to prove abortive. He wrote: "The *Fulton* did not bring our money but the mails the *Glasgow* brings is expected tomorrow. All promise well—but we shall see."

July 11. To McHenry: "From letters of the 25th we presume the bills covering the £12,000 drafts are in the *Arabia*, which reached Halifax yesterday but her mails from Boston may not be here before tomorrow. You may well suppose I am quite nervous about it. I dare not *telegraph* the Doctor until I know they are safe at hand. I was at Bank of Sing Sing yesterday; no money there. We go today to the American Ex. Bank today for our packages of bonds. How we shall succeed is in the future entirely. . . . Hallett saying he will be ready to pay $20,000 next week, but you know he cannot so there is nothing in that at all. . . . I have had two very satisfactory interviews with Merrill. I now promised him a full brief of our . . . testimony (relative to the suit of Morton vs. Penna. company) which you said you would prepare. . . . I have just learned another trouble about the iron. 4,000 bars here are below the New York standard of 56 lbs., being only a little over 50 lbs. The punch for the Waldron Chair is not yet shipped from Holyoke."

July 13. Church: "No word of the bills from McHenry yet. Expected by the *City of Baltimore* tonight."

"I find more perplexity to get rid of the Hallett subscription than to obtain it. . . . We are preparing to fix the offence of forgery and embezzlement on poor Hallett. . . . Is it not a wonder any in Europe trust us when we are in so bad repute at home—contractors and all."

July 17. "Still here. It is supposed the *Africa*, due tomorrow, will bring our credit. . . . The lithographers are preparing the Penna. certificates of shares. . . . McHenry wants all the bonds before he puts them on the market. We should give him no more unless he indemnifies the company. I can easily see how a designing man could sell our road out in spite of us."

At this time the Ohio company gave an order for the delivery of 600 tons of iron consigned to them on payment of freight and deposit of $20,000 of New York bonds as security for delivery of a like quantity of rails to the Ohio Co. when required.

July 18. Went over the work at [Jamestown]. The quicksand cut is nearly finished and the masonry for the bridge over the outlet is in a forward state. At 10, with Allen and Streator, I drove to Ashville, where we were joined by Williams and went on the line to secure right of way with good success. The day was very stormy, and we returned in the rain at nine and found Thorp and Purdon at hotel.

Financial Headaches

The work is progressing well on the line, but our business matters are as usual in a very unsatisfactory condition. Kennard is not here, and I have concluded to leave in the morning for New York and make another effort to place matters right. In fact, if we do not give great care and constant supervision everything would end in disaster. I sometimes feel discouraged with the constant effort to prevent the evil likely to result from the manner that others over whom we have no control manage business.

July 23. With Streator left for New York by Chautauqua Lake, Westfield and Dunkirk. Heavy rain on the lake.

July 24. Breakfasted at Port Jervis and arrived at New York at 10:30. Sent baggage to 5th Avenue Hotel and with Streator went to Thallon's where we met Church and Kennard. The money has not come yet. A telegram from Halifax states that it was sent by the *North Britain* whose mails will be due tomorrow from St. John.

July 25. Money not yet at hand. All in status quo. At Hallett's request called at his office in Beaver Street and had a long talk about his connection with the McHenry negotiation, he claiming that all the European negotiations were originated by himself before McHenry was known in the European arrangements.

July 26. No word from the *North Britain* mails.

July 27. Called on Marsh, trustee, and obtained $20,000 of the New York company bonds and gave them to [Henry] Kent and received order for the 600 tons Ohio iron in bond. Met Brink, agent of Dean, Kuhle & Co., who are supplying chairs. They refuse to forward the chairs unless Streator will give his notes for the price, which he refuses to do. Copy of letter of credit for £6,500 was today received by the *Vigo*.

I wrote McHenry in reply to his letter of June 29, forwarded to me from Meadville, the extracts from mine will give the tenor of his.

"I was surprised at your proposed limit of the present issue to the bonds of the New York company, as all your previous letters indicated the intention to place *all* the bonds on the market simultaneously. . . . I was more than disappointed by the failure to receive the promised statement of the Pennsylvania bonds. You will bear in mind that for a year past this has been constantly asked of you, and from time to time promised. In your last letter you state that you hope to send it by the *Persia* and you now virtually *decline* to furnish it, on the allegation 'that until a regular issue of your bonds is made we are acting rather for the contractors than the companies,' and therefore our returns should be addressed to the contractors. When your bonds are realized we are then bound to account to you for the proceeds and place them at your disposal. . . .

"I am utterly at a loss to see the force of your reasoning. There is certainly a serious misunderstanding between us in relation to the position you occupy with regard to the company.

"The company made a contract with Doolittle and Streator for the building and equipment of the road in the state of Pennsylvania. The bonds under that contract were placed in the hands of Meron and Goddard as trustees for both parties, and could only be drawn upon compliance with certain conditions.

"You contracted with Doolittle to furnish money and iron to a certain extent. After much time and effort you applied to the company for an investment of authority to carry out this contract. In other words, you asked a power of attorney direct from the company.

"This the company granted, giving very ample powers. With this power of attorney instructions of a very definite character were sent, and you accepted the agency with the accompanying instructions. One of the essential requirements of those instructions was *monthly returns of negotiations of the bonds of the company.*

"Now, I cannot conceive what 'a regular public issue' has to do with your monthly return to the company. To them it makes no difference whether the sale is a *private* one or a *public* issue. They wish to know how many bonds have been disposed of and for what purposes. They desire this simply as an ordinary business transaction that their records may show their financial condition. And upon this return being promptly made, the company will insist. Every confidence has been reposed in you. The bonds have been freely placed at your disposal and from time to time changes and modifications have been made at your suggestion in the plans. Yet thus far no act has been performed on your part in strict compliance with your instructions. Neither money nor iron has been forwarded as required by them. . . .

"I did not in any manner alter or change your relations or duties to the company as you seem to indicate in the following: 'The matter of shipment and remittances in proper form has been overcome by your arrangement with Thallon and Kennard.' . . . With over $2,000,000 of bonds out, not one of us can inform a stockholder of the specific disposition of them. Your report of the past winter shows the expenditure of $160,000 for money, freight and iron, but neither the amount nor quantity of either item."

July 30. Arranged with Belmont & Co. for an overdraft of $20,000 by deposit of $40,000 New York company bonds, to guard against irregularity of receiving remittances.

July 31. Found engine at Bucktooth. At Randolph, Hill met me with a carriage.

July 21. McHenry: "I have now great satisfaction in addressing that I have *almost* completed arrangements with Denniston, Cross & Co. to issue the New York loan. They write to Denniston, Wood & Co. of New York this mail and I shall be glad if you can see Wood immediately in order to afford to him every information. A successful issue to the public of the New York section will enable me to proceed to Dayton without a day's delay hence the vast importance of making every arrangement most securely. I hope you have forwarded the $400,000 [New York] bonds ($600,000 received) and the official cancellation of the surplus."

Aug. 7. I wrote to McHenry advising him that I had forwarded to New York the balance of the $1,000,000 of New York bonds to be forwarded to him when the board should so direct. At the same time notifying him that the $400,000 were by terms of the contract specifically applied to the contract, and although sent with their consent, they were sent with special and modified instructions to the trustees. "I sincerely hope you will be able to make arrangements by which we can have remittances here at least thirty days in advance, to guard our contractors against accidental contingencies in the arrival of funds."

The Instructions to Trustees provided, "You will deliver these bonds to J. McHenry, agent and attorney of said company upon his delivery to you therefor of cash or satisfactory bankers' bills or such evidence of absolute sale of said bonds for cash or bankers' bills on account of the said company as shall be satisfactory." Owing to the opposition of Prudon, attorney for Doolittle, the bonds were not sent forward until authorized by resolution of New York board August 18. Prudon served a formal notice forbidding sending them forward.

Aug. 9. Thallon: "I have not the balance of the money yet as McHenry has not been able to strike Salamanca, who was wandering about. Fallon was here yesterday and he and Church fixed up everything nicely."

McHenry, under the date of Aug. 26: "The only unpleasant part of my position is non access to Salamanca who is daily expected in Lisbon, Madrid, and Paris, and the £6,000 hangs fire until he can be communicated with. The £12,000 has gone forward and I doubt not in a few days all will be duly honored. I have no doubt I can manage the additional £10,000."

Aug. 14. Walked to [Jamestown] depot grounds with Streator. Spent most of the morning in arrangements of damage and fencing claims and contracts. With Allen and Streator arranged with the Chautauqua Co. Bank for an advance of $20,000 on deposit of New York Bonds as collateral. After dinner drove to Kennedyville and found the track layers and locomotive at that point. At five started on the engine taking Waldron at Randolph. At Bucktooth telegraphed to Dunkirk for cars to stop, and left at midnight.

Aug. 15. Breakfast at Deposit.[12] Met Tindell on train. Reached New York, sent baggage to 5th Ave Hotel and went direct to Thallon's. Found no money. All the 7,000 tons of iron has arrived. The letters from Europe give very faint hope of receipts in time to save us from trouble. Found the 5th Ave full and went to St. Dennis. Called at New York Hotel to see Kennard without success. Prospects certainly look very gloomy. For diversion of thought went to Niblo's,[13] but could take no interest and left.

Aug. 16. Slept little from thinking of our difficulties. Not finding Kennard at the New York Hotel went to Thallon's. Kennard came in and we there had a full talk over the prospects. It is proposed to relieve the present pressure to raise money on such portion of the iron as not immediately needed for the New York portion of road. I am not fully satisfied of the policy. From examination of the letters it seems very certain that the Salamanca remittance will come sooner or later, but some-

Henry A. Kent, a New York banker, director, and supporter of the A &GW in NY; also brother of Marvin Kent, president of the A&GW of Ohio. Photo by C. Silvis, London. *(Reynolds Collection, Allegheny College)*

thing must be done in the meanwhile to pay the contractors and sustain the credit of the enterprise. Called at the Erie RR office to see Marsh relative to the payment of freights. He is much annoyed by our failure of payment as arranged, and I promised to see that it should be paid without delay. Also talked with him and Minot about furnishing cars for our present business at a fixed price and asking a loan of platform cars for present use.

The Erie RR wish to operate the road on a percentage of the earnings. This I told Marsh we could not agree to. They will probably accede to my proposal.

Aug. 17. Met Kennard at Thallon's and on further consultation we determined to raise money for our emergencies on the iron. Kennard saw Duncan, Sherman & Co. who referred him to Stewart, but they declined to make the advance. Thallon at last arranged with Newman & Co., flour merchants, for $50,000. An order of Waldron and Tindell for $900 for chairs was presented to Thallon but is not yet accepted. It to be drawn on the company.

Church and I remain at St. Dennis and dine at 5th Ave. Hotel.

Aug. 18. In the morning met Fallon and Kennard at Thallon's. At 12 we attended board meeting on Broad Street and adjourned at four. Henry Kent [was] present.

Aug. 20. Met Church at Thallon's and we held an executive committee meeting at Kent's on Broad Street, at which due authority was given me to raise money on the iron. I then went with Thallon to Newman & Co. to arrange for an advance on 200 tons of rails.

Aug. 21. To Thallon's and to Erie RR office to urge immediate shipment 1,780 tons of rails.

Jamestown Opening

Aug. 24. Left home by express to Conneautville with General Dick, Church, and [James] Dick. Spent the evening with Kennard, Church and others arranging programme for tomorrow.

Aug. 25. Drove with Thallon and Goddard to Cheeny's and returned on the south side. We had two showers but a pleasant drive. On our return we found the track layers crossing Main Street and the town in a state of excitement awaiting the arrival of the cars from Salamanca. The train arrived in the afternoon with a large number of guests and officials of the Erie RR Co. and the road was formally opened to this place with one or two short speeches.

In the evening a dinner was given at the Jamestown House in compliment to Kennard. The room was crowded and the dinner as good as could be expected at such hotel. The green turtle soup had been sent by Mr. and Mrs. McHenry for the occasion, and toasts and responses occupied to a late hour. Wm. Lowrie responded to a toast to Jamestown in a witty impromptu rhyme. Altogether it was a success. To the public all appeared promising and bright for the road. To those behind the scenes there was much to damp the triumph in the financial embarrass

The first train into Jamestown, New York, on the A&GW, August 25, 1860.
(Reynolds Collection, Allegheny College)

ments. Among those present were Marsh, president, and Minot, superintendent of the Erie RR, John Goddard of London, son of our trustee, Navarro of Spain, representative of Duke Rianzares.

Aug. 31. McHenry: "I have now the highest satisfaction in stating that I have sold all the bonds of New York subject to certain guarantees being had from Salamanca, the Ebbw Vale Co. and Bailey Bros. for the immediate completion of the road to Warren in Ohio. . . .

"I shall, of course, hold myself in readiness to lay the whole matter in reference to a prolonged negotiation before you. . . . The deadly hostility of various houses in New York and rival interests assumed proportions which astounded me. In fact, gentlemen came over here to show the absolute folly of building the road, and had no difficulty in finding converts and sympathy amongst our leading brokers.

"Edgar Thomson[14] of Phila. may be considered our most active enemy (and he will regret it). Dunniston and Wiggins and other houses to whom I applied for assistance as agents were alarmed by the reports from the correspondents and declined the association. Baffled everywhere I then assumed the name of the company and determined in its name to open offices and rely on my own *force* to defeat what assumed the proportions of a conspiracy to keep me out of the London market.

"The United States Naval Agency came opportunely to my aid with its prestige and valuable business, and elevated myself personally to a position rather to dictate than to beg; and with an entire new combination I have triumphed. . . . I have said I submitted to very serious discount in order to assure success. . . . I recognize freely that I had no justifiable right under my instructions to sell under 75,[15] and at this rate I shall account to the company who will not lose by my personal sacrifices and I submit to you that this should confirm to you my single minded determinations to carry through this enterprise without any selfish consideration whatsoever. I am sure you can appreciate this rather chivalrous idea and give me your . . . confidence when I state facts or demand new powers. The short delay in remittances appears to have caused doubts of my position and forgetfulness of my labors for which I was not prepared. I hoped I had been better appreciated. I beg to say emphatically you are dealing with a man who has had some experience and is thoroughly in earnest, and is totally incapable of anything mean or treacherous; who appreciates loyalty and can distinguish it from suspicion and incapacity. . . . *Support me to end unhesitatingly, blindly,* if such be necessary and I will carry the road to Dayton before midsummer next. Please let me know whether you prepared to go through to Warren and in what ratio do you require money and iron? Can you reach Warren by Xmas if we do our duty here in means? I have now secured for the A&GW the most powerful and active capitalists in England, France, and Spain, which, if properly administered, will raise it to the very front rank of American Railroads. But there must be no suspicions or jealousies intervene to prevent a consummation which I shall lead you to. If there be, I am but responsible."

Again on the 31st McHenry: "I have omitted to call your attention to the fact of my inserting Evans in list of Directors [in New York] without waiting for formal election or authority. I am sure you will make this in order. It was indispensable to give us position here and I have to suggest that a similar position is made for Evans in Ohio and Penna. . . .

"I deem it necessary to say that Kennard is merely an engineer paid by me to superintend the construction of the road and the finances, and I do not wish him to have any powers granted by vote of the board or otherwise. He is paid by me, and it is for all our interests, and his own that he have no powers except through me. Kennard is fond of intrigue and has given me much trouble by interference very unhandsomely with Salamanca, to whom he was introduced by me and I am thus frank in order to avoid any new complications in which so much time has been spent. Kennard, nor his family, have never advanced a penny to the A&GW railroad. I alone have found all the means and assumed all responsibility. . . . With me alone must remain the power until our great work is complete."

Kennard returned to Europe, sailing on the last of the month.

The advices of the opening [to] Jamestown gave a new impetus in Europe and the accounts were extensively copied and published in England, Paris, and was for the German papers. Kennard's reports were satisfactory.

Sept. 1. I received from McHenry a statement of the Penna. bonds and New York bonds, but not in such detail as desired. Thallon's letter states "I have no money yet, but am promised it next week. Sold $5,000 Newman's paper; had to pay 1 per cent per m. All absorbed in freight. I find it is not doing us any good to have this paper on the street so I will try to do without putting it there."

Seizure of Iron

Sept. 3. Thallon telegraphed Church: "Hurry to New York. Custom House threatening to seize iron for want of proper invoice."

Sept. 4. Thallon: "Have got the £6,000 have sent $10,000 to bank at Jamestown. Tell Streator to hurry on the work. Have sold another £5,000 Newman paper." Next day: "Get the Dr. to put on more men and let us get to Union Mills."

Sept. 7. Church from New York: "No sooner is one trouble out of the way until another comes. It is said misfortunes never come single; but with us it is well otherwise we should be wholly played out before this. The same day the news came from McHenry that Salamanca was all right, Thallon was notified that his invoice and entry of iron in bond was fraudulent and a seizure threatened. . . . This is undoubtedly the work of Ward. . . . We can of course get no more money on the pledge of iron." We received news of the death of Doolittle.

Sept. 8. Church: "This has been a blue day. I have had an interview with the Custom House officers about the iron. There is danger of a seizure. They have appointed Monday to meet me again. The facts are that there was no invoice with the cargoes, and Thallon under instructions from McHenry made out invoices here instead of entering as the act of Congress authorized."

Sept. 11. The County Fair commenced today at Jamestown. We had a train of flat cars to run from Salamanca. It came in at 9 but owing to the cold and wet morning brought few passengers.

Sept. 12. The train brought about one hundred to the Fair, but a small number of those expected if the day had been pleasant. We are busy with arrangements for building a telegraph line to this point and the morning was spent with the accounts of the workmen and for supplies and for fencing. Also had a long consultation with Calhoun as to forms of blanks and books.

Church from New York: "Last hearing at the Custom House and are promised a decision of Friday." I wrote to Thallon: "In much perplexity with regard to finances and how to meet our estimate. Remittance to Chautauqua Co. Bk. does not meet account for advances, and a large part of this deposit is needed for fencing and other expenditure. The contractors can get $3,000 at the Crawford County Bank but the Dr. needs $20,000." With reference to the Custom House trouble: "But there is no need to be discouraged. We have had difficulties from the first and we are not at this late hour to be blocked in our progress by the efforts of our enemies, with one of whom this iron difficulty no doubt originated."

I also wrote to McHenry in relation to the probable effect the death of Doolittle would have on the contracts for construction and "I regret to say that the financial condition of our company is not in a very satisfactory condition. We are some thirty days behind in our funds which places us under great embarrassment. We have succeeded in keeping the credit of the company good thus far yet it is by such personal exertion on the part of all of us. And I fear that we may not at all times have the ability to borrow to meet our emergencies. . . . Let me urge upon you the importance, if possible, to place us in funds at least thirty days in advance. I am well aware of the difficulties under which you have labored but have never the less full confidence that with your ability and with the assistance of Kennard you will be able to accomplish it."

Sept. 13. Drove with Hill and Coolman and obtained privilege of a gravel pit from Faulkner. Returned on the cars which were well filled with visitors to the Fair, the day being pleasant. Found the town crowded and numbers waiting at the office to see me on business.

Sept. 14. We are without funds to pay estimate. Streator has gone to Ohio to endeavor to make a loan and wishes me to raise $3,000 from the Crawford County Bank. The Chautauqua County Bank have advanced very generously and we will not ask for more. I decided to leave for New York and see what could be done. I entrusted the general charge of the fencing and telegraph to Calhoun and instructed him to close with Judge Foote for release of way. Left on excursion train at 10 with four cars well filled. I picniced [*sic*] with the party at Salamanca. We tried to run to Great Valley, but were obliged to return on account of gravel train. Telegraphed to Robinson at Dunkirk to stop the Erie RR train at Salamanca. Spent the afternoon watching the laying of water pipe across the creek to supply the tank, and at 6 left for New York.

[Again from New York Church writes regarding the Custom House problems]: "No arrangements made. Can have possession pending proceedings on security given."

Sept. 15. Arrived at New York at 10:30. Met Church at the 5th Ave. Hotel. No money has come, but is expected on next steamer. No room in 5th Ave. Hotel. Went to St. Dennis. A grand union torch light procession in evening.

Sept. 18. Went to Thallon's. No news. Paid Robertson and Seibert, engravers. Received telegram from Streator for money. Sent him Thallon's check on Corn [Exchange] Bank. Letters from McHenry show that we shall have our £12,500 in a few days. Church states: "I think we shall make the iron matter all right, with perhaps the payment of a higher rate of duty than heretofore."

Sept. 19. To Thallon's to hear the unwelcome, "No news." Very strange. Crow writes in a mail or two plenty of money. (Crow was McHenry's Liverpool partner.) Cut coupons off bonds to be sent to Europe. Spent the evening with Church discussing the outlook.

Sept. 21. We found the train waiting at Salamanca at 10:00 and reached Jamestown 12:30. Spent the afternoon with Streator discussing the question of the contractors operating the road as they have the right under their contract. The European parties are averse to this from some cause, and insist on a surrender of privilege. (The reason was shown on the arrival of Splatt and Evans, who used every effort to transfer the operating to the Erie RR as will be seen in future.) Streator at last consented to yield the right.

Church had sent his nephew to Jamestown to take oversight of the operating of the road. [Streator] refused to permit him to interfere. He demanded access to the accounts of the company and Calhoun declined to let him have the books but offered to give him any information. I sustained both the contractor and Calhoun in their course, and [Church] was very much offended. Thorp and General Dick arrived in the evening and the executive committee met and passed bills, but nothing was concluded about operating the road. The discussion was warm and the committee adjourned at 11:00 P.M.

Sept. 22. Nothing having been done by the executive committee I wrote a note to Streator stating that the company would assume the operating of the road, and that I would appoint the officers placed in charge by the contractors to act for the company until further arrangements should be made.

Returned home with General Dick, Church, and Thorp. While in New York I forwarded $82,400 of Penna. bonds to Meron and Goddard "Subject to the instructions heretofore given."

I also wrote to McHenry in answer to his letter of Aug. 21, only received at New York, giving reasons for his disappointment in the delay of opening to Jamestown.

1st. The too sanguine anticipations of Kennard and consequent promises which could not be redeemed.

2nd. Unforeseen contingencies not taken into account by him in his expectation.

3rd. Inadequate supply of money from late acquisitions, and delayed remittance.

4th. Great loss of time by adopting and experimenting on a new patent chair for the manufacture of which the patentee was unprepared. Whatever may be the advantages of the chair, the experiment with it so early in the work was in my opinion injudicious.

With regard to Kennard: "We have been on the most friendly relations, and his efforts have been for the success of the work; but apart from his province as engineer, we can carry out the necessary negotiations and arrangements here much more satisfactorily than he can with his limited experience with our railway companies. . . . To reach Warren by Christmas is impracticable. Winter will be here, and the light work would be expensive and badly done. . . . My advice is to progress with all suitable work and for this purpose be prepared to supply the cash as fast as it can be judiciously expended. Lay iron to the S&E road and be prepared to lay track west by April 1. Commence to forward iron in February, during April it can be sent west by Erie RR and be distributed by canal to different points at each of which track laying can be carried forward."

Thallon: "Received £4,000. . . . Kennard has reached Liverpool and gone to London with McHenry. . . . Evans and Splatt leave for here on [September] 22 and have letters for us. The Ebbw Vale guarantee to go on with 10,000 tons rail and Salamanca was to be in Paris [on September] 15 so that and everything was looking first rate."

Sept. 24. Thallon: "I have a most satisfactory letter from Kennard. . . . Was to start next day for Spain to see Salamanca. He proposes coming out again on *Great Eastern* on the 17th of October. . . . One of the conditions with Evans and Splatt is that the contractor is *not to be allowed to work the road.* . . . I also paid today Danforth, Cook & Co.

the first installment $3,166 and the locomotive left this morning. They grumbled a good deal at getting only this and they said the Judge had promised them all. . . . I also saw Shell (the collector). He has promised not to do anything until [Church] returns."

Sept. 28. Thallon: "Will . . . pay Belmont $6,000 tomorrow. . . . I am very glad you arranged so easily with the Doctor, as it had got to be done, whether easily or not . . . As arranged with you, I paid Danforth, Cook & Co. the one third on their assurance that the locomotive had gone. Imagine my surprise and indignation to be told by them yesterday that they had detained it for the balance."

Streator: "I am much annoyed about the cars. [Merrill and Bowers] have shipped 10 flats which we have got and there is ten house [cars] ready, but they are like Danforth, Cook & Co. They do not like to deliver a great deal without some settlement according to agreement. I cannot comply with the agreement under my present circumstances. What can we do? The cars are wanted for the business of the road. . . .

"We have had the best reputation as a company so far since we commenced that any co. ever enjoyed, but what must we expect if we do not meet our engagements?"

Sept. 22. McHenry: "I came here to see Splatt before he sailed. Evans will join at Cork and you will see them immediately after arrival. Splatt has paid me in cash the first installment for the bonds. . . . The sale of 600 bonds is positive, of 400 contingent. . . . Opposition continues severe. . . . I made a new contract with Salamanca, viz: to reimburse the present outlay made by him in installments, and to receive from him a new subscription of $400,000 at the rate of $80,000 per month. I have made a similar contract for rails. These arrangements with our other resources enable me to supply you with cash and material to reach Warren in Ohio without a day's cessation. Kennard leaves in three weeks to join you in pushing forward the works and will go with renewed vigor as he is now made acquainted with my plan. . . . I shall send you about $20,000 weekly in cash and I commence to move 2,000 tons rails at once. I have taken an office in *London* so that I shall be able with some comfort to myself to keep you more regularly advised than heretofore (office heretofore Liverpool)."

Oct. 2. Church wrote to me from New York that the Custom House had formally seized the iron. To take the iron from the Custom House would require collateral security of $65,000. Church remained in New York for a number of days in order to make some satisfactory adjustment, but without success.

Evans and Splatt of London arrived the first week of the month, and owing to the delay of the Custom House arrangements, Evans purchased from Decker 450 tons to be sent forward for immediate use. This was ill advised as it was not sufficient for extension to any available point and absorbed money needed for other purposes.

Oct. 7. I went to Jamestown to supervise the opening of the books of the Co. in New York and get the accounts placed in shape for the information of Evans and Splatt. I remained at Jamestown until October 9 having on 7th arranged for the location of the station at Salamanca. I then went to New York, where I met Evans and Splatt, who professed to be desirous for the most rapid progress of the work. The following extract from one of my letters gives my impressions at the time: "The road is now beginning to do a very good business. We carry daily a fair number of passengers and we have already enlarged our freight house (at Jamestown). The eastern travel from Warren now passes over our line. We will next week commence running two trains each way. Our first locomotive is now on the road, and two more are finished, which we will forward this week. McHenry writes very satisfactorily. Says his arrangements for completing to Warren are perfected and remittances of cash will be punctually made."

Oct. 10. We expect to forward part of our iron at once, and are now prepared to lay track and expect to complete to the S&E RR by December 1.

Oct. 11. The arrival of the Prince of Wales and his reception at New York prevented the accomplishment of much business. I remained some days in New York with Evans and Splatt and in consultation with the Erie RR Company and returned home on October 20.

Oct. 25. Appraisers were appointed to appraise the iron at the Custom House. On the 27th Thallon: "We are digging away at this horrible C.H. business. The appraisement is on Monday. . . . Did you get the

Doctor's abandonment of the Penna. contract? . . . I must have that settled before anything is done beyond Union Mills." It will be proper to state that McHenry had since Doolittle's death desired to secure the control of the Penna. construction [contract] but the overtures to Streator had not been satisfactory, and no result favorable to McHenry. Evans and [Church] and Thallon were very anxious that Streator should transfer the contract to McHenry. I, on the other hand, had sustained Streator against what I thought an unfair attempt at coercion by embarrassment of his financial matters as connected with the road. I insisted that he should be treated with perfect fairness and justice and not driven into terms.

Oct. 28. A telegram from McHenry: "The issue commenced yesterday. Is wonderfully successful. All the bonds will be sold before the directors (Evans and Splatt) return."

Oct. 30. Thallon: "We are working at the horrid iron business and I think will get the first lot out tomorrow."

Nov. 1. I [had written] to McHenry in reply to his of Oct. 9: "I fear you have been misled by some error in the calculations of Kennard as to our true position financially. September 22 you state that your arrangements were made and you would send $20,000 per week. This amount if regularly remitted would accomplish all we wish. . . . But for two weeks we have had no remittance and you say that Kennard stated that we *were not in immediate necessity.* Now, Kennard must have made a great error in his estimate of our finances.

"At the time he left we had arranged to [borrow] on security of our iron $50,000, which sum it was estimated would carry us through the next month (September), and leaving the amount overdue at Belmont's to be paid from the first of your remittances. Owing to the difficulties at the Custom House we did not realize on our loan on the iron security more than $35,000. This amount is now due and must be paid to release the iron for the use of the road. We are in arrears for advances made to the contractors by the Chautauqua Co. Bank to meet estimate $23,000. We are yet back on September payments $7,000 on rolling stock etc., etc., a sum total of near $70,000."

Nov. 2. Remittance of £4,000, $19,000. Expect 350 tons of the iron from the Custom House. Church and Thallon have bought 360 tons of American iron at Danville at $45 per ton at Elmira. Thallon: "You didn't say whether you have the Doctor's resignation. Evans . . . is anxious on the subject. . . . The fact is it has got to be done, and quickly, too, by fair means, certainly if possible; if not—by coercion. . . . Henry Kent and the Judge have given the security for the first iron, say $12,000. Myself and friends here will manage an equal quantity. . . . Let some of the rest do their portion and not leave everything to you, the Judge and myself."

Nov. 6. (Extracts from my reply to the above): "The contract [of Doolittle and Streator] can be cancelled by the assent of the proper parties. [Streator] wishes a contract for the 60 miles west of Union [Mills] including everything except iron rails, chairs, spikes, frogs, and switch irons at a new and much reduced rate of prices. . . . A meeting of the board has been called to consider the whole matter. . . . It is useless to talk of coercion. . . . I am sure that the directors do not sympathize with Church in his distrust of the Doctor's integrity . . .

"With regard to an arrangement for the Erie RR Company to run our road for the time being . . . Evans conversed with me on the subject at Dunkirk and I have given it much thought since, and have only been confirmed in my opinion of its utter inexpediency." I received at length the inducements offered and gave my reasons for dissent.

Nov. 12. Left home in lumber wagon with Peter who carried a marble mantel from Linesville. Thorp accompanied me as far as Westfield. At Dunkirk met Hill. Also Captain Alden on his way to Cuba, New York, to bore for oil. At Salamanca was joined by Streator and [Henry] Kent. [Arrived New York City the next day.]

Nov. 14. After breakfast consulted with Streator as to the proposal by the Erie RR to operate our road and at 10 met Church, Kent, Streator, and Evans at the Broad St. office [in New York City], and discussed the policy very fully. It was agreed that Evans should ascertain the terms which could be obtained from the Erie RR Company, and that Kent, Church, and I should make arrangements with the [Cleveland &] Mahoning RR (C&M RR) for access to Cleveland.

The Southern secession movement has created a panic which

threatens to become serious. Stocks are down and exchange worthless.

Nov. 15. At 9 o'clock Splatt called for me to visit Long Dock and make with the Erie RR Directors the first trip through the Bergen Tunnel. The platform cars on which we made the trip were lighted with "wide awake" lanterns. On our return we found a collation spread in the ferry house. Some speeches were made and we returned to the Erie RR office where with Marsh, Evans, Church, Kent, and Streator the proposal and terms of operating the road was talked over, and Church was instructed to place the proposed terms in form for future consideration. Delivered to H. A. Kent $14,000 company bonds as collateral security.

Nov. 16. No remittance received by the *Canada*. Streator has a note falling due tomorrow, and he is very uneasy. I advised him to reduce his force until finances improve. I countermanded the order for the last two locomotives.

Nov. 17. Called at the Claredon to bid goodbye to Splatt who sailed by the *Atlantic*. He promised to see that funds are provided for our necessities. At one o'clock met Evans at Thallon's. Times are very blue. Streator's note of $5,000 went to protest. Financial outlook gloomy in the extreme.

Nov 19. The Penna. and New York companies authorized me to agree with McHenry that in consideration of the present financial difficulties they would arrange with him a fair and equitable basis for any loss he might necessarily sustain in arrangements for construction means for immediate use.

Nov. 20. By appointment met Hartshorn at Thallon's. He agrees to pay $35,000 for the $70,000 package in the Exchange Bank. Thallon also to give him our order for the $109,000 package to be paid $10,000 on Thursday, one-half the balance on Monday and the residue on Monday next.

Nov. 22. Hartshorn arrived and declined to complete the agreement as arranged. Although we are sorely in need of the money, I am yet well pleased with the result of the negotiation. Evans returned from Jamestown with Hill and expresses himself well pleased with the road. Left for home in the evening.

When the question of the Erie RR Co. operating the road was under discussion I submitted in writing the conditions of my assent, viz:

"The Erie Co. propose to operate the line of the A&GW RR Co. at say 40 cents mileage. If this is agreed to it will be on my part on the following conditions:

1st. The amount due the company by McHenry according to his engagements to the present time shall be paid to liquidate our liabilities for work done on the line of road.

2nd. That means shall be at once provided to complete to the S&E RR.

3rd. That means shall be provided for the work *west* of the S&E RR at not less than $40,000 per month for the actual construction on the line, the first payment of which shall be paid before January 1.

4th. The Erie RR Co. to purchase or use our box cars on fair terms. We to retain the residue of our rolling stock."

Nov. 26. A meeting of the Penna. company was held at Meadville at which I repeated my interview with Splatt and Evans in New York, and that it was their earnest desire that the several corporations should make arrangements with the Erie RR Company to operate the line, thereby to save the cost of rolling stock to the Penna. and New York companies. After a very full discussion it was deemed inexpedient to take definite action at that time although the opinion of all except one was decidedly adverse to the arrangement.

On the afternoon of the same day I received a telegram from New York from Evans. "Minot will be in Jamestown on Thursday (29th) with that agreement (Erie RR operating) I have asked the favor of Church to meet you there in order to make the necessary arrangements." I replied that I could meet Minot on Friday afternoon and not earlier. On the 27th Thallon telegraphed, "Meet Minot at Jamestown on Thursday to sign agreement."

It will be remembered that at the meeting at the Erie RR office on the [November] 14th, Church was instructed to place in form the proposition of the Erie RR Co. and details that they might be submitted for consideration. After I left New York, instead of this being done, a contract was prepared and this was the paper referred to in the above telegrams. I had not seen it nor had it been submitted to the companies for action.

On November 26 I wrote to Marsh (Receiver of Erie RR), "I have received a telegram stating that Minot would be at Jamestown on Thursday with the contracts for the operation the A&GW RR. . . . I telegraphed I cannot be there before Friday evening. There seems to be . . . a misapprehension of the necessary methods of making this arrangement. You are well aware that corporations are restricted . . . as to the manner in which their powers shall be exercised. Neither the president of a railroad company or the Executive Committee . . . have the power to transfer the right to operate the line of road. . . . While I therefore will do all in my power to advance the mutual interests of the companies, [I] of course, can only do it under the forms prescribed by law. As the proposed contract has not yet been submitted to me for mature examination I cannot say whether I have any suggestions to make. As soon as I have the opportunity to examine it, I will call a meeting of the Board Directors for the requisite action in the matter."

Nov. 29, Judge Converse of Parkman [Ohio] called to ask if the A&GW would entertain propositions for the purchase of the Clinton Line. I could give him no encouragement.

Rejection of Erie RR Plan

Dec. 1. Executive Committee met at the office and discussed the contract for operating the road by the Erie RR Company, and on motion of Church it was decided to be inexpedient for the present. After dinner examined accounts of the company and in the evening met and accepted contractor's orders $6000.

Dec. 3. Spent the morning at the office examining accounts and making disposition of our limited means to meet the most urgent demands. In the afternoon I left for New York. Streator and Hill accompanied me as far as Olean to return to Ohio.

To McHenry from Jamestown: "I have received no letters from you since those informing me of your definite arrangements to forward to us $20,000 per week and urging the work forward to Warren. Upon your positive assurance of remittances I have given my personal influence to assist the contractors through various banks. Your failure to remit has placed me in a very embarrassing position . . . I, some weeks since, wrote you a full statement of our situation and informed you of the disastrous result to arise on failure of the October estimate. The estimate yet remains unpaid and another is due. Winter is on us and there are now hundreds of laborers who are without clothing suitable for the inclement season, without money, and what is worse, destitute of food for their families."

Dec. 4. Arrived at the city 12:30. Sent baggage to St. Nicholas and went direct to Thallon's. Thallon was very much dissatisfied with my refusal to sign the Erie contract. Says "It has killed the road." Evans called at 3 o'clock and was disappointed that the agreement had not been signed, but not like Thallon, out of humor.

Dec. 5. Went to Jersey City to see Evans off. He left in fine spirits and promised to see our finances set right. Left for home.

Dec. 8. Thallon, in a very despondent mood: "I can only repeat what I said to yourself, that whether you were right or wrong in the view you took that *you have killed the road.*"

Dec. 11. To McHenry: "Thallon sends me copy of the following extracts from your letters to him. . . . You say you are without contracts promised. I have most carefully read your letters to me and in no one of them do I find any reference to any such contracts. . . . I am the only person authorized by the companies to act in relation to the European negotiations and it is therefore desirable that all official letters or letters referring to the state of our negotiations should be addressed to me as president of the company. . . . After the first estimate we have never been without embarrassment in our finances. . . . The great mistake committed from the beginning has been the error of forcing our work beyond our means. It has always been contrary to my judgment but in this I have been overruled. I shall not be in future. . . . You must be your own judge of the amount you will be able to furnish weekly. Whether large or small we will work to it."

Dec. 14. Streator [quotes one of the workers]: "There is a large number of men discharged waiting for their pay. As yet they are quiet, but

Heaven only knows how long they will remain so." [Streator adds]: "We are in a bad fix. *What can be done?*" With regard to Thallon's letters: "The [devil] is to pay but I am satisfied we are right. We must get money enough out of them to pay our debts."

Dec. 19. To McHenry in relation to letters of Thallon: "If Evans considers the action of the executive committee a cause of withdrawal from the board, I can assure you I regret his determination . . . our opinions did not agree . . . [in the case of the New York contract with Doolittle and Streator] which gave to the contractors the right to use and operate the road for three years and receive the proceeds thereof. It was afterward decided that the company had not the power to transfer to the contractors or any other party the right to operate the road. . . . I wish to again say that I am the only person authorized to manage the foreign negotiations or give suggestions and instructions to the agents of the company. . . . All correspondence in any degree of an official character should be addressed to me direct as president of the company."

Dec. 27. At a meeting of the Penna. company at Meadville, Reynolds, Shryock, and Church were appointed a committee to make a final settlement with the surviving contractor (Streator) upon an equitable basis, and after such settlement to negotiate a new contract with responsible parties.

Very great bitterness was manifested toward me by [Church] and [Thallon] on account of my determined opposition and successful defeat of the Erie plan for securing the control of our road. Knowledge in future proved the wisdom of the refusal and the admission of this fact was made by Thallon and McHenry. The direction of all the boards sustained me with two or three individual exceptions.

The year 1860 closed with far from flattering prospects for the future. Much work had been accomplished yet not what had been anticipated, and the political complications were very discouraging in every view.

At a meeting of the board of directors of the Pa. company of November 11, 1860, I presented a written report from which I extract as follows: "On August 11, 1858, Doolittle made a contract with McHenry to furnish 31,000 tons of rails and 193,000 pounds of cash. Ward, agent of the co., assenting thereto. . . . This contract according to my information has never been complied with according to its terms, has not been renewed, and has expired by limitation. . . . There is at present no existing contract for supply of money and iron in force other than by sufferance. McHenry has from time to time forwarded money and iron but not in accordance with either the contract with Doolittle or in compliance with the instructions of the president of the company. . . . I would recommend that the company should take some immediate action to rescind the contract with Doolittle and Streator if the same can be done in a perfectly legal manner, and make new contracts for construction and for money and iron."

Committee was appointed by the board, which committee reported in favor of a new contract upon more favorable terms.

On December 27, Reynolds, Shryock, and Church were appointed a committee to make a final settlement with Streator the surviving partner upon an equitable basis, and upon such settlement negotiate a new contract with responsible parties. Also to settle with McHenry according to contract of McHenry with Doolittle.

4. Challenges and More Challenges, 1861

The contract with Doolittle and Streator was terminated and a new one with McHenry was approved. McHenry and his people began to press for more European representation and authority in the American companies as foreign investment increased. Meanwhile, Reynolds cried out for more efficient management. The money crunch and concerns over the manner in which McHenry was disposing of the securities compelled Reynolds to travel to Europe. He met with Salamanca, who expressed dissatisfaction with the slow progress of the A&GW RR. To compound matters, the Civil War was creating a weakness in the money markets and a growing reluctance to invest in America. Back home, Reynolds emphasized the need to tap into the emerging oil market. He also accused Erie and Cleveland interests of trying to prevent construction of the A&GW west of Corry, Pennsylvania.

Financial Crisis and the Coming of War

The year opened under very inauspicious circumstances. The companies of New York and Penna. were in arrears to the contractors $75,000. Streator, trusting to the promises of McHenry, had strained his credit to the utmost and was a large borrower at the Portage County Bank and at the Chautauqua County Bank at Jamestown. Payments were due to men and many of the laborers were in much distress.

The terms were by no means amicable between the company and McHenry. He had failed in his promises and did not furnish satisfactory reports of his disposition of the bonds and shares given him by the trustees. He was moreover very anxious to secure the contract of Doolittle and Streator exclusively for himself, and was disposed to embarrass the contractors to compel them to submit to his terms. He had engaged the services of John Fallon, Esq., of Philadelphia, to aid his agent Thallon, and Church who for a long time had not been in cordial sympathy with the other directors, threw his influence to forward McHenry's plans.

Jan. 2. General Dick, Shryock, and I left in the morning by stage to Linesville, thence to Girard, Dunkirk, Salamanca to Jamestown, where we met Hill and Thorp. I here received letter from McHenry saying: "I hope my recent letters have reassured you as to the question of my ability . . . I repeat, I am ready to go to Warren. . . . I am sorry you did not sign the Erie contract (lease). I hope you will have done so, as your refusal gives me some difficulty with Evans."

Fallon wrote that he would not be able to meet us at Jamestown, and Church also failed to make his appearance and Kent was ill. Not having a quorum, the board adjourned to meet at New York January 10. One item of business was the consummation of the details of the E&NY City RR contract which had to be deferred. I ascertained that our contractors were indebted to the Chautauqua Co. Bank $25,700, an amount which caused them some uneasiness. Many creditors and claimants called for dues which we were unable to pay, and it was with much satisfaction I left for New York with Streator, General Dick, and Shryock.

Jan. 4. I had a long interview with Thallon and demanded a payment of the $20,000 forwarded by McHenry with instructions not to pay it over until the contract (Doolittle and Streator) should have been transferred to him. I stated that the company would not object to making a reasonable contract with McHenry, but would enter into no negotiations while the money arising from negotiations of the company's securities was retained. Also telegraphed Fallon and Church to meet me in New York.

Jan. 5. Streator needs $2,000 today. Thallon under instructions refused to pay over. I read him the power of attorney to McHenry and he showed me the very positive instructions of McHenry. He telegraphed Fallon for advice but without reply.

Church and Fallon arrived in the evening and we spent the night investigating accounts and estimating the amount required to finish to Columbus. Kennard's estimate proved very erroneous, more money being now needed than by his estimate of August. Thallon urged contract for McHenry for the Penna. road and evidently wished to control the New York road. After a long consultation it was decided to obtain accurate reports of the work done in New York and the amount required to complete the same, also amount required to reach the S&E RR and Warren, Ohio, and meet at Jamestown on January 22. Thallon would not under his instructions pay any money to Streator, but consented to give me $5,000 to pay the men discharged from work.

Jan. 7. A meeting of the New York board at the Broad Street office. Shryock was elected in the board to fill vacancy caused by the death of Doolittle. Streator tendered his resignation and Col. Wm. Hall of Jamestown was elected in his place. We decided to make an effort to borrow money for present emergencies on the security of the iron now in the Custom House. A committee was appointed to report on the condition of the work and settle the account of Hill, Engineer.

Prall, of Danforth, Cook & Co. called for payment for note given by contractors for the last locomotive. Not having the money, I arranged for an extension for 60 days on the acceptance of the company. Thallon gave me draft for $5,000 to pay discharged hands, order for $373 for right of way note and agreed to protect note of the contractors at the Crawford County Bank due 10th for $1,500, and note at Ravenna Bank for $5,000, and to accept my draft if necessary for $1,500 more.

Jan. 11. Streator came from Columbus in the night with letters from Calhoun giving very discouraging account of situation of affairs on the line. The Irishmen in a state of mutiny and threatening much unless paid. At least $5,000 more needed at once. Telegraphed Thallon without response. John Dick, Shryock, and I arranged for the money with J. R. Dick on our personal security and I sent Streator back to Columbus.

Jan. 21. Went to Jamestown with Gen. Dick, Shryock, and Thorp. On the next day, Fallon arrived from Philadelphia. I spent the day in a fruitless discussion of McHenry's connection in the past and that proposed for the future. His claims for McHenry were entirely inadmissible.

Spent the next day with like result. Left with Fallon and Streator to meet Church at Salamanca. We all went to Olean and spent the night without any result. Church advocated the acceptance of the basis of arrangement proposed by Fallon. Streator and I absolutely refused to entertain any proposition [other] than such as was based on the well understood agreement when the New York contract was made.

Jan. 24. We returned from Olean; met Kent, Shryock, and [General] Dick at Salamanca on [their] return home but induced them to return to Jamestown where I convened a meeting of the directors and laid before them the state of affairs with McHenry. With the exception of Church my course was fully sustained.

No satisfactory results having been effected by the personal interview, Thallon and Fallon wrote intimating a desire for further interview in New York and indicating a concession of terms proposed, but I declined to treat except on the basis of the contracts.

Jan. 29. To Thallon: "I can see no advantage to result from another visit to New York. Fallon is aware of the position I have taken. I know precisely what can be done, or at least what *could* have been done. I have in no respect concealed my views and in consultation with our directors find that my course meets with their unqualified approval. I stated to Fallon that all my offers were withdrawn that night unless he gave his assent to the money now on hand being at once placed at the command of the company. Unless assured therefore that the programme as proposed by me to Fallon will be carried out substantially, and as a condition precedent that the money raised from sale of our bonds be placed at the disposal of the company, I feel it my duty to say, that there is no hope of any arrangement with the Penna. company and consequently there will be no benefit to raise from further interviews in this matter."

I received a letter from Fallon of date of January 29, enclosing a copy of his communication to McHenry of some 25 pages, to which I replied in full, giving a condensed statement of relations between the companies and McHenry and sent a copy to McHenry.

Jan. 31. The directors of the Penna. company passed the following: "Resolved, That the president be instructed to take immediate and efficient measures to obtain from James McHenry the full avails of the aforesaid bonds and shares as reported in his hands, also that he be authorized to recall and place in the treasury of the company all such bonds as shall not be represented by the cash or iron, at the specified rates, in the mentioned contracts, and that he be further authorized to revoke the power of attorney heretofore granted to the said James McHenry; and to employ such counsel as in his opinion may be necessary to attain the ends specified."

Thallon writes on February 1 referring to a letter received from Fallon. He says: "If this thing is to [be] fixed at all, *we must do it ourselves.* The New York branch is to be settled on the basis of the contract with such reasonable modifications as our greater experience of the working may warrant. . . . I think it will obviate all objections. Come on to New York, Church and yourself . . . and let us try to settle it fairly. I see no difficulty in the way myself and if we can do so I will accept it settled absolutely or conditionally for McHenry either with or without Fallon's concurrence."

After further correspondence at the request also of Fallon, I went to New York with Gen. Dick and Shryock where, on February 12th, we met Church, Kent, and Streator, Thallon, and Fallon also on the part of McHenry.

Feb. 13. Went to 56 Broad St. where met Kent, Church, Dick, Shryock, Streator, Thallon, and Fallon. Spent the morning and afternoon in the discussion of the proposed arrangements with McHenry. Fallon insisting on a division of the New York contract profits in addition to his commissions with McHenry, which I persistently refused to assent to.

This was at last waived by Fallon and we adjourned to meet in the evening at the St. Nicholas to arrange the basis of a contract with McHenry for the Penna. company.

Streator made a proposition at double the sum proposed at Olean and was not disposed to make concession. Thallon dined with us and in the evening he with Church, Shryock, and myself met at Fallon's room and agreed upon a general basis of new contract for the Penna. company. All points being arranged as I wished.

Feb. 14. We all met and spent the afternoon in the examination of the contract now in force and those proposed. We at length arranged to meet all our views on a fair basis in so far as the company was concerned. Thallon endeavored to make a settlement with Streator, but without coming to final arrangements, Streator demanding much more than at Olean, which we all think unreasonable. Spent the evening at the St. Nicholas with Fallon, Thallon, Kent, and Church in drawing the programme for the Ohio contract to McHenry, which was made satisfactory. All that remains to be done is a settlement with the contractors Doolittle and Streator.

Feb. 15. Met Fallon and Church at Thallon's office, Hanover Square, and talked over the Ohio contract with Doolittle and Streator with Hill. We afterwards met Streator, Kent, Dick, and Shryock at the Broad Street Office, where all the terms of the Penna. and Ohio contracts to McHenry were adjusted only subject to the final arrangement with Streator for the abandonment of the Doolittle and Streator contract.

The amount of cash here is not sufficient to meet the wishes of Streator who wants $15,000, while we can only give him five thousand. Thallon promises $5,000 more the first of the week. Fallon, Church, Hill, Dick, and Shryock left for home. Hartshorn called relative to the subscription to the Hallett-McHenry bonds, but I told him the company could take no part in the matter.

Feb. 16. In the morning went to Thallon's to close arrangements with Streator and Thallon. Thallon does not today promise more than $5,000 cash, but offers his note for $5,000 at 30 and 60 days. This of course does not suit Streator. [He] demands $12,000 for one year's services as Superintendent. Thallon offers only $6,000. I ask written consent to use Penna. bonds to pay salaries. Nothing was definitely arranged, but postponed to Monday.

Feb. 18. Presented to Thallon:

1st. Agreement on the part of McHenry to pay the contractors the balance due on estimate in 30 & 60 days.

2nd. Assumption by McHenry to the Penna. company for the cash portion of the settlement with Streator.

3rd. Agreement on the part of McHenry to comply and pay Streator as superintendent.

4th. Assent to payment of 1st mortgage Penna. bonds for salaries when money is deficient.

Thallon agreed substantially except the time in the 1st and the amount claimed by Streator in the 3rd.

The proposed terms will not suit Streator who insists on $15,000 down. All in status quo for another day. Confidence in the ability of the European parties much impaired.

Feb. 19. Met Streator at Thallon's and after a long talk all matters were satisfactorily arranged. At Broad St. office we met Kent. Thallon gave me a check for $5,000 which I paid Streator on contract and I am authorized to draw on Thallon for $8,000 on forwarding the contract. Sent Danforth, Cook & Co. agreement for retention of their lien on the locomotive "Salamanca" until purchase money shall be paid. Thus have terminated these long and vexatious negotiations.

Feb. 22. At a meeting of the directors of the Penna. company held at Meadville, the old contract with Doolittle and Streator declared abandoned, and the new contract with McHenry submitted and approved.

Feb. 25. Left for New York with Church. At Salamanca were joined by Streator.

Feb. 26. We went direct to Thallon's where we met Kennard. He says he is prepared to go on with the work, but finds fault with the estimate for the contractors. He is however satisfied with the arrangements made with Thallon for McHenry. Spent an hour with Church and Merrill. Signed petition to the Secretary of the Treasury for release of the iron from the seizure at the Custom House.

Feb 28. Met the directors of the Ohio board at the Weddell House in the evening. Gen. Dick joined us at Girard. On March 1 the contract with McHenry for the Ohio division as agreed on at New York was approved and confirmed by the company, and the president instructed to execute same.

March 4. Kennard arrived here [in Meadville] last evening having come over the proposed line with Hill, Engineer. He seems to prefer the line over the flats opposite the lime-kiln for entrance to the town [of Meadville,] but will make further examination before deciding the route.

March 5. Went over the two routes as far as Bemustown[1] with Kennard and Hill and have decided to locate on the east side of the creek. Arranged to meet him at Erie and if possible effect an arrangement with the Erie Canal Company for occupation of the towing path. He has arranged with Hill to remain in charge as assistant engineer.

March 19. Went to Erie with General Dick and Shryock to attend board meeting of the New York company. Met Kent at Girard. Hall, Allen, Streator, and Thorp arrived after dinner from Jamestown. The directors meeting occupied the afternoon and the morning of March 20 and was not satisfactory. It was evident that undue influences were at work the object of which we could only surmise. But the impression from many circumstances was that the [Erie RR] influence and that of Splatt and Evans was being brought to bear on the completion of the line to the junction with the S&E road [at Corry, PA], and give the operating of this part to the [Erie RR]. A mutual running arrangement to be effected with the S&E RR for a Lake Shore connection at Erie and the ultimate completion of the A&GW west of the junction to await the results of the future. Subsequent events have confirmed this surmise. At least one influential director was in this interest, and the scheme was thwarted with dissention in the several boards by the efforts of one director and the persistent efforts of interested parties. Had the concession been made it is doubtful if the A&GW would have been completed west of the junction.[2]

The statement of the accounts of the contractors and the balancing of the books of the New York company occupied the month. Kennard remained in New York. Thallon, on the March 14: "We have very good accounts from the other side and Kennard and I are at the old trade of trying to raise some money in the meantime 'til we get it from abroad. They tell us we can have plenty if we only put things in a satisfactory shape, which we have done, though they don't know it yet."

Kennard writes for details: "I am most anxious to explain to them in England how my estimate has been exceeded."

McHenry to Thallon: "I have an excellent and satisfactory letter from Reynolds, a real practical business letter, the first to touch on the bad earnings at Jamestown and to give me any light on the future prospects, which I could fairly use here."

March 26. Thallon: "I paid Allen's notes for $1,200 and have been applied to by the Erie RR Company. Shall I pay them? I have received Thorp's account. . . . I paid the Danville iron and have the notes I had to borrow from another party giving as much iron at $20 per ton as would make up the amount. The accounts from Europe are good and we have arranged for money and will have it soon now, and that makes a good start."

March 27. Extracts from my letter to McHenry: "Our company has suffered much in credit on account of its utter inability to meet its obligations. And the restoration of this credit will be of the most [importance] in the prosecution of the work. . . . Anxious as I am for the rapid advance of the line, . . . I am nevertheless fully convinced your *persona* will be greatly enhanced by now starting with the prestige of public confidence in the solvency and the ability of the A&GW company. We have many interested against the enterprise who make the most of every mishap.

"It will be important to all interests that a settlement at the present time should be made between you and the New York company. . . . I have nothing to say about the iron difficulties [at the Custom House]. I have not interfered except when desired for assistance. If the present proposed arrangements fail, I think I can perhaps be of some service with the Treasury Department."

The company had been obliged from the failure of McHenry to remit as promised to me as collateral for various purposes $107,000 of bonds, besides the $45,000 which were wrongfully in the [hands] of McHenry. He had repeatedly promised to send back the $45,000 New York and $107,000 of Pa. [bonds] that all adjustments could be made, but had to this time failed to do so, greatly to our embarrassment. My advances to this date reached $10,529.68.

A full settlement was made between Streator and Kennard for McHenry

Crediting contractors Doolittle and Streator contract price	$1,650,000.00
Extras agreed	4,206.45
Discount on bonds	11,476.66
Total	$1,665,683.11

McHenry agreeing to pay the amounts yet due by the contractors or assumed by the company. This arrangement was ratified by the New York company at a meeting held at Jamestown the same day. Church, Thorp, and Shryock went with me from Meadville. Gen. Dick arrived from Washington, and Fallon from Philadelphia.

April 11. Kennard writes that he has received £4,000 from McHenry and expects more next mail. Will send forward rails, chairs and spikes as fast as they can be laid. Wishes my opinion as to letting the Erie RR Co. operate when line reaches the Junction in deference to the wishes of Splatt.

Attack on Fort Sumter

The news of the bombardment of Fort Sumter received on April 12 with the consequent popular excitement almost paralyzed every enterprise in the Country.

April 15. [Kennard] writes, "I intend if possible to run a train up to the Junction (Corry) on May 1." Hill, Engineer, of same date says he has explored the route from Muddy Creek to Columbus south of Union Mills, but reports unfavorably. The chairs and spikes are arriving, and the rails are expected in a few days. Has started the construction trains west to prepare the track. Everything moving in good shape.

April 23. Thallon: "1,000 tons of iron have left here and the balance to Columbus goes tomorrow. Say to the Judge I feel sure of getting the . . . iron. I was at the Custom House about it today. Is it not awful times? Here the enthusiasm is tremendous. Thousands leaving every day to fight the traitors. I go for the old stars and stripes with all my heart."

May 7. Thallon: "Accounts from the other side keep good. Evans and McHenry are going over to meet Salamanca in Paris. We expect pretty soon to be in full force."

At this date the track was within one and one half miles east of Columbus and awaiting spikes.

May 15. We left Jamestown with an invited party of about 150 on seated flat cars and one passenger car on an excursion to the S&E Junction, to which point the track had just been laid. The afternoon was delightful and the ride very pleasant. The S&E train stopped for a few minutes when I met Gay, Vice President, Black, Superintendent, also Camp and Sterritt of Erie. On our return, we encountered a severe storm of wind and rain which drove the ladies into the covered cars. Gen. Dick, Thorp, Shryock, Mr. and Mrs. Church left us at Columbus. Kennard arrived in Jamestown in the evening.

May 27. Left home with Gen. Dick in Taylor's carriage for election at Jamestown. The Klecknerville[3] bridge being down, were compelled to go by Marvin's Mills on the plank road and reached Waterford just in time for cars. There met Judge Church and daughter, and Superintendent Black. Found the turntable at the Junction finished and Bennett laying the sills for an eating house. Reached Jamestown at 3 and held the election. Kennard arrived from New York.

Finances and Oil

May 28. I left with Kennard for New York. The Jamestown volunteer company for the seat of war left on the train accompanied to Salamanca by some two hundred friends.

McHenry: "I received a published notice of opening to Columbus on 15th. I have succeeded in raising cash equal to Kennard's requisitions to reach Akron. Short delay pending some advices . . . meantime I shall proceed with shipment of rails. The Bank of London has advised Duncan, Sherman & Co. to honor coupons of New York due July 1."

May 29. The city is filled with troops. The City Hall Park and the Battery are covered with encampments and regiments are quartered in different parts of the city. Met Kennard and Thallon. Letters encouraging. Kennard sent authority to the Chautauqua Co. Bank to draw on McHenry for $15,000. Hill arrived to make arrangements with Erie RR Co. for cars for oil.

June 18. Letter of [Jules] Levita, [attorney] from Paris: "The examination of the oil shows a splendid result for the purpose of fabrication of gas."

June 20. McHenry: "I have just returned from Paris. I have made final arrangements for one million dollars subject to the report of Kennard which should be in my hands this week."

June 28. Extract from [my] letter to Kennard: "Under the circumstances . . . your presence without money would have been . . . of no benefit but perhaps the contrary. The course of McHenry is to me inexplicable. I can readily appreciate his difficulties and excuse delays arising from unforeseen causes, but I cannot so easily excuse him for the constant and positive assurances by which his friends are led into such serious embarrassments. . . . I will submit your suggestion relative to the pledge of the iron in the Custom House . . . to relieve from present trouble."

Same date to McHenry: "Under the arrangements made on your behalf with Doolittle and Streator, Fallon and Thallon stipulated that the indebtedness for work done should be paid in 30- 60- 90 days. This time has expired with a large proportion yet unpaid.

"[On April 26] you write: 'the remittances made to Kennard will enable you to reach the state line free from debt, . . . and thus reinstate the credit of the company,' but from some cause the requisite amount has not yet been received. I have had much difficulty to prevent the disastrous results of numerous suits by persons whose just claims have from time to time been postponed on assurances of settlement. . . . I would strongly advise that . . . you should carry out the terms of arrangement made with the former contractors . . . pay the debts by which the contractors, Doolittle and Streator are embarrassed. . . . I would next suggest that, until you are fully prepared with means to promptly meet all further engagements, that the work should be suspended . . . Under no circumstances would I advise the pushing of the work beyond the means of prompt payment."

July 1. To Thallon: "Please to hold what iron you have received from McHenry . . . as it may be necessary for him [Kennard] to negotiate a loan for the company using the iron as collateral in accordance with the authority of the company as per resolution herewith given."

June 29. McHenry: "At length I have pleasure to send accounts with many apologies for delays. . . . I hope tomorrow to receive the documents from Kennard and in a few days announce that I have ample funds to proceed into Cleveland without any halt."

July 12. Met Kennard at Thallon's [in New York]. The iron has not been released as I supposed, but will probably be in the course of next week. We have no money yet. Kennard has drawn on McHenry for £6,000 and proposes to obtain £10,000 from Duncan, Sherman & Co. on the iron as collateral.

July 15. With Church and Kennard and Thallon finished list of Penna. and Ohio coupons. Gave Thallon authority to hold the iron subject to the order of Kennard, Engineer in Chief, for loan of £10,000. The iron is not yet released from the Custom House, but the arrangements are nearly made for that purpose.

Aug. 2. Kennard, from New York: "McHenry is in Madrid and has telegraphed today all is arranged, and that the bill I drew on him for £6,000 will be paid. We have not yet got possession of the iron but hope to do so every day, when I shall have as much money in hand as we want. I hope we are now at the end of our troubles."

Aug 3. McHenry writes: "There need not have been any trouble in finance had there not been some misapprehension between me and Kennard. I sent him about $100,000 which I understood was all he required to reach the Junction free of debt. Here he was to rest until I had received the money arranged for with Salamanca. Several circumstances have delayed this . . . though it will be paid shortly. The remittance made today should meet every demand but I am quite in the dark and should not be. . . . I can overcome everything by your continued support. . . . I can complete the road to Dayton with gradually decreasing trouble."

Aug. 6. From Hill, Jamestown: "Were it not for the two months pay due the men by the contractors on the first of July, and which still remains unpaid, we should not have any difficulty in reducing expenses to the lowest possible limit consistent with efficiency. Since the receipt of your letter I . . . have [sent] the gravel train and all the men who could be spared into Penna. so that this large expense may be returned to contractor's office. I have directed one party to commence grading west of S&E RR.[4] . . . Everything connected with our operation is moving along in very good shape. Freight increasing and I think we are now transporting eight tenths of all the "Oil Creek" oil now moving eastward, and our prospects are very fair for getting it all."[5]

Aug. 13. McHenry: "I enclose a letter from Paris about oil. . . . I have sent over to Paris samples and a lamp received from Thallon."

Aug. 19. McHenry: "I am anxious to know what arrangements have been made at the junction with the S&E. Whether we have to make an independent line to Union Mills. . . . I have no trouble about finances when properly supported and kept regularly advised. . . . The non-completion of my New York settlement has caused me serious loss and anxiety. . . . I see my way clearly to success in spite of the controversy arising, political, financial and other difficulties, and in order to reach it I claim your continued support."

Left home on Am. Ex. stage via Waterford. Church in company to Jamestown en route for Warren. Dined at Bennett's at Junction and rode on locomotive to Jamestown. Found the track in good condition. Went direct to office where I found Hill and J. M. Dick. Saw Kennard but deferred business with him until morning and spent the afternoon in examination of accounts. At tea met Mr. and Mrs. Keeling (the latter a sister of Mrs. Kennard). The Jamestown directors met in the evening to manage for a reduction of assessment in some townships.

Cutting Back

Aug. 20. With Kennard and Streator made a thorough investigation of company accounts. We decided to at once pay and discharge all gravel train men and carpenters; do away with telegraph superintendent and road agent. Track master to discharge former duty. To reduce repair force in this state to thirty men. Give freight engine to York and allow Badger to resign. Estimate reduction for coming month $1,500.

Kennard brought for payments $13,000 which we distributed to meet the present necessities in this state and Ohio. $40,000 Ohio bonds collateral by contractors to Beskell are advertised for sale on Friday. Kennard to leave for New York and arrange for delay.

Aug. 21. After breakfast left Jamestown on hand car with Keeling, Hill, and Allen to meet Stewart at his farm for settlement of right of way. Church met us coming on freight. Stewart returned to Jamestown with us and a settlement was effected at $500. Found a large quantity of oil awaiting transit. Kennard writes from New York that he had settled with Beskell and sends me a check for $2,000 for payments leaving only $600 to our credit in New York.

Aug. 27. McHenry: "I am waiting patiently . . . [for] information from Kennard. . . . Evans will sail in a few days and will no doubt be able to give matters a more animated prospective. . . . I therefore urge on Kennard to arrange with you for a tramway to the oil springs of 20 or 25 miles. I will find all the money and material if you will make a fair arrangement with me under this contract."

Treasury department, Washington: "I have had under consideration the petition of the A&GW RR Co of Pa. for remission of the forfeiture of a quantity of railroad iron, and being satisfied that no fraud upon the revenue was intended, have decided to remit the forfeiture.

S. P. Chase, Secy. of Treasury."

Aug 31. Kennard, from New York: "I hope we are now almost at the end of our difficulties and that I shall be able in the course of next week to make all our accounts for the completion of our line to Meadville. I have arranged with my friend Duncan a loan of $100,000 as proposed, and with this we can at all counts complete the grading during the fine weather. I have advised McHenry that I shall require $250,000 in all and that he must place me in funds as the grading proceeds. I regret however to inform you that the style of his letters to me is very bad, and in place of thanks, he has positively the impudence to abuse me."

The A&GW Company of Pennsylvania by resolution authorized a pledge of the iron in New York as collateral for loan of $1,000 from Duncan, Sherman & Co. Kennard to draw on McHenry at 60 days and pledge the iron for collateral on draft. Kennard: "I propose to put 3,000 men at work as soon as this is done."

Sept. 6. Streator, from New York: "Kennard is quite out of patience with McHenry, although McHenry says he will send him all the money he wants. There is something *not right* with McHenry. I am certain the company must look to their own interests for McHenry will only look to his."

Relative to oil traffic, "The yield of some of the late wells is truly wonderful, forcing from a depth of 600 feet from 200 to 800 bbls per day, with such power as to throw the oil like a vast fountain to a greater height than the surrounding forest trees.

"We have secured the oil sent to the eastern market by rail from Union [Mills] and other points on the S&E RR, but as stated in my last, a very large quantity is wagoned to and shipped from a point on the canal five miles south of Meadville (2½ miles from our line.) This averages from 300 to 500 bbls per day although on Monday reaching 1,800. Our line if completed to Meadville would secure that now taken by canal, and a large proportion of that sent by the river. The quantity now sent daily from the wells exceeds 2,000 bbls and I am assured this does not exceed one fourth part of the quantity actually yielded by the wells, the other three fourths being stored in tanks in the ground await- ing better prices. Some wells have from 40 to 60 tanks full averaging from 200 to 500 bbls. Owing to present low prices few of the pumping wells are in operation. You can therefore estimate the present capacity of the oil region if stimulated by advanced prices on those now ranging at from four to five cents per gallon at the well. It may from eighteen months experience be safely assumed that the business is permanent and may enter into future estimates of the profits of the road. Each month has produced wells surpassing those previously drilled until many of those a year since considered a fortune, are now regarded as small affairs."[6]

Sept. 9. To McHenry: "I have just received from the Trustees their accounts for June and July. I am at a loss to understand why such a large portion of Penna. 1st mortgage bonds should have been withdrawn from their hands in consideration of the amount of work done in this state. Will you please give me an explanation that we may understand for what purpose they have been appropriated. . . .

"To control this oil business the line must be extended at least to Meadville, and a cheap side line to Franklin would in case of the permanence of the oil fields, be a profitable investment and would secure all western as well as eastern transportation. The amount carried by the canal to the last of the past week was over 7,000 bbls and is increasing."

Sept. 12. Kennard: "I hope today to sell a bill for $25,000 and another tomorrow for the same amount. This first $25,000 will be fully absorbed in payment of duties."

Sept. 18. Kennard: "I fear after all that our troubles are not over, and that we must immediately take steps to place the company on a sure footing as against the conduct and actions of our contractor. Our bonds must be checked and . . . placed in the hands of unbiased trustees. Accounts must be produced on the other side and all future money must be remitted direct through a [London] banker. . . . I fancy from the copy of Salamanca contract that I shall have to go to Europe to settle matters, but before I go I must see you all and settle upon a definite course of proceeding. . . . The time for action has I think arrived. . . . I expect Evans over in a few days."

Sept. 19. Left home to attend meeting with Kennard in Jamestown. On arrival was disappointed by telegram from Kennard wishing me to meet him in New York. I instructed Hill to discharge all engineers on Saturday.

Sept 20. Arrived in New York and met Kennard, Thallon, and Streator at the Hanover building. Kennard read a letter just received from Fallon of a most extraordinary character. McHenry has failed to remit money and appears anxious to cover his irregularities by a quarrel with Kennard, and Fallon seems desirous to again place our affairs in confusion. Kennard has decided to go to Europe and wishes me to go with him. As the European mail was expected tonight we accepted Kennard's invitation to dine at Delmonico's and then adjourned to Thallon's for letters, but received nothing of importance for our present necessities.

Remained in New York until September 23 but no satisfactory letters. All urge me to go to Europe with Kennard, and it is also proposed that Thallon and Henry A. Kent accompany us with all requisite authority from the several companies to act as we shall find best for the interests of the companies.

A European Trip

Sept. 24. From Kennard, New York: "The *Persia* has passed Cape Race. She will be here tomorrow and . . . I hope to be on board of her with yourself, Kent and Thallon. I am more than ever anxious as to the oil charter to the oil wells. . . . We could arrange for the iron in Europe."

NOTE: This was an old charter controlled by Struthers but needed additional legislation to be available. Struthers proposed to obtain this and join interests with us in its construction, and did secure the requisite legislation, and so advised us when in Europe. The letter was received by Kennard at Madrid but was neglected by him and unanswered. Receiving no authority to act from McHenry and Kennard, Struthers and Streator secured the charter and afterwards constructed the road. I made arrangements with them on two different occasions for a transfer of the line to the A&GW on favorable terms but could not secure the cooperation of McHenry and his agents, notwithstanding every effort on my part. The control of this road for many years secured the lion's share of the oil traffic.[7]

Sept. 28. Kennard from New York: "Evans is here, but I regret to say he does not bring any money with him. I also regret to inform you that McHenry has obtained more money on our New York securities than I at first anticipated. . . . I am utterly at a loss to know what he has done with it. Under these circumstances it is more than ever necessary to go without . . . delay, and I have this day taken your passage [on board] the *Persia*. . . . I fancy Evans is very much under the thumb of McHenry. . . . He has advised McHenry by this post that we are going. . . . I find McHenry paid him £500 before he started."

Oct. 3. COPY OF RESOLUTION A&GW of Pa. "The consideration of the bond account of the trustees and the contract relations with James McHenry, Esq. laid over from last meeting of September 28, 1861, was resumed, and on full discussion it was RESOLVED: that John Dick and the Secretary be and they are hereby authorized and directed to execute under the seal of the company and deliver a power of attorney to William Reynolds, Robert Thallon, and Henry A. Kent, authorizing them or a majority of them if the three fail to concur, To revoke all powers heretofore granted by this company to any person or persons as attorney or attorneys, agents or trustees, and such revocation to have all the force and effect as if the said revocation was made direct by this company; and in behalf of this company to exercise all the power vested in the company to revoke, cancel or annul any or all contracts for the construction and equipment of this road. To demand and receive from all former agents, attorneys and trustees, if they so deem necessary, all bonds, certificates of stock, bills and any papers in any way appertaining to any negotiation hitherto made on behalf of the company, and belonging to them. Also to demand and receive all bills of lading for iron, all bankers bills or money received by any agent of the company for sale of the bonds or stock of the company.

"And in case the foregoing powers or contracts be revoked or annulled, the said agents be authorized and empowered to make any new contract or contracts for the finishing and furnishing of the road.

"RESOLVED: that the solicitor of the company be directed to prepare a form of power of attorney embracing the foregoing authority."

The power of attorney above mentioned was prepared in form and executed and delivered by John Dick. Attested by Wm. Thorp, and witnessed by A. M. Fuller and J. D. Gill. The said power of attorney with certified copies of proceedings of the A&GW companies of PA and Ohio for adoption of the A&GW in NY as a connecting road and the guaranty of $1,000,000 of the first mortgage bonds were delivered, to the committee before leaving for Europe.

At the meetings of the Penna. company in relation to the mission to Europe, very decided opposition was made by Church who for some time had been in sympathy with Fallon, McHenry's attorney. Fallon had for some time given us much trouble by his advice to McHenry, thus thwarting our plans without our being able to definitely know where the trouble existed. With the exception of Church the board was unanimous as to the propriety of our visit to and personal investigation of matters in London.

Oct. 7. With wife and [son] Henry started for New York via Linesville. At Salamanca met Hill and gave instructions as to the side track at the station. We reached New York and stopped at Astor House. Met Kennard, Thallon, Streator, and Church at Thallon's office. There found a note from Fallon to prevent our departure by threats of suit by McHenry: "It is but proper that I should add that but for the fact that I expect him (McHenry) here, I should have taken decided action on his behalf, and would do so now by resorting to legal measures to protect his interests. . . . I may consider it necessary to take the responsibility at once of acting on his behalf as the state of things seems to me to re-quire. I would therefore, request . . . in case you should be absent, who would be your legal representative with whom I could communicate."

Evans came in about two o'clock and is very averse to our going and predicts mischief from it. Church was evidently in league with them. It was apparent that they all had some motive to prevent our investiga-tion.

Oct. 9. With wife and Henry [son] went on board the *Persia* at 8:45. At 11 the steamer started on her voyage.

Oct. 19. We were aroused by the cry of land being in sight of the Irish coast. We entered Cork Harbor for mails. Sunday, October 20, dropped anchor in the Mersey and went on shore and dined at the Adelphi in Liverpool.

Oct 22. London. We breakfasted with Kennard at his house in Sus-sex Gardens. Greenfield called and we walked to the office Great George Street through Hyde, Green, and St. James Parks. Owing to the exasperation of McHenry against Kennard, it was deemed better that they should not yet meet. Kent and I therefore called at his office, Unity Building. He was evidently expecting us. We here found John Goddard, one of the trustees. McHenry expressed himself pleased to see us, but was evidently excited (probably from letters received from U.S.). I stated the object of our visit, for the perfect adjustment of all differences which had hitherto so much embarrassed us, and the full investigation into all accounts, but did not then propose more than a friendly interview. I imagine he was anticipating a different attitude on our part. Our interview and conversation was very pleasant except for his bitterness against Kennard. I was favorably impressed by the slight acquaintance with Goddard. After an hour's conversation McHenry requested us to go with him to see Elsay at the Bank of England, who he said, wished to see us. Elsay received us with much cordiality and spoke in most exalted terms of McHenry from long acquaintance; advised a full investigation into all proceedings of McHenry and the trustees, which he predicted would result in renewed confidence between all parties. McHenry acquiesced and express his desire for a full examination, which he would aid to the utmost. We parted the best of friends, we accepting an invitation to dine tomorrow. McHenry read me Fallon's letter to him inclosing a copy of his (Fallon's) note to me stating "he did not intend to carry out his threat but wrote for effect on me."

Oct. 23. After breakfast Kent and I went to McHenry's office where we met Thallon, from whom we parted at Birmingham. Kent did not remain and Thallon and I went into a general examination of the Penna. bond accounts, and I obtained a statement of them so far as out of the custody of the trustees. The account shows that most are deposited in various banks either as collateral for advances or for basis of advances on sudden emergency. A large part of the latter being subject to call. Of the New York bonds the last $400,000 have not been yet sold, but are unavailable, being with Splatt under an arrangement with McHenry. Splatt has instituted legal proceedings against McHenry to recover back £30,000 on allegations of non-completion of the road as agreed, and McHenry has commenced Chancery[8] proceedings to restrain him.

Less money has been realized than we had supposed, while of this amount payment of outside commissions made great reduction of net results. McHenry read me letters of Salamanca and Lillo to contradict the assertion made by Kennard that Salamanca was brought into the contract by his influence. At two P.M. met Kent and Kennard at the banking house of Haywood, Kennard & Co. and was introduced to the Kennards, who expressed much interest in the enterprise. At three P.M. Kent, Thallon and I, with McHenry, left London Bridge on boat for Westminster, thence drove through parts of West End to Richmond, and then to Oak Lodge to dine with McHenry, where we met Elsay, Goddard, and Moran of the Legation of U.S., and Sanson of the *Times*. After an excellent dinner and delightful evening, we left for the hotel at eleven o'clock.

Oct. 24. Breakfasted with Kennard; went to the City and spent most of the day at the office with Thallon and McHenry. Thallon and I engaged rooms at Fenton's for the party for tomorrow.

Oct. 26. Removed to Fenton's Hotel and then went to the Canaen St. office, where we went into the arrangement of materials for the settlement of the New York account. Thallon brought Kennard to the office, where a full reconciliation was effected with McHenry.

McHenry read letters from Evans written after his arrival in the U.S. and before our sailing giving most unfair and untrue representations of our motives in coming here, and stating that Kennard and I were very unpopular with the Erie RR Company. We have all come to the conclusion he is not to be trusted.

All I have learned here convinces me that Splatt and Evans with Marsh and others are in conspiracy with Stone, of the Lake Shore [Railroad], to stop our work at Columbus, and make an outlet via Erie. I have fully posted McHenry of this scheme, and its ultimate effect if successful. I think it is dead.

Oct 27. Kennard breakfasted with us. We afterwards prepared a full statement of settlement of the New York accounts with McHenry and submitted it to him for examination.

PARIS, Hôtel de Louvre

Nov. 1. Thallon and I left for Paris via Bologne. Day disagreeable and rainy. The passage of the channel unpleasant in the extreme although (said) not rough. Boat small and the accommodations bad. At Bologne went to cars by omnibus and arrived at Paris 6:30 P.M. where we found Kent at the Hôtel de Louvre. Kennard is at another hotel. He has four children in the city at school, and one with Mrs. Kennard in New York.

Nov. 4. We were advised today that Salamanca would arrive in Paris tomorrow. We accordingly telegraphed McHenry to meet us tomorrow morning without fail.

Visit with Salamanca

Nov. 5. Salamanca arrived this morning and Kennard called to see him. We were disappointed in not seeing McHenry, as Salamanca leaves in the evening. By appointment Kennard, Kent, Thallon and self met him at three o'clock and had an interview of half an hour, Levita acting as interpreter. Salamanca is dissatisfied with the progress of the work and says that under McHenry's agreement with him the work should have been completed to Akron. McHenry furnishing the rest of the funds, and that he (Salamanca) was then to provide funds to complete to Dayton. A misunderstanding of such importance renders the failure of meeting very unfortunate. Salamanca stated that if McHenry could not comply with his engagements to complete to Akron, that he would agree to take the whole line, furnish all the money, and complete at once,— but only with the understanding that he was himself to be the managing contractor. He left with his agent, Quadra, authority to make statement of account from McHenry and report the same to him.

Salamanca is a fine looking man with ease of manner and pleasing address. He is said to be the greatest railway builder of the age. That the profits on his present contracts in Italy will reach five millions of dollars. I am informed by those who pretend to know, that he has

40,000 men on his many works. Levita was to have dined with us, but we received his regrets and acceptance for breakfast in the morning.

Nov. 6. McHenry arrived this morning. Levita breakfasted with us, and we had the pleasure of the attendance of his brother at dinner. The day was spent in the examination and preparation of accounts for Quadra.

Nov. 11. This morning by appointment called on Quadra and saw his report to Salamanca which was satisfactory. As Salamanca is to return to Madrid in a few days we have decided to meet him there and if practicable, bring all negotiations to a conclusion.

Nov. 13. We left Paris this morning, with Edward as courier, and interpreter, via Orleans, Blois, Poitiers, and arrived at Bordeaux 9:50 P.M. [We] remained for the night at Hôtel de France [while] McHenry and Kennard remained in Paris [but] are to meet us here tomorrow.

Nov. 14. Bordeaux. We have spent the day here awaiting McHenry and Kennard. At 2:30 Edward left for Bayonne to make arrangements for our journey to Madrid. On our return from the opera in the evening, received a telegram from McHenry postponing arrival of himself and Kennard for twenty-four hours.

Nov. 15. McHenry and Kennard did not arrive as was expected much to our disappointment. We shall leave for Bayonne in the morning, having word that they will meet us on the train.

Nov. 16. We left the hotel expecting to meet McHenry and Kennard at depot, and were much disappointed at not seeing them, but were most agreeably surprised after a journey of some miles, to see them with Levita on the platform, we having missed each other on the train. The day was rainy and the country for a large part of the way a flat pine covered morass with few inhabitants occupied in production of turpentine and resin. We arrived at Bayonne with Levita and Thallon went to Bieritz [*sic*] to meet us in the morning.

Nov. 17. Left Bieritz at 6 A.M. in a diligence[9] specially chartered for the party. Thallon and Levita joined us from Bieritz. Passed some handsome grounds pertaining to private residences near the city, and met numbers of market women with their little donkeys. We soon entered among the hills and passed the dividing stream and entered

Spain. Our passports were examined both on the French and Spanish side of the stream, and a soldier or gendarme [was] sent on the diligence to the Custom House some miles in the [interior]. Our road passed over mountains with picturesque scenes and well cultivated farms in the valleys or hillsides. Saw the women for the first time with black mantillas and black plume in front. The men wore large blue flat caps and scarlet sash. We reached the Custom House in a most desolate and antiquated village with large stone houses, the lower or ground story used for stable purposes. The church dated back to the 16th Century containing in its tower four discordant cracked bells. Excutcheons [*sic*] on the front of the town hall recorded the deaths of the several alcaldes of the city. We were detained two hours in this village. The afternoon ride was very interesting amid high and rugged mountains. Late in the evening we reached the highest summit with a magnificent view. At 9 P.M. rested at the Hotel de Infanta in Pamplona [*sic*]. Tired and hungry we ordered a simple but substantial dinner and were greatly surprised to be soon seated at a most sumptuous repast with choice wines, which had been ordered by Lillo from Paris.

Nov. 18. Left Pampelona on cars, our diligence being mounted on one of the flat cars. At Tudela we again took the diligence. The country to this place was good, the road well constructed, but curves abrupt. After leaving Tudela passed large plantations of olives, but as we commenced the ascent of the Sierra, the hills became barren and sterile to an extreme, the only cultivated portions being a narrow strip in the village. For miles neither house nor tree was visible, and the hills covered with rock and black heath. The weather was rainy and disagreeable and the Sierra Nevada covered with snow. The inhabitants look like brigands with striped ragged blankets, red turbans and sandals. Every stopping place was infested with most, most miserable beggars.

The Spanish villages are the most dreary imaginable. Gendarmes patrol the highways and towns to protect against banditti. We reached Soria where we supped in a cheerless room only warmed by a large brazier of coals under the table, which warmed our knees, while our feet and backs were freezing.

Nov 19. The ride from Soria was cold and uncomfortable. We did not reach Jadraque until 11 A.M. too late for the cars. We telegraphed to Madrid and the company ordered a special train, but we were again detained, by the breaking down of the engine and did not leave until 5:30 and arrived at Madrid at 9:25 and after vexatious delay by Custom House officials established ourselves in comfortable quarters at the Hotel de Engletine. (The old Court of the Inquisition).

Nov. 21. With Levita and McHenry called on Salamanca when we met Kennard who had preceded us an hour. Salamanca did not seem disposed for a further advance on reasonable terms, but said he did not fully understand Quadra's report, and wished further information on points submitted in writing. We arranged that Kennard and Levita should return with written answers in the afternoon.

Nov. 22. Levita and Kennard called again on Salamanca at his request for further explanations and affairs are assuming a more favorable shape, as he more perfectly understands the state of the enterprise. We are all invited to dine with him tomorrow.

Nov. 23. Kennard and Levita spent the morning with Salamanca with very satisfactory progress. We dined with him at his residence. The party included several agreeable gentlemen and ladies many of whom could converse in English. His superb house was brilliantly lighted and his picture gallery thrown open.

Nov. 24. By invitation of Salamanca we visited his country residence a few miles from the city. A beautiful place with handsome grounds and expensive house containing valuable statuary and a large collection of paintings. On our return we occupied his private box at the Plaza del Teros and witnessed the brutal and disgusting national amusement, a bull fight. The building was crowded a large portion of the spectators being handsomely dressed ladies who seemed to take great delight in the cruel sport. We left Madrid by rail for Jadraque, where we again changed to the uncomfortable night ride on the diligence.

Nov. 25. Spent the night in the diligence as also all of today until six o'clock this evening. We breakfasted at Soria at a wretched hotel. The town is very ancient and dilapidated. The fountain in the plaza in front of the hotel was surrounded by women filling their water casks. At Tudela we had a good supper at the station and left by rail and arrived at Sarragassa [*sic*] where at the Hôtel d'Europe we have comfortable quarters.

Kennard, Kent, and McHenry parted from us at Tudela. We left Levita at Madrid enroute for the South of Spain. Thallon and I with Edward for our courier return to Paris via Barcelona.

Nov. 26. We left Sarragassa. The moon was shining brightly and the street appeared well built. We crossed the Ebro on a fine stone bridge, the river being as wide as the Allegheny at Franklin. The first part of the ride was through a plain bordered by mountains, the more distant covered with snows. The land in some parts well cultivated and fruitful in others a sterile clay washed in gullies and ravines by the rains. Mont Serat was in view for many hours, a collection of rocky pinnacles. Montzen and Lerida are strongly fortified. We arrived at Barcelona at six in the evening and are well lodged at the hotel of the Four Nations.

Nov. 27. Spent the day riding about the city and visiting the fort on the promontory overlooking the Mediterranean. We were permitted to go through the fortification and officer detailed to accompany us. The commandant was very courteous and invited us to take a glass of wine with him. We left Barcelona at five in the evening by rail, and at eight o'clock were transferred to a diligence for a night ride over the mountains.

Nov. 28. We passed a comfortable night in the diligence and reached the frontier at Bellegarde where we passed the usual Custom House examination. The fortification on the French side is very strong and perfectly commands the pass. We almost immediately began the descent of the Pyrenees and I enjoyed the ride exceedingly. The scenery in the mountains was wild and grand and after the descent the road passed through a beautiful highly cultivated plain. For miles overarching sycamores shaded the roadway. We reached Perpignan at 10 and remained until three visiting its old churches and its castle now used for a military prison.

Nov. 29. We arrived at Avignon this morning. After breakfast we visited the Palace of the Popes and many of the churches. The view from the Palace is extensive and comprises in its limits fourteen villages within a radius of 20 to 30 miles. At one o'clock we left on the cars for Paris.

The road passes through the valley of the Rhone where the olive groves of Spain and the south of France have given place to the mulberry and vine. Dined at Lyons where we saw notice in the paper of the capture of Mason and Slidell by U.S. Steamship *San Jacinto*.[10] We are very apprehensive that trouble with England may result and as the least of evils feel that all of our negotiations may be jeopardized by the uncertainty of the political future.

Nov. 30. Arrived at Paris. We found McHenry, Kent, and Kennard at the Hôtel de Louvre. McHenry and Thallon left for London.

Dec. 1. There is much excitement over the capture of Mason and Slidell and by many war with England is predicted as the result. We feel very blue over the disastrous prospect of our financial negotiations.

Dec. 3. Kent and I left Paris this morning. Left Bologne and arrived at Folkstone and [later] at London. Came to Fenton's Hotel where we met Train.

Dec. 4. Spent most of the day at the office where I met Kennard and Evans. War is the general topic of conversation and prospects look very gloomy.

Dec. 5. Spent most of the day at the office arranging accounts. Called on Elsay at the Bank of England, who thinks time unpropitious for financial ventures. Am invited to dine with McHenry tomorrow and with Howard Kennard on Saturday.

Dec. 6. Breakfasted with Train and two gentlemen whom I suspect being in the secession interest. In the evening dined with McHenry, Howard Kennard and wife, Goddard, T. W. Kennard, Thallon, and Kent.

Dec. 10. Kent and I left London [and] reached Dublin at 6 P.M. Next day to Belfast.

Dec. 13. Spent the morning in looking at points of interest in [Londonderry], and in the afternoon embarked on the [ship], where we again met Thallon. We have few passengers and those wives of officers sent to Canada and Canadians. Most of them, Thallon says, sympathize with secession.

After a stormy passage of fourteen days we entered Portland Harbor.

Peto Joins the Ranks

Dec. 14. McHenry: "I have just seen Sir Morton Peto. He is disposed to take up the whole affair. In some way I shall manage it soon as daylight appears in politics."

Dec. 20. McHenry: "Sir Morton Peto has given me $25,000 this week, . . . and I have transferred them to rails to be held only in case of war. . . . In case peace is assured the rails will be at once devoted to our road and ample means be places at your disposal. . . . Kennard hopes to sail next week. . . . I am well inclined for an immediate branch to Titusville and another to Franklin."[11]

Dec. 21. McHenry [to Thallon]: "You may consider our all money secure in case of peace, and we shall be ready for immediate operations. Church writes to Evans that he can buy from Struthers a charter from any point on the S&E RR to the oil wells. . . . Church says it can be had for $3,000 but I would pay much more to secure its privileges. . . . Lose no time in securing it so that we can run at once a tramway to Titusville of our own gauge to be worked by horses from Corry or locomotives if you prefer. A much more peaceful feeling today and all stocks are up."

Dec. 27. Levita, from Paris: "On my return from Cadiz to Paris I was staying a few days in Madrid in order to complete some arrangements with Salamanca. Salamanca is ready to conclude definitely the arrangements which had been provisionally agreed to during your presence in Madrid, in case McHenry has assured elsewhere £200,000. McHenry informs me that the said amount has been provided for subordinate only to maintenance of peace."

Dec. 28. McHenry: "I have my arrangements complete for instant progress to Akron, as soon as peace is made assured. In view of this please hasten forward the New York bonds and . . . endeavor to extract from Hallett the Penna. bonds which it becomes so important I should have."

Conditions at Close of Year

On May 27, the line had opened to Corry. The line in both states operated by the A&GW in NY under the superintendence of Hill. Owing to financial difficulties work on the extension of the road in Penna. was virtually suspended, although a small force was employed west of Corry. McHenry had become embarrassed in his negotiations and while constantly promising remittances failed to meet his engagements. Distrust naturally arose and this was promoted by interested parties. It became evident that there was a scheme entertained by the English representatives of the Erie RR, the officers of the latter company and the Cleveland and Erie interests, to make a connection from Columbus or Corry with the Lake Shore at Erie, and stop all further building of the A&GW west of Corry.

The Erie RR Company coveted the control of the A&GW and by representations to English creditors of their company enlisted them in the project. At least one prominent director of the A&GW was suspected of being employed by them to further the plan. Foreign negotiations were rendered difficult by the Civil War and from all these causes the business affairs of the company grew daily more embarrassed. And to add to this arose the quarrel between McHenry and Kennard. At last it was deemed important that a representative committee should go to Europe. This was a wise and, as the event proved, a fortunate movement, although for a time paralyzed by the *Trent* troubles. The interview restored confidence between the various parties in interest.

During the absence of the committee Evans, Fallon, and one of the A&GW directors did much to discourage and embarrass the directors of the A&GW. An effort was made to remove Hill. It was at one time deemed necessary to forward $400,000 of the New York 2nd mortgage when they were all prepared for signature. On December 3 the trustee, Marsh, declined to sign them, after having promised to do so.

The year closed with a line to [the] junction with S&E RR and all construction forces disbanded.

5. Difficulties Continue, 1862

With a boom in the oil market, Reynolds and Robert Thallon urged that the A&GW run a branch line into the oil region. McHenry agreed, but he also pleaded for additional securities and threatened to hold back on sending cash until he received them. Reynolds warned that this would be counterproductive. He insisted that the company was meeting its obligations under the contract, that McHenry was being capricious in his financial dealing with European investors, and that his actions underscored the need for better accounting and management. A shortage of cash was causing strikes by the workers on the line. Cash problems and disgruntled workers did not prevent the company from negotiating for new lines to Franklin and Sharon in Pennsylvania, and to Cleveland and Cincinnati in Ohio.

Oil Traffic Increases

Jan. 1. McHenry: "Hope that I shall be able to arrange for Kennard's departure next week well provided with means to go right on to Akron."

Jan. 4. Thallon, New York, relative to Oil Creek charter: "I wrote to McHenry relative to the building into the oil region. From what I have seen and learned since my return, I am fully of the opinion that it will be expedient if not absolutely necessary to build to the oil region to or near Titusville. The S&E now owned by the PRR Co. contemplate the same, and it is important our line should be located and commenced first. . . . It will be advisable to secure the Struthers charter in preference to obtaining a new one, as much valuable time would be saved, and the trouble of legislation avoided. . . . I fear to secure the control of this valuable traffic it may also be necessary to build to Franklin. . . . The Lake Shore Company proposes to build from Jamestown on the S&E RR to Franklin. When I tell you that at this time two hundred wagons laden with oil pass through Meadville daily for the P&E besides those which pass south of this place, you can form some idea of effort to secure this traffic."[1]

Jan. 10. A letter was received from a committee of Franklin gentlemen. Bissell, Whittaker, Heydrick, McCalmont, and C. V. Culver, appointed by a public meeting of the citizens asking the A&GW RR Co. to extend a branch to that place.

Jan. 11. McHenry: "The settlement of the *Trent* affair clears the track. As at present arranged, Kennard sails next Cunarder with credits complete. . . . Kennard is in Paris today. Salamanca will be there also."

Jan. 13. To Thallon: "Our town is filled with oil wagons every day, from the oil region to Linesville on the P&E RR. While only a portion take this route, many going south of us to other points on the same road. . . . We have appointed a meeting with the committee (from Franklin) on Friday, when we will endeavor to set matters in proper shape."

Church saw Struthers in Philadelphia and is of the opinion that his Titusville charter can be secured at less than the sum suggested in his letter to McHenry. We all concur in the importance of securing its control.

Jan. 17. I wrote a very full letter to McHenry relative to the oil traffic and the proposed road to Titusville and Franklin, with a map of the region and the proposed outlets. At the present time it is estimated that more than 2000 wagons are employed in hauling oil and one half of these delivering to the P&E at Linesville and Jamestown, PA.

Jan. 21. McHenry, Paris: "I am here to close our negotiation with Duke Rianzares and Salamanca, and all looks well for Kennard sailing on Saturday (25th) with his papers in order for a speedy termination of the A&GW to Akron. We won't stop short of this, but our program will be aided by an immediate branch to Titusville, and one also to Franklin, soon as we reach Meadville."

Jan 22. The PRR Co. assent to terms for crossing the S&E track.

Jan. 30. Left Meadville in my sleigh. At Union [Mills] found vast quantity of oil awaiting transportation, said to be 20,000 bbls. At Corry 7,000 bbls. Kent arrived tonight.

Jan. 31. All hands have been busy moving to the new office. Hill's absence causes much annoyance. Church and Shryock arrived and in evening, board met at the office.

Feb. 1. Board meeting at 9. At noon Thorp, Dick, and Shryock left for home. Church, Kent, and I left for New York.

Feb. 2. Near Port Jervis (west) on the precipice we had a narrow escape from serious accident by the breaking of a rail. We left the car and rode to Port Jervis in the baggage car.

Feb. 7. Went with J. M. Dick, Treasurer, and Church to office of Marsh and cancelled all over $1,000,000 of New York 1st mortgage bonds. I signed $100,000 New York 2nd and Marsh Trustee, the $400,000 New York 2nd mortgage.

Feb. 8. No arrival of Kennard, but expect him next steamer. Spent the morning at Thallon's where, with Church, drew a form of contract for extension of contract of the Penna. bonus to submit to the Erie RR Company. Streator arrived.

Kennard, London: "My place had been taken in the *Edinburgh*, . . . but I could not go by it. . . . It is most important that we complete the Titusville branch at once. . . . We must lay the rails [on] the surface even if the grades are 150 feet to the mile. . . . Time is everything. . . . I hope to get our engines through in six weeks after my arrival. Our subscription list is now complete, but we must have a traffic to encourage our friends. . . . The *Trent* affair has caused a vast amount of ill feeling."

In 1860, August 21, the A&GW in New York [had] borrowed from the A&GW of Ohio 879 tons of rails, agreeing to return the like quantity when needed, and deposited with Henry A. Kent $20,000 of New

York 1st mortgage bonds. It has become necessary to have these bonds for negotiation, and in order to obtain them Church and I gave a personal guaranty to Kent for the delivery of the iron within sixty days, a guaranty which was the cause of much inconvenience in the future.

Feb. 9. McHenry: "I am pleased you have arranged to send [2nd Mortgage] New York bonds. . . .

"I regret much that Kennard remains very ill and today is confined to bed, but the doctor says he has no doubt of being able to sail on the 13th. He will have £20,000 with him and my whole finance will be easy if satisfactory progress may be made westward, as well as to the [oil] wells, in order to stimulate receipts.

"The Duke of Rianzares has paid me £20,000 on . . . his subscription of £100,000 and each two months he is to pay same amount, provided Navarro goes on your board and gives him assurance that all is going well. Sir Morton Peto subscribed £50,000 but will not pay for some time. Heywood, Kennard & Co. and Barnard & Co. each subscribe £75,000 in installments same as the Duke. . . .

"I am very desirous to see good relations reestablished between you and Fallon. It is many reasons. . . . Part of the onerous conditions made with the Duke is the purchase by me of the American estates now managed by Fallon."

Feb. 12. Went with Church and Streator [to] Philadelphia. Called at PRR office and arranged terms for the crossing at Corry. Then met Morehead at S&E RR office. On return to hotel met Struthers and had a talk about the Titusville charter. It can be secured to the interest of the A&GW on terms to be submitted to Kennard by Streator. Streator and I returned to New York, Church remaining.

Feb. 13. Went to Thallon's with Streator where he fully explained to Thallon the situation of the Titusville charter. Went back with Streator to office 54 Broad St. where he read his letters to Kennard relative to the Struthers (Titusville) charter. Went to Erie RR office and consulted with Minot about road equipment. Spent an hour and a half with Marsh talking over the interests of the road and urged the renewal of the bonus contract with Penna. company. His remarks relative to the proposed plan for a third rail from Corry to Erie as proposed by Stone, convinced me that had it been done our future prospects for the building of the A&GW would have been blasted.

McHenry: "Kennard improves daily but we have decided it will be safe for him to start out on the 19th by *City of New York.* You may look for him by that ship. We have read over carefully your valuable letters of 21st January with diagram. . . . I have to say that the Titusville Branch is a *financial necessity* to enable me by this early development of a great traffic to secure the continued support of my friends."

Feb. 15. Spent the morning at Thallon's and Kent's. In the afternoon called on Marsh relative to the proposed bonus contract. I have in hand the renewal of the old contract with the Erie RR for a percentage of receipts on our traffic. The executive committee of that company were favorably disposed, but the percentage on westward bound business would be objectionable.

Feb. 17. Had a short interview with Minot who introduced me to J. C. Blasdel, of Boston, who proposes to furnish freight cars. In the afternoon had a long and satisfactory interview with Marsh at the Erie RR office. Left for home.

Feb. 19. Jamestown. Spent the morning at office with Calhoun, Hill, and J. M. Dick. Hill's resignation to take effect the 20th has been received, and it is arranged that for the present Calhoun shall act as Superintendent. Hill's course is not satisfactory.

McHenry: "I fear it will be ten days before [Kennard] sails. I saw him this morning. . . . If Kennard cannot sail [on] *China,* I will send then £20,000 bank credits which are already prepared. . . . The finance question is sound. I have £300,000 to go to Akron with, payable as we proceed. I am bound to be in Meadville in June and Akron in October. See copy of contract in hands of Fallon. I send Thallon orders for 500 tons rails for your immediate use, and shall send you more by *China* if Kennard cannot go."

Feb. 20. McHenry: "I find Kennard much the same today. Very feeble. I think we must make up our minds to proceed without him at present, and you must arrange accordingly. Peto's engineer won't be ready for a fortnight. I must therefore depend on your able administration, and I shall send the credits in your name and Thallon's if it be de-cided Kennard don't go [by] *China.* I shall send also an order for bal-ance of rails. . . . I am under heavy responsibilities to be at Meadville in June and Akron in October."

Feb. 22. McHenry: "I . . . have duly received the $400,000 (bonds). . . . I am happy to state that Kennard is rapidly improving and beyond a doubt will sail on the *China* on 1st March. I have arranged to send the balance of rails and £20,000 to you in case he had not. . . . *The road must be at Akron in October.* . . . I think a horse railway to Titusville will answer every purpose and save much cost."

Feb. 28. Contracts with S&E RR Co. for a crossing at Corry execut-ed and sent to Thomson, president PRR.

March 1. Thallon: "The bonds were forwarded last night by express ($400,000 New York 2nd to McHenry). . . . Expect *City of New York* Tuesday. . . . Enclosed is a note from Fallon about electing Navarro (representing Duke Rianzares). Will you have that done on Mon-day? . . . I hope you have ordered rolling stock. . . . I consider that we are all safe to go through to Akron."

March 3. Left home in carriage with Dick, Church, Shryock, and Thorp. Found great accumulation of oil at Union [Mills] and Corry.

March 4. Meeting of board authorized the issue to the contractors of $100,000 2nd mortgage instead of 1st mortgage. Accepted resignation of Evans and elected Navarro to the board.

March 6. Left Corry for Erie, and in the afternoon left for Cleveland. Met Merrill at the hotel and talked over terms for building twenty cattle cars.

Thallon: "You will be sorry to see that Kennard has been very sick. . . . Mrs. Kennard has a letter from her sister dated 17th, advising the same. I have today however telegram from Halifax dated the 22nd in which McHenry says Kennard is much better and will sail positively in the *China.* She . . . will be here next Tuesday or Wednesday."

March 7. In the morning rode with Merrill to his car factory and arranged for the purchase of twenty cars. Left Cleveland, dined at Erie, returned to Girard and to Linesville by P&E RR and home by stage.

March 12. Arrived at St. Nicholas, New York. Called at Hanover

Square on Thallon and read his letters. Little hope of Kennard's arrival for two weeks.

March 14. Met Streator at Thallon's and completed arrangements for commencement of work. McHenry sends credits for £10,000. Thallon gave Streator cheque for amount of McHenry's indebtedness. Called on Marsh at Erie RR office relative to the bonus contract. He wishes to cut it down to five years. I remonstrated and hope he will not insist. He will have it drawn in full tomorrow.

March 17. McHenry: "Sir Morton Peto has made it one of his conditions that Rose should be on the line under Kennard in some way as engineer, and I am sure this will be agreeable to all concerned."

March 18. Jamestown. Streator and C. Coolman [Engineer] arrived from Corry. I arranged with Coolman for the commencement of the location west of Corry, and settled all contract accounts with [Streator].

March 25. Coolman reports: "I am happy to inform you that I have succeeded in finding a location for our line keeping entirely on the south side of French Creek which meets our most sanguine expectations."

March 27. Kennard has arrived and will be out on Sunday. Goddard sent letter of introduction of J. H. R. Rose, who has been appointed by my friend Sir Morton Peto as his confidential agent, as well as to employ his engineering talents for the A&GW RR. Also a letter of introduction of Lawrence Johnston, who has been engaged by McHenry to assist keeping him posted as to the accounts of the railway, having had great experience in the Railway Clearing House for the past nine years.

March 31. Left home in buggy with Peter. Met Peter Young at Corry who is to take charge of a construction gang as soon as work shall be ready. Arranged with Baldwin of S&E RR for a platform at Corry. Also met Coolman at Corry and spent the evening at Jamestown office with Calhoun and J. M. Dick.

April 1. Streator and Calhoun came from Corry. Kennard did not arrive as expected. Church returned from New York. Kennard telegraphed wishing us to go to New York. Had full talk with Coolman relative to the engineering, and in the evening gave instructions to Newham, track-master, with regard to the track. Merrill came with

Streator and I arranged with him to build ten flat cars instead of cattle cars, for gravel train.

April 8. Spent the day at Jamestown settling rights of way and negotiating with Baker, Allen, Hall, and Shaws for depot grounds from Baker. Baker asked $3,000 for land south of road to the creek, payable June 1st. We offer payment 1, 2, and 3 years. No conclusion. Kennard telegraphed that he would leave New York tonight. Streator came from Corry in the morning and in the evening read me the correspondence relative to the oil road.

Thallon: "Kennard has left me to go to the train. . . . He has with him Rose, an assistant engineer, and Johnston, book-keeper, both from London. This will relieve Flagg from that post, but I have arranged with Kennard that he will take the post of paymaster instead. . . . If Kennard and the Doctor can settle about this oil road, we can go to work vigorously. I am sending you 64 tons rails, and chairs will go next week."

April 9. Kennard, with Rose and Johnston, arrived from New York and a full conference was held relative to the oil road, resulting in an agreement written by me and signed by Kennard for McHenry of the first part, and Streator contractor, of the second part:

"The said first party in consideration of the location and construction of the said railroad from Corry to the oil region, with a continuous six-feet-gauge from the Atlantic & Great Western RR and other considerations hereafter mentioned, contracts to furnish to second party for such construction 2,600 tons of iron rails to be delivered at Corry, and the sum of $75,000 cash according to following terms:

"Second party shall deposit with Henry A. Kent, of the city of New York, $375,000 1st Mortgage of the said company bonds 7 per cent interest. . . . Upon the deposit with Kent of an order for 2,600 tons of iron [and] . . . $50,000 cash. . . . The remaining $25,000 . . . to be paid . . . as required for completion and stocking of the road to Titusville.

"Upon the completion . . . second party . . . to pay first party . . . $50,000 in shares . . . of road. . . . The issue of stock limited to $16,000 per mile finished, and 20 per cent of net earnings reserved for a sinking fund.

"Office of A&GW Ry. Co. Hanover Building, Hanover Square."

April 12. Kennard's estimate of cost to complete from Corry to Akron exclusive of rolling stock, and including 25 miles oil branch $799,150.[2] Cash on hand $140,000.

April 16. Thallon: "You will be pleased I am sure, with the energetic way Kennard is proceeding to work. At the rate Kennard is progressing he will soon use up money. I therefore enclose to you for your signature the first of £10,000."

Labor Shortages during the War

April 19. Kennard: "I am here hard at work. . . . I have secured 2,000 fresh laborers here—that is to say, I have made contracts with agents who agree to find them in 20 days. This looks well and it is my intention to be at Akron on 30th August in a locomotive, and I hope to have you with me. . . . I have bought . . . furniture (for house at Meadville). The Dr. will have to look out sharp for shovels."

NOTE: The men sent from New York by Kennard's agent were very unsatisfactory, as will be seen from To Kennard: "I am sure you will come out loser in the transaction unless you can provide against the impositions practiced. A large proportion of those sent never come on the works, or if they do, cause disturbance and dissatisfaction among those at work. Many are the very off-scourings of the City, their countenances stamped with vice and degradation, and in many cases utterly unfit for work. In a party which arrived today were two boys not more than ten or twelve years of age. All claim they were engaged under the ten hour rule, and some refuse to work at all. Of the first party of sixty, twenty left after two days . . . (with good to the OC RR.) I feel sure that efforts are making and influences exerted which if successful will not contribute to the interest of the A&GW.[3]

"Eighty men arrived this morning and after breakfast a gang of twenty-five desperadoes started over the line to compel the working parties to quit. Of the party of 140 who came previously, none are at work at this time. Many are induced by unprincipled contractors on the S&E

RR to leave to you the [cost of] transportation out and go to [work on] that road. The only profit to result from this method of forcing the work will be to the Erie RR Company for transportation."

April 22. Met Streator at Corry, who informed me of his interview with Reed, Superintendent of Feeder,[4] relative to occupation of towing path by A&GW.

April 23. Jamestown. Saw Allen and others of E&NY City RR and submitted the McHenry proposition to retain the $45,000 New York bonds (which were to have long since been returned) and pay for them £140 per bond. They will give an answer after consideration.

April 25. To McHenry: "We have had great difficulty in obtaining the number of laborers necessary for the work, but Kennard is sending a large number from New York, and they are coming in from all quarters, and I think by the middle of May we will have all . . . we want."

April 29. Left home with my horse and buggy for Waterford. At Corry met B. Wells foreman for the Oil Creek R.R. (OC RR) The work on that road has not yet been commenced. Newham informed me that the chairs will not fit the rails, and I telegraphed Kennard to stop shipments until the same was made right. At Jamestown I met the Committee of the E&NY City RR relative to McHenry's proposition to pay them for the $45,000 of New York bonds which should have been returned by him. Their board met in the evening and agreed to the proposition.

More Financial Difficulties

April 30. I closed the long standing and vexatious question of the $45,000 New York Bonds retained by McHenry with the E&NY City RR Co by drawing the necessary orders for cash and stock under authority of the executive committee. On return found some sixty or seventy laborers on train sent from New York by Kennard's agent; a hard looking lot.

May 1. Kennard: "I have just time to tell you I have settled with Hallett." The above settlement was delusive as much trouble was experienced for some time in closing the transaction with Hallett by Kennard and McHenry. The companies were only interested in so far as Hallett should embarrass McHenry by attachments on bonds.

May 5. McHenry was authorized and empowered as agent of the company, to make the necessary detailed arrangements in Europe for securing and perfecting the objects and purposes set forth.

May 7. McHenry: "I think you will agree with me the company is bound to find me the securities I require. My arrangements for cash and rails are complete to take us to Akron . . . based upon my contracts, which entitle me as a right, not as a favor, . . . to certain issues of bonds and shares. . . . I shall go on with remittances under Kennard's requisitions."

May 8. Left home with my horse and buggy; crossed at Pollock's bridge, and arrived at LeBeouf,[5] whence took cars (S&E RR). Thorp, Rose, and Flagg joined at Union [Mills]; the two latter left at Concord to go over the line. At Corry met Struthers and Wells, who informed me a commencement of work on the OC RR. At Jamestown found treasury depleted by payments to Erie RR Co. on iron. Telegraphed Kennard and wrote Thallon on the subject.

May 9. Gangs of men were at work on the line and making good progress.

May 10. McHenry: "I am going on with rails and shall have cash in New York to meet Kennard's requisitions for June, but hope you will have seen the justice of my demand for securities to be lodged with the trustees as per contract. . . . I had a long conversation with the Duke of Rianzares yesterday. He is here with the Queen to see the exhibition. . . . I translated to him Kennard's last letters and he assured me I shall have more money than the contract calls for if I require it."

May 14. McHenry: "I have not yet decided as to issuing the bonds. My cash arrangements are complete without actual sales, and my losses in the New York division now so severe that I must make what I can out of the remainder of my work. . . . My chief and only fears have been want of securities to deposit. . . . During this month I shall have 6,000 tons [of rails] afloat, and the balance of Kennard's requisition will follow without delay. The Duke assures me that he will supply me with more money than his contract in case of need, but we will not want it."

May 18. McHenry: "I make a large remittance today to cover the June payments, and am pushing forward the rails. . . . I have not yet brought forward the Penna. bonds. Waiting for the documents written for and for a favorable opportunity."

May 28. McHenry: "Nothing can be more satisfactory than your letters. I am entirely satisfied. Judge Thompson of your country was here with me this morning. He knows you and highly regards you. He did not know I had any connection with the A&GW RR and was astonished at its sound position. He quite agrees with all our friends that when built it would be the most profitable railway in the United States. . . . I shall not cease until I send 11,000 tons [rails]."

May 31. McHenry: "I have yours of 12th. Nothing could be more satisfactory, as I now know my wants are understood, and you are determined to meet them."

Note on foregoing letters:

McHenry's complaints of the failure of the companies to furnish securities was without foundation, as the companies had done all they agreed to do. But McHenry was constantly making and changing his financial arrangements in Europe according to the exigencies of the time, without the knowledge or consultation with the companies, and in the [end] many of his schemes would promise what could not be performed by the companies, without a longer time than he arranged for. To this impetuous and vacillating method a great part of his trouble was due.

May 14. Kennard: "I am coming out tonight with Navarro." Kennard at this time has taken his residence in Meadville in the Shippen House, and removed the construction offices to this place in the Corinthian Block.

On May 16 the A&GW RR Co. of Penna authorized a second mortgage of $1,000,000 of date of July 1, 1862.

May 20. Left this morning with Kennard and Coolman in Kennard's carriage. Arrived at LeBeouf 30 minutes before the S&E cars. Reached Warren. Streator and Merrill arrived in the evening train. Streator, Kennard, and I spent the evening with Struthers, discussing the question guaranty for OC RR bonds. He objects to a contract with the company, but made a supplemental contract with Streator which may suit our purpose.

To McHenry: "Kennard works indefatigably and is in the best of spirits. We are pleased with Rose. If your expectations are [realized] as to cash, all on this side will do well."

May 22. Penna. company takes preliminary action relative to a guaranty of the OC RR bonds under certain conditions.

May 27. [Jamestown]. The board of the New York Co. elected yesterday organized and authorized sending to London $200,000 New York 2nd mortgage for hypothecation for purchase of rolling stock. The question of guarantee of OC RR bonds was discussed and referred to a committee to report. Kennard, Shryock, Dick, and Thorp, returned to [Meadville]. Church and I go to New York.

May 28. Arrived at St. Nicholas having been detained by the burning of the bridge at Narrowsburg. Called to see Thallon.

June 7. Board meeting of the A&GW of Penna. committee Reynolds, Church, and Finney reporting in favor of guaranty for OC RR bonds which report was approved and adopted by the board. Finney tendered his resignation as director of the company.

June 12. To McHenry: "We today forward $48,000 1st Penna. bonds." The rest of New York 2nd are of small denominations and time is required for signature of the secretary. We will work at them until the Penna. 2nd mortgage is ready, when being of $1,000 denominations we will be able to prepare more rapidly and send, and then resume work on balance of New York 2nd. The work is progressing finely."

Franklin Branch

June 17. [At the] board meeting of the A&GW of Penna. the engineer was instructed to survey the eastern coal fields branch and extension (Franklin Branch) and make full report and estimate.

June 18. McHenry: "I feel much indebted. . . . We shall not stumble again. . . . I am loading rails . . . and will remit further cash soon as the bulk of the bonds arrive."

June 23. Left in buggy with Church for Jamestown to arrange for depot. Met the Jamestown directors who presented their plans, and we agreed to submit them to the board. At Corry with Downer examined location for a side track for his proposed oil works. Also met Potts, Superintendent S&E RR and Baldwin, relative [to] mutual interests of the companies in oil transportation.

June 28. McHenry: "The bonds arrive in due order and my machinery will now work smoothly. I send bank credits next week for £10,000 and £20,000 and will go on steadily. I have already shipped . . . 8,900 tons rails, and will have 3,000 more during July."[6]

July 5. To McHenry: "The treasurer will forward to the trustees next week $900,000 of 2nd mortgage of Penna. The residue of New York 2nd mortgage will be sent by the following steamer. This will be all of the bonds of Penna. and New York unappropriated, except $50,000 of small bonds retained for the exigencies of home use.

"I received yours of the 18th June and must confess that it greatly puzzled me and at the same time has caused me great solicitude. You say that you will forward more money when the bulk of bonds arrive. I am utterly at a loss to understand this. So far as the Penna. company is concerned it has certainly not been in any degree derelict to its obligations under the contract, or under any understood arrangements with you. When I left London it was fully understood by me that you had the control of sufficient 1st mortgage bonds for all early exigencies, and you gave me a statement showing over $400,000 in England subject to your control, beside the Ohio bonds.

"I had no idea to the contrary until your most urgent letters to forward 2nd mortgage. This we have done as rapidly as time would permit. A very considerable portion of bonds have already reached your hands, including some of those released from the Hallett difficulty and the New York 2nd mortgage.

"All of our 1st mortgage Penna. you have except the $50,000 to the contractors and I cannot understand why at this early stage of the work money should be short until the *bulk* of the residue of the bonds should arrive.

"Now, as the bulk of these bonds will not reach you before this letter, and as there is not any cash on hand for the payment for the past month (not taking into consideration the present month), the time for payment is next week, when at least $50,000 will be required. Can you doubt our uneasiness as to the future?

"We have had some serious consultations as to the course to adopt, but difficulties surround on all sides. Should the payment be delayed, most disastrous results must follow. Yet, where can means be obtained on such short notice? The very effort to borrow at this early stage must have a most damaging effect on the credit you wish to establish for launching your bonds on the market.

"It seems a great pity to disband your forces which have been collected at much expense and trouble, and could not be again recollected without great cost. Yet if funds do not arrive, I see no alternative. . . .

"This is rather a blue letter, and I still hope that the coming mail will prove that I have not properly interpreted your meaning as written in your letter."

July 11. At Corry met Struthers and left with him the proposed plan for station and track location for the OC RR. At Jamestown met Allen and Shaw, and arranged for closing the E&NY City RR contract with the A&GW in NY.

It will be seen by To McHenry of July 5 that he had utterly failed in his remittance for the early part of the month and the prospect was that his remittance would await the receipt of more bonds. More than a thousand men were at work between Meadville and Corry, many of them of a bad character, and who would stop at no excess if their passion was aroused. The indebtedness of the contractors to these men, and to contractors for ties, etc. exceeded $60,000. Pay day was at hand and no money, and worse, no immediate prospect.

July 13. The situation was desperate, and it was deemed absolutely necessary that I should again visit London and see personally to placing our finances on a secure basis for the future.

July 15. Arrived at Astor House [New York] and secured the only remaining state room on *Scotia*.

July 16. We left the Astor House for Jersey City and were just in time for the last tug to the *Scotia*. The day is delightful and our stateroom though small is well located. The ocean is calm.

July 25. The Irish coast was in full view this morning. Day beautiful and ocean smooth. Arrived at Queenstown and [went to] the Imperial Hotel, Cork.

July 30. London. Secured room at the Terminus Hotel and went at once to meet McHenry at the old Broad St. office. Was greatly relieved to find that our affairs were in an improved condition, and that a remittance passed me on the ocean.

July 31. Spent the morning at the office with McHenry adjusting the accounts of bonds and arranged for the settlement of all balances of the New York company.

Aug. 2. Went to the office and executed a power of attorney to Thorp to sign bills of lading and for me bills conjointly with Thallon. Received a letter two days since from Thallon, Liverpool, who returned to U.S. on *Scotia*. Was sorry to have missed him.

Aug. 15. Left London, and boarded the *Great Eastern* at Liverpool.

The following extracts will show the state of affairs on the road during my absence.

July 16. McHenry: "You will be apprised of a change of agency at New York, which has for a long time appeared to be necessary. My interviews with Thallon made this more and more clear."

McAndrew and Wann from this time acted as McHenry's agents in New York.

July 18. Kennard: "After you left we were plunged in great trouble by a messenger from the west telling us that all the men had struck owing to the delay in the pay, and that they intended to come into town in a body and demand their money. Anticipating trouble in this quarter, I had, as you are aware, drawn upon McHenry for £1,000. . . . I therefore got the money from Dick and started Flagg off without a moment's delay. This saved us for one day. . . . In the evening of that day Streator came in from the east and found the men all along the line very uneasy and on the point of striking.

"We received that night the long promised credits on Barnards for

£10,000. These however were made out to your order as well as my own . . . and placed me for a moment in a terrible fix. . . . Your father . . . signed them for you. I [sent] . . . Rose to New York with credits . . . [and] £3,000 extra on McHenry . . . with instructions to Wann to sell the same if possible.

"The next day I was inundated with contractors for ties after their pay, and I had a pretty hard time with them, but fortunately Bittenbenner . . . came in with $5,000 currency in his pocket, and he lent me $4,500 on a ten day check on Duncan. I am now expecting to have a telegram from Rose. . . . It is very hard to show a bold front in face of all these difficulties, but still we have got along much better than might have been expected. . . .

"I consider it is quite providential that you have gone. You must explain to McHenry the consequences of not sending us money in time for the monthly pay."

July 22. Shryock: "I have just returned from a general survey of the line north as far as Millers looking after road crossings and with a very few exceptions found all in a very satisfactory condition. The work is in a closing state. The Pendleton cut and the plank road at McGuffins is all that will probably detain them beyond next week. . . . Young commences to lay iron today. . . . The day after you left here was rather a blue day with us. The force east and west of this was on the point of striking . . . and the line men were chasing up the contractors. . . . This all shows the great necessity of your trip over, that a case of this kind may not happen again. . . . Our government difficulties makes people suspicious, and expect a break down and consequently they will not give scarce one day's time over the regular pay day."

July 23. Thorpe: "After you left . . . there came very near being a regular stampede. Out west, a report got into circulation that the company had broke up and no more payments would be made."

July 26. Kennard: "Since my last I have received from McHenry . . . bills for £10,000 which has made me quite comfortable for a few days. He also advises me that a further issue of £20,000 will be sent off during this month. This will pay wages due on August 1, and pay £6,000 due on rolling stock, but it will not cover the duty on rails, which will be coming early in the month. I really think McHenry is demented on the subject of money. He desires to think I ought to be able to raise all the money I want here *on air.*"

Aug 23. [At the] board meeting of the A&GW of Penna. Kennard reported the survey and location of the eastern coal field branch and extension (Franklin Br.) completed and the executive committee was authorized to make arrangements with McHenry for construction of the same.

NOTE: The PRR Co. questioned the authority of the A&GW to build the branch to Franklin under their charter, and the question was referred to Church, who on September 22 filed his opinion with the company, asserting full, legal power to construct the Branch.[7]

Aug. 26. McHenry: "I am told active measures are in progress to prevent our having a third rail fro. Dayton to Cincinnati Junction with the Ohio & Mississippi R.R. (O&M RR). I shall be at Dayton, all contracts complete, during 1863. I have shipped all the rails to reach Akron."

Sept. 3. McHenry: "The Philadelphians are becoming alarmed for their communication with Cleveland owing to your energetic and decisive action. . . . How have you decided to reach Cleveland?"

Sept. 6. McHenry: "I send Thallon an important report on the oil traffic which I wish you to see. I am endeavoring to secure conscription on various parts of the continent, . . . to develop the traffic of our railway. Of course the conscription can only be large if price be kept moderate, say 12½ cents per gallon including packages at the wells. With this traffic developed [we] shall gross $5,000 weekly. . . . The tramway . . . should be an integral part of your line. . . . The A&GW should have the monopoly of this traffic."

Sept. 24. McHenry: "The Franklin rails go per Steam and will be in New York by November 1."

Sept. 27. McHenry: "I am running short of securities, especially 1st mortgage. I hope this has had your attention. Kent should send us a large parcel of Ohio, and the 1st mortgage of the Franklin Branch would come in well. 2nd Mortgage and shares had also better be hastened forward."

NOTE: During the month of September negotiations were opened by [Marvin] Kent, President of the A&GW of Ohio, with George Carlisle and S. S. L'Hommedieu for a connection to Cincinnati from our terminus at Dayton.

Negotiations were also opened with J. H. McCullough of the Cleveland & Pittsburg Co. for a third rail to Cleveland, and with the C&M RR Co. for an entrance into Cleveland. I went to Cleveland with Minot, Superintendent of the Erie RR, and Kennard, to ascertain the views and wishes of the various interests in Cleveland as to some permanent arrangement. We found much jealousy, but a desire to accomplish the object with the Cleveland people.

Henry F. Sweetser was at the close of this month appointed superintendent of the operating of the road. He had some years been assistant superintendent of the eastern division of the Erie RR at Jersey City. It was proposed to give Brooks, Superintendent of the Erie RR shops at Dunkirk the charge of shops on this road, but objection was made by the Erie RR Company. The construction east of Meadville was completed this month ready for the track, but the iron could not be pushed forward as fast as needed.

Oct. 1. McHenry: "In my present scarcity of securities I feel the want of the small things. I hope there will be no delay in sending me 1st mortgage Ohio and Franklin, and as many 2nd mortgage as possible."

Oct. 8. McHenry: "Your Cleveland negotiations are interesting and I have also good advices from Kent about Cincinnati. *I am badly in want of securities.* I cannot too urgently insist on this and I beg your earnest and prompt attention."

Oct. 11. McHenry: "Evans . . . is in correspondence with Drew about buying in this market a large parcel of bonds. I am much pleased with Piermont for an oil depot. . . . I am glad you make Franklin 1st mortgage bonds. I am very deficient in securities. At close of this month I shall have remitted cash £200,000 and about 14,000 tons rails since Kennard sailed, equal to an absorption of three millions of bonds. . . . I remit £10,000 per week pretty regularly. This should do. . . . *But I must have bonds in full supply.*"

Oct. 25. An excursion train left Meadville for Jamestown at 7:30 A.M. Kennard sent out invitations: "To accompany the directors and officers on an Examination Excursion on the line east of Meadville."

On the same evening I wrote McHenry: "We have returned from an excursion trip over the line from this place to Jamestown. You will therefore see that the road to this place is an accomplished fact . . . . It has required a longer time than we anticipated, but to those of us who are acquainted with all the adverse circumstances which have embarrassed us . . . the accomplishment is a cause of great gratification. . . . I can see that no work of such magnitude has ever been done so quickly under such difficulties, and all of our most intelligent railway men are greatly surprised at our success."

Nov. 8. To McHenry: "I have just returned from a board meeting of the Ohio company at Cleveland. The steamer which carries this letter will I trust convey you a remittance of Ohio 1st mortgage, and I trust a few days will place in your possession bonds of the Franklin Branch. . . . I am sure you will be well satisfied with the provision of the Franklin Branch contract. . . . We have also in contemplation a short but very important branch to the coal fields of Mercer county, of which I shall write you when arrangements shall be perfected."

Nov. 10. Road opened to Meadville for business.

Nov. 14. To McHenry: "I am sorry to say that we have not been able to pay in the entire amount for the January coupons as soon as you proposed, but will do so within a very few days. . . . Kennard . . . (was unable) to assist as he was much strained to meet his pay rolls. . . . Our work still progresses well, but difficulties on account of labor are very great."

Nov. 17. To McHenry: "The Franklin bonds are now being printed and I hope will be ready the first of the week to be signed and sent by steamer of Saturday of next week. . . . The weather is not good for the railroad work but I hope will improve as I am very anxious that the line will be open to Warren at the earliest possible time."

Nov. 18. McHenry: "I have no advice of the settlement made in Meadville by Thallon and Kennard. Where are my $65,000 shares sent to Thallon? I have not a single share in Pennsylvania and I wish you would send me something like my proportion. . . . I am a little vexed about the remittance to Heywood not taking the shape I required, considering my enormous sacrifices to carry out my engagements."

Nov. 19. McHenry: "I hope you have now the trains regularly in motion to Meadville. . . . It was only by your cordial support at all times afforded us, that enabled our work to prosper. To you therefore, belongs, of right, the credit in a great measure."

Nov. 24. To W. L. Scott relative to third rail to Cleveland: "I have just received a telegram from Sweetser stating that he has satisfactorily arranged the question of the crossing [of the P&E RR] near Greenville with Brown."

NOTE: The Cleveland, Zanesville & Cincinnati R.R. Co. (CZ&C RR) made overtures for a connection over their line to Cincinnati through F. Vost, New York and R. Buchanan, of Cincinnati.

Nov. 25. McHenry: "Am much obliged for . . . the bonds. I am glad you have decided on the little branch to Sharon. I am very busy with my Penna. bonds. Hard work."

Nov. 29. McHenry: "I have had a very successful launch of Penna. bonds in face of a very, very strong opposition."[8]

Dec. 6. To McHenry: "The treasurer (of A&GW of Pa.) sends to the trustees the Franklin Branch bonds. Next steamer I will send the contract as agreed upon, between the company and Kennard, acting for you; together with instructions to the trustees to be carried out upon the execution of the contract. . . . In your letter of November 12, you say, 'as the Penna. division is now about complete, you will be able to send me shares and bonds to a point.' I have requested Kennard to send you a statement of the work actually done and yet remaining to be done on your contract in this division. The line although nearly ready to be opened, is not by any means completed. The banks are narrow and the cuts not near so wide as necessary for the completed work, and a great deal of masonry remains to be done having been substituted by trestle, until the line should be open . . . for the transportation for the stones. . . . Besides this, you are aware that a large part of the rolling stock and engines are not on the road yet, and those delivered (are not paid for). . . .

"As it is necessary that shops for the use of the road should be built here before the road shall be in full operation, I have proposed to incorporate the same in a contract with you, to which he [Kennard] has assented, thus making all the arrangements for the entire completion of the enterprise with you."

Dec. 12. From [Marvin] Kent: "Kennard telegraphs me [that] McHenry wants $500,000 Ohio stock. . . . I cannot understand the object of so large an issue. . . . $600,000 would be the probable amount due upon his contract when completed to Akron, of which $280,000 are now with the trustees, leaving a balance of $320,000."

Dec. 13. To McHenry: "We send $500,000 of certificates of stock of the A&GW of Pa, by steamer of next week and will send forward the residue of the stock to complete the account due on completion of the contract as soon as the account is designated on estimate. I trust that these remittances with the Ohio bonds sent forward will relieve you from embarrassment."

Dec. 27. To McHenry: "The road is progressing well in spite of very unfavorable weather, and the connection to Ravenna will be made before the end of next week. . . .

"I was at Cleveland last week with Kennard. I went with the intention of making a contract . . . with the C&M RR but on our arrival overtures were made on the part of the C&P RR which in some respects are more advantageous than . . . we have heretofore had. We accordingly have adjourned the arrangements until to January 8th. . . . We will be able to make good arrangements with either party. Minot and others of the Erie RR Company were out here last week and were well satisfied with matters."

Dec. 30. To F.G. Navarro: "It is expected that the track will be laid to make the connection with Ravenna this week. . . . As a complimentary manifestation to our European friends, a reunion of those engaged in the enterprise is proposed at this place on Tuesday, January 6, at 7 P.M."

The above was in accordance with a resolution of the A&GW of Pa. board of December 26, viz: on motion of J. J. Shryock, "RESOLVED: That a complimentary dinner be tendered to T. W. Kennard, Esq., Engineer in Chief, and representative of James McHenry on the occasion of the road being finished sufficiently to run a train through to Ohio." Reynolds, Church, Shryock, and James E. McFarland appointed committee of arrangements. (The banquet was held at the Barton House, S. Water St.)

6. Pressing On, 1863

The Civil War created distrust of American investments, thus making it difficult for McHenry to raise capital. Nonetheless, he continued to demand more securities. Reynolds remained puzzled by McHenry's position and maintained that the Pennsylvania company, for example, had forwarded securities far in excess of the work performed to date. The ongoing arguments between the two men did not stall expansion plans that raised new questions of management. While Reynolds insisted upon tighter control, McHenry and Kennard sought to increase their authority. And while he charged McHenry with mismanagement, Reynolds accused Kennard of incompetence in dealing with railroad leaders. Unless his colleagues changed their manner of conducting business, Reynolds threatened to resign. This internal strife did not prevent company officials from celebrating the running of the line to Meadville and Cleveland.

Tightening Control of Management

Jan. 1. The line was opened to Warren.

Jan. 5. The contract with McHenry for the Eastern Coalfields Branch (Franklin Branch) was approved, and the president was authorized to deliver (by consent of Kennard, acting for McHenry) $65,000 of bonds of same as settlement between Thallon and McHenry, to Thallon, the trustees being instructed to retain a like amount in London.

Jan. 6. The president reported execution of the above contract with McHenry, and the delivery of the $65,000 of bonds to Thallon.

On same date the contract with the OC RR Co. for joint depot and track at Corry was approved.

Jan 12. The capital stock of the Penna. company was increased 18,000 shares making an aggregate of 20,000 shares, $1,000,000.

McHenry became very impertinent for additional securities for negotiation. The war necessarily created great distrust of American investments, and great difficulty was experienced in obtaining money. The enormous rise in the value of gold and our bond coupons being payable in New York in legal currency, caused the European holders to urge the payment in sterling.McHenry urged such payment. I opposed on the ground that the companies had no legal authority to make such change. It was shown that Ward had in the early negotiation made such promise, but in doing so exceeded his authority.

About the middle of the month Kent sent forward $200,000 Ohio bonds to the trustees, being much in excess of what was due McHenry on work. Negotiations were opened for extension of the broad gauge to Toledo via Sandusky, which for a time promised successful result.

Jan. 29. Kennard had for some time been sick at New York, and I this date left for that city, where I remained until February 8 in efforts to perfect the bonus contract with the Erie RR Co. and also negotiation with Struthers and Streator of the OC RR.

The question of the construction of the machine shops at Meadville was at this time important. The executive committee met a committee of the citizens and proposed that the citizens should make subscription towards their erection. It was agreed that the citizens should subscribe $14,000 towards the same. (It may here be stated that very little was ever paid.)

Extracts from letter to Kennard. January 21:

"I am much perplexed with McHenry being now short of securities. The Ohio company, from Kent's statements which I sent you, are in advance of the stipulations of their contract $480,000, and but a comparatively small portion of their road finished. . . . As a *plain, straightforward business transaction* between a company and their contractor, it is certainly asking of the company a very bold step, to make an increased advance of their securities. . . . Here (in Pennsylvania) the track is laid the entire distance. . . . Yet even here the company has forwarded securities to the trustees far in excess of the work performed under the contract.

"McHenry with his contract completed would be entitled for

91 miles main track at $33,000	$3,003,000
say 5 miles side track at $28,000	140,000
Total completed	$3,143,000
The company has paid 1st mortgage	$2,450,000
1st mortgage paid to Streator for transfer of PA contract	50,000
2nd mortgage sent forward	900,000
2nd mortgage to Streator as agreed	50,000
	$3,450,000
"This, at 75 is	$2,587,500
Stock sent forward (trustees)	500,000
Stock sent McHenry	65,000
	$3,152,500
"Being an overpayment on completed road	$9,500
"Now, we are all well aware that the contract is not finished within a very large amount of graduation and masonry, say	$50,000
A deficit of eleven engines	132,000
Only three of 21 passenger cars	45,000
But on all this stock much is to be paid	$227,000

leaving in round numbers not less than $250,000 for completion.

"With the Franklin Branch, partially completed, not only all the bonds have been sent forward to the trustees, which will be done on completions, but in addition, the company has deposited with Thallon $65,000. I do not take into account the $200,000 New York bonds for hypothecation, on which the first rolling stock was to apply.

"The account stands . . .

Advance over work done, Ohio company	$480,000
Penna company	250,000
New York company	150,000
Over advance	$880,000

"In some of his [McHenry's] recent letters he intimates that he has not been properly sustained by the companies. This intimation is not just."

A contract was this month (February) made with McHenry for the construction of shops on the island west of the [Meadville] Station, also for an increased amount of rolling stock.

Finances were again in very unsatisfactory shape, and the question of payment of coupons in sterling strenuously urged by McHenry as also a large advance of Ohio securities.

March 6. Owing to the complications arising from the independent action of the three companies on questions of common interest, it was decided to concentrate the general powers of the three companies into a Central Board, which should have full control of all questions of mutual interest. This board was accordingly organized on March 6. [Wm.] Reynolds and Allen of New York, [Wm.] Reynolds, John Dick and Shryock of PA, M. Kent, and Streator of Ohio and Kennard, Engineer in Chief.[1]

March 12. At the urgent request of McHenry the Penna. company passed a resolution making the coupons of the 1st mortgage payable in sterling, notice of the fact to be given the holders of the 2nd mortgage. This I deemed to be contrary to the legal powers of the company, and so represented to the company, and explained at length in my letters to McHenry and his agents.

The coupons of the 2nd mortgage were to be paid by McHenry and he to receive shares in payment of his advance for such purposes. At his request Kennard was elected Vice President of the A&GW of Pa.

A bridge on the Franklin Branch. The ornate brass fixtures on the boiler and wheels of the locomotive are normal for the era. Note the split rail fencing in the foreground. Much of the right-of-way was fenced at the railroad's expense. *(J. F. Ryder survey, Reynolds Collection, Allegheny College)*

March 21. To McHenry: "We are now beginning to carry oil to Cleveland via Ravenna and will no doubt be able in a very short time . . . [to] secure all the oil destined for that market. This oil for the west and lumber will give a most valuable western freight as they will be carried on cars which will return with coal from the west, thus being freighted both ways.

"Assuming that the daily yield of the oil wells is 5,000 barrels per day (which from the best information I can gather is below the fact), the A&GW at the present time controls only ¼ part of the transportation of the oil. . . .

"Now with the line completed to . . . Oil City I see no reason why we should not control at least three fourths of the traffic. . . . All exertion should be made to be prepared by the coming fall to do all this business either west or east without delay. If so prepared we will secure the traffic against danger of competition and if *not*, we may rest assured that other roads will be built with which we will have to share the business. . . . With the requisite number of cars for the past six months for this business we could as well have made a daily average of 2,500 bbls.

"I regret to say that our line has not yet reached Akron. . . . The delay is a matter of great disappointment, as . . . we could have a fair business in flour to help to increase our revenue.

"The Franklin Branch is in very unsatisfactory condition. There is no doubt that there was a great mistake in the pattern of the iron. It is entirely too light for the uses required, and in my opinion will have to be changed to a 56 lb. rail."[2]

April 1. To McHenry: "I have only to report that I think if you could spare the time, it would be for your interests to come over as early as possible in the spring. . . . Kennard is in New York. . . . I think however that the interests of the companies would be promoted if he would leave all their arrangements *exclusively* to the proper officers. . . . I think him devoted to the interests of the road but in railway negotiations it is not well to have too many parties acting independently."

April 4. To McHenry: "Much dissatisfaction exists along the line from delay in payment. . . . [Kennard] has drawn some $70,000 from a banker at this place with the expectation that the account should have been made good long since. This should not be, as it seriously affects the credit which may be necessary hereafter."

It became evident that greater facilities were required for interchange of business with the Erie RR at the terminus at Salamanca. It was proposed by the Erie RR Company that a lease should be made from the Indians[3] of a large territory east of the present junction at the joint expense to the two companies.

April 17. To McHenry: "I returned from Ravenna yesterday where I attended a meeting of the Ohio board at Ravenna. Kent had an Act passed authorizing a second mortgage . . . [of] $4,000,000. . . . I understand that the iron was laid to Akron yesterday."

April 27. To McHenry: "The river is in good boating order, and im-

Photo of the station at the Franklin Petroleum Oil Works. The string of broad-gauge box cars are being loaded with oil barrels for transport. *(J. F. Ryder survey, Reynolds Collection, Allegheny College)*

mense quantities of oil are now carried to Pittsburg that route. If our line was completed to Franklin we would secure a large amount, but as we are not there, we must wait patiently until the low water. . . . We are not prepared for any large business. Our transfer facilities at Ravenna are very incomplete and our sidings along the road entirely insufficient for any large business. There seems to be a deficiency of iron for this purpose."

May 1. To McHenry: "I returned from Buffalo last night where I attended a Railway convention." I there met Marsh and had a long interview with Stone in relation to Kennard's plan of a broad gauge connection to Ashtabula and Cleveland.

May 11. Kennard wishes me to go with him and Ogden to Brady's Bend, Pittsburg, and Cleveland, relative to a scheme of extending a branch to the Allegheny River at Brady's.

May 16. To McAndrew and Wann: "I have your enclosed memorandum of McHenry's account with the Penna Co. It is surprising to me how McHenry should have fallen into such mistakes in the details of contract prices, and the amount received. His first error is the supposition 'that the Penna. division is complete.' . . . The next error is in the length of the road in Penna. . . . He has not given credit for either a portion of the Hallett bonds or the $100,000 paid Streator. . . . In his credit for shares he has omitted the $68,000 of the Ward stock sent through you.

"With regards to the contract for the Franklin Branch, the errors are yet greater. Instead of being 30 miles it is less than 27 miles including sidings. The contract price is $16,000 per mile *not* $33,000 as in statement of account. This [branch] is far from complete, [track] being laid for little more than half the distance, and not any rolling stock provided.

"You will see that . . . the Penna. company not only is not indebted for the works done, but is in advance even with the road completed according to contract."

To McHenry, same date: "It is strange we should differ to an amount of more than a million of dollars, yet such is the fact. I can only account for the errors you have made in your statement by supposing that you have trusted to your recollection and have not referred to the contracts and accounts. . . . I fear that the A&GW has only been made the whip by which our rivals interests have been made to join their interests. I can only say, as I said before, that such negotiations can be better managed by others than by Kennard, who relies too much on the professions of those with whom he negotiates. . . . These thoughts I give you in confidence. . . . I do not wish in any way to be responsible on failure of plans with which I have had no part. . . . Kent . . . assures me that no time shall be lost."

May 21. The Franklin & Oil Creek Turnpike Company of 114 shares of $50 each, offer to sell their stock at $70 per share. This road occupied the most available route for R.R. between Franklin and Oil City, to which point it was proposed to extend the Franklin Branch.

A&GW in NY Length of line 47.87 miles. Cost $67,641.00.

May 26. Rhodes: "Kennard proposed to elect McAndrew and Wann into the New York board instead of Shaw and Marvin. This was not done, much to the irritation of [Kennard], notwithstanding that the proposed gentlemen were not eligible under the New York laws."[4]

June 1. The rails were laid to Franklin, but the line was in very unsatisfactory condition. The rail was too light for our engines, being only 28 lbs.,[5] with very bad fish plate joints.

June 12. McHenry: "Kennard's . . . operation in the Cleveland & Toledo (C&T RR) business if successful, will be in the highest degree advantageous; but it is right to remember that [Kennard] is measuring his strength with some of the most shrewd railway men in the country, and although all, everything by his representations, appears of the most flattering I yet am not sanguine in such cases until the results reduce to certainty. The Mahoning project . . . I think well of. . . . I do not estimate the value . . . so high as [Kennard], but regard the control of that line of vast importance to the A&GW, even if it should cost so much more than the rent proposed, $300,000 per annum. The net income for the past two years averages $225,000, and the control of the road and the terminal facilities and right of way at the City of Cleveland are worth more than the $75,000. I have no hesitation in advising the consummation of the lease as soon as possible."

The Penna. company have sent you all the stock they are authorized at present to issue, and until increased by vote of stockholders. I am desirous before my connection with the company shall cease, that its business should be well settled. It can be done better while I am connected with the company, as no other person will be so conversant with the business in the progress of the road.

June 4. Contract for building [machine shops at Meadville] with McHenry at $250,000, also contract for additional rolling stock; and $400,000 shares authorized to be sent to the Trustees, subject to the ratification of above contract by McHenry.

June 18. To McHenry: "I have to say that we differ entirely in our views. So far as to any companies I represent, there has been no injustice done you by delay in sending securities. They have done all they were required to do, and as much more as was within the range of possibility to accord to your wishes. . . . Our ideas of business management in these matters appear to be very opposite. While using every effort to forward your interests, I wish it now and hereafter to be most distinctly understood that it must be done according to my views of what shall be just and right for all parties. I have no personal ends to attain while I remain connected with the road, beyond the success of the enterprise as the result of a fair and straight-forward administration of my department. There are other parties in interest besides the company and yourself, . . . and justice . . . demands that all the business transactions of the company should be conducted on that system which will bear the closest scrutiny. . . . The fact that there will be a large amount due in Penna. sooner or later is not the basis upon which the company should issue securities.

"If the amicable relations so long and pleasantly existing between us are to be maintained only by a sacrifice on my part of my opinion of what is right in the transaction of the business of the company, it must terminate; and no one would regret it more than myself."

June 19. Kennard telegraphed: "I put the contract through all right and have a certificate it passed a unanimous vote of the stockholders. McHenry is hurrying for securities."

June 22. Went to Franklin with Sweetser. The station [house] at Cochranton has been commenced, but no work has been done on the one at Franklin nor the turntable completed.

June 29. Went to Corry with Henry, and arranged with Struthers and Streator for right of way from Franklin to Oil City, under the franchise of the OC RR Co. Kennard telegraphs he has decided to push the work forward to Urbanna [sic] without delay. Rails laid to Akron.

July 2. Contract ratified with McHenry for construction of Machine Shops at Meadville.

July 3. Stockholders called to meet on July 14 to act on C&M RR contract, Toledo RR, and OC RR contracts, and the increase of the stock to $1,500,000.

Trestle near Akron, Ohio. It is interesting that the construction displayed here is much more substantial than that shown in Pennsylvania and New York. Even the fencing seems more finely crafted. *(J. F. Ryder survey, Reynolds Collection, Allegheny College)*

July 7. With Kennard, Shryock, and others went to Franklin and from there drove to Oil City to examine proposed location of the line through to Oil City.

July 10. Rhodes V.P. of the C&M RR Co. advises me of the satisfaction of the lease of the road to the A&GW. Ayes 11,971 Nays 424.

July 17. To McHenry: "The company is ready and has been to issue the shares for the bonds you have paid and sent forward but McAndrew and Wann refused to receive except at a discount, which the company has no right to make on capital stock. Kennard informs me that the remittance of Ohio bonds progresses satisfactorily. Our treasurer will send $100,000 shares to the trustees to make up the residue of the last contract for shops, etc. and will also send you 90 per cent of the coupon account sent by you to McAndrew and Wann. Much trouble rises in the adjustment of this account from the fact that Kennard has not furnished the company with the requisite certificates of work done upon which to base the amount of the bonds due you under the provisions of the contract.

"The C&T RR arrangement will probably save us a fair proportion of the Cleveland business. We are bringing our central organization into good working shape. I feel sanguine that we will have a system of management not surpassed in the country. My great object is perfect system in every department, and that most rigid economy may be exacted."

July 24. Above contracts ratified and stock increased to $1,500,000 and a contract of the A&GW Company of Ohio, with the Cincinnati, Hamilton & Dayton RR Co. assented to July 15. The eastern coal fields Branch and extension (Franklin Branch) authorized to be extended to Oil City. A resolution of thanks to Kennard for his services in securing the C&M lease. (This was done at the wish of Kennard to give him some eclat in England. His services in this arrangement were no more important than those of others, except the agreement for construction). Authority was given to send to trustees 90 per cent of account rendered by McHenry in certificates of shares, pending settlement of same by proper vouchers.

July 27. To McHenry: "The company have no data from which to ascertain the time and amounts due to you on the shipments of the iron." These are absolutely essential for the precise entries on the construction accounts, which cannot be made without them.

Aug. 10. With Allen, Hall, and Shaw went to Salamanca to meet the Indian council [Seneca Nation]. We there met the attorney of the Erie RR Co. but the survey of the proposed new location having been left behind, we could not make our arrangements and we adjourned to meet at Perryville [on] August 20th.

Aug. 15. To McHenry: I think it well to say, "that if I continue at the head of the management, . . . it must be with a most explicit understanding that the duties of the office are not to be interfered with by any outside negotiations by other parties. This is of most imperative necessity for the interests of all concerned. There cannot be two heads acting independently without disastrous results. I am satisfied that we have not gained credit with good railway men for shrewdness in some of the negotiations which have been made, but have lost prestige.

"My connection with the enterprise, if it shall continue, will be only for the credit which may arise from a discreet and economical administration of the business of the company for the benefit of the stockholders in interest, and I cannot consent to be committed by my position to any arrangement which I do not conceive will contribute to that end."[6]

Aug. 17. To McHenry: "These contracts may be or may be not advantageous. I do not believe they will be carried out in good faith. My opinions heretofore expressed are unchanged, that these negotiations should be left to the proper officers of the company. With the exception of the Mahoning [lease], they have been unwise. The result proves that Kennard is not safe in measuring his strength with such men as he has had to deal."

Shortcomings of Kennard and McHenry

Aug. 19. To McHenry: "Under your contract, the authority to receive bonds from the trustees is upon presentation of bills of lading and the monthly estimate of the [engineer] for work done. Now, as I sit in my office, I can momentarily see the passing of engines upon the road; yet in the office of the company there is not an *official paper to show that any work has ever been done by you on the line of road, or that you have furnished a pound of iron or a dollar of money since your contract took effect.* And yet you have apparent or seeming cause of complaint for delay in settlement.

"You may readily imagine the vexation this has given me. The fault, as you will see, is not that of the company, but that of the engineer in not doing as he is required by the contract, viz: to furnish monthly estimates. The construction office has given us nothing even in the form of a statement. I have from the beginning used every effort to correct this evil, but without success.

"Had it not been that I could not in justice leave business in such unsettled state which would have caused discredit to all interested, I should have long since retired from all connection with the road. I am most happy to say that as far as the company has had control, the accounts are in perfect order, and will bear any investigation. My great desire has been, that when I shall terminate my connection wish the road it will be with credit to myself and with a satisfactory exhibit to those in interest.

"I am not at all satisfied with the manner in which your business is conducted here. To a certain extent this is not an affair of mine, as I have no interest direct or indirect in the profits of the contract but as connected with the management of the road, I have some pride in the reputation it will in future have for an economical as well as thorough construction. . . . On this account I have so repeatedly urged you to visit the work, that you might judge for yourself. . . . Despairing of your coming, I cannot fail to give you my opinion that the business might be managed much better than it is.

"Rose, who is placed in charge of the entire engineering department by Kennard, is *not* the man for the place. The duties require a greater business capacity than he possesses.

"Of Kennard, I can only say that you know him as well as I do. He has energy, and in many respects most excellent talent, but his desire to assume the duties and manage the business of all the departments of the company leads to great trouble. He is not by nature fitted for railway management, however he may excell [*sic*] as a railway builder."

Aug. 20. Left home on special train. At Salamanca met St. John, the treasurer of the Senecas, a fine looking and very intelligent Indian. At noon we went to Perryville, where we met Allen, Brooks (of Erie Co.) and others. The Council assembled in the afternoon and evening, and all negotiations were satisfactorily closed, and a contract for the lease of the new grounds signed. Brooks held a freight train, and we left at 10:30 P.M. for Salamanca, where we took a special, arriving at Meadville at 6 A.M.

Sept. 4. To McHenry: "We have just completed some very important arrangements for the oil traffic of our road, and I am busy drawing up the papers. . . . We have arranged to secure a charter for the transportation of oil from the wells by pipe. This charter is secured for the

Detail from an 1870 lithograph of Meadville, showing the A&GW shop complex (bottom). *(Crawford County Historical Society Collection)*

mutual benefit of the A&GW and the OC RR. The title is the 'Oil Creek Transportation Company,' and has full corporate powers. The interest and directions will be equal between the two companies. The oil will be carried to the terminus of each road by pipe, through which it will be forced by steam power at a cost far less than by railroad." Under our arrangement we hope to identify the interests of the OC RR with our own, and virtually control the monopoly of the oil traffic.[7]

Sept. 9. To McHenry: "I am surprised to hear that you are short of Ohio shares . . . as Kennard assured me that an ample supply had been sent forward. Since the transfer of the construction offices to Akron, I am not so well posted on Ohio business. . . . I wish to again caution you against making too high estimate of traffic returns for the present. The amount of our traffic receipts is in no degree an index to the business which the road could command . . . with full facilities for doing it. We have . . . all of our rolling stock employed. We are not able to take the oil which is now offered and will not be for some time to come. We have now 42 locomotives, but many of them are used on construction. Of the 373 platform cars, 122 are in the service of the construction department. We have not even to the east of this place, sufficient sidings for a large increase of business."

"I am well aware that Kennard insists that we must and will do a business of $50,000 per week, but I know we cannot do as matters now stand, not for want of business offered but for want of means to accomplish the work.

Kennard's intense anxiety to show vast earnings causes him to make over estimates both in the traffic and in the progress of the work. I greatly regret this disposition of his to so estimate as it necessarily results in disappointment. He still insists that he will have the line open to Cleveland on October 1 but do not make any promises of the kind, as I have not the most remote idea of it. I have not yet the statistics from the construction and engineers office to be able to make the settlement of your account. (Relating to pipe Co.) The cost will probably be $125,000, with a capacity of 10,000 bbls per day. Under this arrangement the Branch will probably terminate at Franklin instead of Oil City."

Coal and Oil

Sept. 14. Left home at 7 A.M. Bittenbenner drove me from Greenville to Sharon where I met Gen. Curtis, Coolman, Stewart, and others, and with them discussed the question of the extension of the Hubbard Branch of the C&M RR to Sharon. We dined with Coleman, and afterward drove to the several furnaces and iron mills.

Sept. 15. We left Sharon in carriage. At Greenville the horses ran away, breaking the carriage but injuring no one.

Sept. 21. Left on express. Met Streator and Struthers at Corry, and arranged terms of contract for construction of the oil pipe line.

Sept. 26. To McHenry: "We carry about 2,000 bbls of oil per day. The production is not less than 6,000. We cannot do more from deficiency in cars and the impossibility of making the Erie RR Co. appreciate the magnitude and importance of the traffic. The PRR carries more oil than the Erie RR and New York Central RR. The reason is that the oil which we cannot carry away promptly is stored in tanks instead of barrels and those remain until the rise of water when it is transported in boats to Pittsburg and there by PRR.

"We are about securing some valuable coal fields for the Cleveland trade, which have thus far been undeveloped for want of transportation facilities. . . . It is my desire to secure all the coal for the use of the A&GW within competing distances of Cleveland. The trade is yet only in its infancy, and is destined to be immense in future."

Oct 1. To McHenry: "I have almost despaired of obtaining the information we need to make a settlement of your account. . . . I have accordingly instructed the treasurer to take the account as stated by McAndrew and Wann, reduce it as nearly as possible to the form required for the settlement of the contract requirements, and remit 90 per cent of the full sum to you."

Oct. 2. To McHenry: "The rails are laid to Cleveland, but it will be some weeks before the frogs and switches are in so that cars can run in on broad gauge."

Oct. 8. To McHenry: "I returned yesterday from Franklin Mills where the Board of Directors have recommended to the stockholders [of the Ohio Co.] to increase the capital stock of the company two millions of dollars."

Oct. 14. To McHenry: "The Directors [Pa. Co.] have authorized the issue of stock to you for their proportion of the expenditure on the C&M RR . . . at 25 per cent above actual cost. . . . As the company have already exhausted their 1st and 2nd mortgages, there seems to be no method of reimbursement except by stock or revenue bonds. . . . Kennard thought it better to make no further liens to take precedence of stock. We will forward you next week $400,000 of stock certificates on this account. . . . The New York company will send you stock certificates as security for their proportion of the C&M RR expenditure. I think that company will be able in a period of time three to four years to reimburse you in *cash* with interest."

Oct. 20. Met Mr. and Mrs. Kennard and family and others on a steam tug for an excursion to Kennard's new purchase of Burton's home at Glencove L.I. The day was beautiful. We arrived at Glencove at 11, where we lunched and spent the afternoon in looking over the ground and studying the proposed improvements.

Oct. 28. Kennard and Rhodes of the C&M RR met in Meadville and executed the lease of the Mahoning Road.

Oct. 30. The stock and bonds of the several A&GW RR companies placed on the New York Exchange.

Oct. 31. To McHenry: "I have succeeded in forming two companies of some twenty in each, a majority of whom, including yourself and Kennard, are in the interest of the A&GW, whose object is to lease all the valuable coal lands in each districts in Penna. and Ohio as it may be desirable in the future to extend our road or branches to. One of these companies has already secured some 25,000 acres of excellent coal lands extending from near the town of Mercer toward the Allegheny River near Brady's Bend. . . . The other company has secured about 10,000 acres south of the C&M RR extending to New Lisbon, Ohio. This is not fully organized but it is proposed to lease some 30,000 acres."

Meadville and Cleveland Celebrations

From *Cleveland [Daily] Herald* (no date)

Evening of 3rd was an important era in the history of Cleveland. A train of freight cars from Long Dock, Jersey City, arrived in this city over the Atlantic & Great Western R.R. The train consisted of ten freight cars and the elegant private car of T. W. Kennard, Engineer in Chief. It was drawn by the locomotive No. 2 named "James McHenry." The engineer was Richard D. Poor, the Conductor, Charles Warren.

The party comprised several leading officers of the road. Wm. Reynolds, President of the New York and Penna. division, T. W. Kennard, Engineer in Chief, H. F. Sweetser, General Superintendent, J. H. R. Rose, Resident Engineer, Frank Cummings, Superintendent of the locomotive and car department, C. Blakesley, private secretary of T. W. Kennard, Charles H. Rhodes, Superintendent of the Mahoning and Cleveland Branch, J. Dwight Palmer, General Freight Agent of Cleveland Branch.

The new depot at the junction is nearly completed. It is 160 feet long, and will contain offices and restaurant under charge of Mr. James Caffron.

The prominent features of the railway will in a short time be photographed by J. F. Ryder. The road will formally be opened on the 12th. We would urge upon our citizens the propriety of marking by some public demonstration their sense of the importance of this great enterprise. We think it eminently proper that the arrival of the excursion train should be signalized by bonfire illuminations and other demonstrations of gratification.

Nov. 4. To McHenry: "The important end towards which we have so long directed our efforts has been consummated. We yesterday ran a broad gauge engine, freight train, and passenger car to the new A&GW station into the city of Cleveland without accident or delay. A train laden with beef is now in transit from Cleveland direct to New York. Another era has thus been reached in the history of the A&GW enterprise. The line will be opened for regular business on the 16th."

Nov. 12. To McHenry: "If I, after the next election, retain my position, it will be with the understanding on my part that my authority [as] the principal officer of the company is to be paramount. I cannot consent to assume the responsibility and name, while another shall assume to the title and authority of 'General Manager'. . . . [Kennard] and I have very different views in the matter [of] railway management."

Meadville, Pennsylvania depot (center) with the McHenry House (left), considered one of the finest establishments in the country. *(Editors' collection)*

Nov. 16. To McHenry: "We are all busy with arrangements for the opening celebration to Cleveland, which will no doubt be a very creditable affair."

From the *Crawford Democrat,* Nov. 24, 1863.

Tuesday, Wednesday, Thursday and Friday (17th, 18th, 19th, and 20th) of last week were days long to be remembered in connection with the A&GW Railway. On the first named day a company of gentlemen, especial friends of the enterprise, started from New York, filling five passenger cars, and on the day following at 8 A.M. reached this place. After partaking of the well provided hospitality of the McHenry House, at one P.M. they were joined by a band of some hundred gentlemen from Cleveland, and after a sumptuous dinner at the McHenry House all left for Cleveland at 3 P.M. The train consisted of twelve cars under the direction of Conductor A. G. Croker. It was led by engine 28, the "Marvin Kent," in honor of the president of the Ohio division. The Engineer was Richard D. Poor, fireman H. S. Davis.

From the *Cleveland Herald*.[8]

The engine was the most handsomely decorated that ever went out of Cleveland. Flags of all kinds floated from every available point on engine and tender. The red crosses of England, the tri-color of France, and the yellow and red of Spain, floated amicably by the stars and stripes of the United States, symbolizing the different nationalities whose capital has been invested, in the road. . . . Over all floated a banner, "Atlantic& Great Western Railway." . . .

And so with music and gaiety the train sped along the beautiful country cheered at the several crossings by assembled crowds until it reached Meadville. Here it passed under a triumphal arch on the west side of which was inscribed "Welcome Ohio and New York to the way through our state." Beneath was the inscription "New York, Pennsylvania, and Ohio."

The excursion train which left New York at 1 P.M. Tuesday was under charge of conductor Frank Champlin and was drawn by the locomotive "William Reynolds" named after the President of the New York and Penna. divisions. It brought 165 guests, among whom were Wm. H. Aspinwall, Wm. Evans, C. Minot, R. Dudley, S. Gregory, McAndrew, and Wann, and Col. H. A. Post. In due time the united parties rallied at the table of the McHenry House. . . . The eatables and drinkables were sumptuous; a prince gets no better. With three cheers for Taylor and three cheers for Meadville, the gay company was soon heading westward.

The Reception. The reception of the guests was a grand occasion. The firing of cannon hailed the approach of the train to the depot. At that moment a rocket from the cupola of the Weddell House was the signal for the grandest and most gorgeous display of fireworks ever seen in our city. . . .
In the balcony of the Weddell House was a splendid set piece illuminating the name "Kennard." Across Bank Street at the Angier House was a triumphal arch in which the words "Atlantic & Great Western Railway" were most elaborately and gorgeously illustrated. . . .

The Dinner. The excursionists were escorted to the Angier House, where after time for dress and rest, they were ushered into the dining hall where a sumptuous repast awaited them.

The tables were spread with all the luxuries of the season, and presented a brilliant display. No expense was spared to make it as brilliant an affair as money could procure.

William Reynolds, Esq., President of the New York and Penna. companies, presided over the meeting. After full justice to the good things of the feast, the president read letters of regret from Hon. Geo. M. Dallas and Hon. S. P. Chase. In introducing the regular programme of toasts Mr. Reynolds alluded to the magnitude of the work which the meeting celebrated.

The Ball and Supper. The Academy of Music had been handsomely decorated for the occasion and the result was striking and beautiful.

The entire parquet and stage were covered with a matched floor. The auditorium was gorgeous with flags, banners, pictures and mirrors. The orchestra was built in front of the family circle with the entrance to the ball room beneath it. It was draped with national flags. The pillars of the first floor were wreathed with evergreens in an artistic manner, and hung with festoons of red, white and blue. The paneling above was covered with choice engravings and oil paintings elegantly framed, with large mirrors reflecting the gorgeous scene beneath.

The pillars of the tier above were wreathed with red, white, and blue, and from the capital of each depended a banner with silver and gold stars upon a blue field. Festoons of red and white hung from pillar to pillar, and at intervals gorgeously emblazoned banners of various nations were displayed. The panel above was thickly dotted with small American flags.

The ball room was crowded with a gay and brilliant throng dancing to the music of Leland's full band. Every one was dressed to the height of fashion, and the general appearance of the whole was magnificent. The boxes and galleries were crowded with ladies in full dress, while the floor was packed with the dancers. It was decidedly the greatest success for years.

During the evening Gen. Rosecrans entered the ball room and was conducted to a private box, where he was greeted with enthusiastic applause.

At midnight a splendid supper was served in the dining room; after supper dancing was resumed and it was daylight before the last dancers retired.

Thus terminated one of the greatest railroad openings that ever came off in America.

From the *Crawford Democrat*, Dec. 1, 1863.

An ovation by the citizens to the Atlantic & Great Western Railway Company.

Last week we gave a general account of the opening of the Atlantic & Great Western Railway from New York to Cleveland, the principal features of which were the dinner and ball given at the latter place. . . . If the people of New York and Cleveland did something big, the people of Meadville, under the auspices of their own free will offerings, did something highly creditable. Now, let us see what that was.

No sooner had it been announced that the day had been appointed for the commemoration of the Union of New York and Cleveland by the A&GW Railway, than a number of our most active and enterprising citizens began the work

The dining room at the depot, Meadville, Pennsylvania. *(Reynolds Collection, Allegheny College)*

of preparation. One of the first steps taken was to call a meeting of the business men of the town. At that meeting [several] expressive resolutions were adopted.

Resolved, that the president of said Railway Company, William Reynolds, Esq., and his fellow laborers in the Board of Directors, are entitled to and are hereby tendered our most hearty thanks for the unflinching perseverance and surpassing energy with which they have confronted and overcome the almost overwhelming obstacles with which their enterprise was called upon to contend in its earlier history.

Resolved, that a dinner be procured by the businessmen of Meadville to be served at the McHenry House on Saturday evening next the first at 7:30 P.M., and that the heads of departments of the Railway and the various editors of the press be invited to attend on that occasion.

The committee on banners caused a brilliant display about the depot and grounds. Nearly all the available flags in the town were brought into requisition.

On the northern cupola of the depot was planted the British ensign; on the middle cupola the flag of our own loved Union, while from the southern cupola floated the Spanish red and yellows. And all this was most appropriate and befitting.

The capitalists of England and Spain have contributed at least the greater part of the material aid necessary for the construction of the railway, and our own countrymen connected with the enterprise have contributed their share of diligent labor and means.

At the crossing of Dick Street was extended a banner forty feet in length with "Welcome New York and Ohio to the Way through our State," and beneath the inscription "New York, Pennsylvania, and Ohio." The whole was wreathed with gracefully arranged evergreens interspersed with a large number of small flags and gay colored ribbons, presenting a decidedly brilliant appearance.

And now, one word in conclusion. Why should not the citizens of Meadville rejoice and felicitate themselves on the completion of five hundred miles of the A&GW Railway. This grand project, like many another, flagged in its incipiency, notwithstanding the wonderful energy and expedition that now distinguishes it.

The Ohio interest in great measure became dormant, and New York stood still; but not so with the patrons of the road in Pennsylvania. They put their shoulders to the wheel and they resolved not to abate their efforts. Among those most prominent in this direction were Messrs. J. J. Shryock, Gaylord Church, and William Reynolds. Legislation was required in New York and

Pennsylvania. Money was to be raised and foreign influence secured. All this was accomplished. The needful legislation in both states was secured. Pennsylvania bonds were negotiated in England by James McHenry, Agent for the companies, and the road was commenced, prosecuted, and is finished.

There is every reason why the citizens of Meadville should rejoice, and why they should be proud of the immense artery of commerce which passes through our town, destined ere long to be the leading channel of travel between the Atlantic and Pacific.

Tighter Control Needed

Nov. 26. To McHenry: "I have advised Kennard not to open west of Akron before next spring, even if the road is complete. My reasons I think are good as we are now, and for the winter will be, doing all possible with our equipment of rolling stock. The extending of the line [for operating purposes] could not add to our receipts, while it would add much to transportation expenses. Which facts would not add to our credit abroad, and would take so far from the net earnings for payment of interest. . . . I think it would be well to urge upon Kennard not to make any expenditures not imperatively necessary outside of the railway line, until the road shall be completed to Dayton. You still have a very heavy work before you. . . . I fear that there may be a temptation to expend in these things which may be postponed without detriment for two or three years. Economy is my motto while building the road and build all ornamental buildings and additions from the earnings."

Nov. 30. To McHenry: "It is perfectly useless, however, to base any calculations of the future of the road from the present. . . . Our expenses are so mingled with the construction expenses, and the transportation is in all cases [made] subservient to the necessities of the work of the contractors, that many elements now enter into the operating of the road, which will in future cease to come into account. In my opinion the interests of the road are greatly sacrificed in the effort to hurry forward the work west with undue haste. In concentrating every effort on the new work, instead of taking proper care for the completion of the necessary sidings and buildings on the part already open for convenience of business. Our sidings, at the setting in of winter, are entirely insufficient, and our engines are for the most part unhoused during the present cold nights. I am trying to impress the policy of making all complete as we go along and take care of our business on each portion as it is opened."

Dec. 7. To McHenry: "I have watched all matters closely and am well convinced that the *rushing* principle has already been carried too far for all interests. No single man can watch so many widely separated pieces of work and have all forced forward, without some being greatly neglected. . . . We are now experiencing this truth. Three fourths of our engines now in the commencement of winter are without housing, and some will be all winter. We are short of sidings, and have *very* limited facilities for repairs. . . . I am sorry to say that your accounts with the Penna. and New York companies yet remain in status quo. . . . The only reason I can assign for the delay is that your representatives have not time to attend to them. It is useless to talk of any report until this is done. . . . With a road almost entirely completed, *you* are an immense *debtor* to the company (according to the books), as we have as yet no basis upon which we can enter the proper credits."

Dec. 21. To McHenry: "Kennard is here and . . . your account with the company will at once be taken in hand. . . . I have tried for months to have them attended to without success, and I have feared that before they would receive attention, that all would be in confusion."

Dec. 31. To McHenry: "Palmer [McHenry's agent] has the accounts between the Penna. company and yourself in hand. He finds he has to make a revision of the statements as returned from the construction office. . . . I have arranged matters with Kennard in a manner satisfactory, if he shall abide by the terms which he promises to do. If this cannot be done, I shall withdraw entirely from my connection with the company. . . . One object of my ambition has been realized—the completion of the road. . . . The next object of my ambition is that the enterprise shall not only be remunerative to those who have invested in it but that it should surpass all of our predictions. I am sure this result can only be attained by perfect accord and unity of purpose among those entrusted with the management."

Dec. 31. The track was laid to Galion, 81 miles from Akron,

making total miles constructed	356
Mahoning road leased	78
	434

Between Galion and Dayton ninety per cent of the earth work and masonry completed and most of the bridging and trestle, the ties being distributed, and all the iron received for the track. The main line from Salamanca has been ballasted, except some four miles, and is in good running order throughout. Some ballasting has also been done between Akron and Galion. Commodious stations have been completed at Salamanca, Mill Village, Cleveland, and Meadville. At the two latter places dining arrangements have been added, and at Meadville a first class hotel (McHenry House) under charge of R. M .N. Taylor. At other points temporary but convenient structures have been built, to be hereafter replaced from the earnings of the road.

Repair shops have been built at Corry and temporary shops at Meadville for use until the completion of the large and permanent structures now in process of construction at Meadville and Franklin Mills.

The total rolling stock of the three companies consists of 74 locomotives, 19 first class passenger cars, 14 baggage and mail cars, and 1370 freight cars.

Arrangements have been made for the lease of the Jersey City locomotive works for the construction of 100 engines to be placed on the line in 1864, and an increase of freight cars to 2500.

The Mahoning lease at $300,000 per annum went into effect Oct. 1, 1863.

The sidings of the line are yet insufficient for a very considerable increase of traffic, while the motive power and rolling stock is taxed to its utmost.

Reynolds, Kent, and Kennard helped celebrate the completion of the line to Dayton, Ohio. On the negative side, Reynolds regretted the control of the Oil Creek RR by the combined efforts of the Pennsylvania RR and the New York Central RR. He blamed this disaster on the short-sighted policies of McHenry and Kennard. Reynolds continued to attack Kennard and his lavish lifestyle. More pointedly, he cited Kennard's thirst for power and the appointment of his friends to key positions in the New York company. Reynolds urged and succeeded in getting McHenry to come to America to see what was happening with the company. A warm welcome greeted the Englishman. Shortly thereafter, both Reynolds and Marvin Kent submitted their resignations.

Driving the Last Spike

Jan. 8. Went to Cleveland with Thorp and Shryock where we met Hubbard, Upson, Kennard, and others, and organized the Ohio Coal Company.[1]

Jan. 20–26. At New York with Palmer (McHenry's bookkeeper), Church and Streator and Kennard to make adjustment of the contractor's accounts, but without full success as the books of the contractor appear to be in hopeless confusion, if the abstracts furnished by Palmer are taken as tests. I also endeavored to impress on Kennard the importance of securing the OC RR on the basis proposed by Streator, but was unsuccessful, as Kennard is full of visionary schemes which engross his attention to the exclusion of really important objects.

Feb. 17. Meetings of the Control Board and of the A&GW of Pa. to settle the accounts with Ward. All matters closed with Ward.

March 25 to 28. At New York to arrange financial basis for advance by McHenry of funds for payment for supplies and expenses outside transportation, for which the company have paid. Arranged for oil pipe company to take my stock.

April 20 and 21. At Cleveland, organization of the New Lisbon RR.

May 20. Franklin Mills, meeting of New Lisbon Coal Company.

May 23. Jamestown. Annual election. Kennard most unwisely made

View of A&GW Engine No. 71, built by the Jersey City Locomotive Works in January of 1864. Of special interest are the six-foot-broad-gauge box cars in the background. *(Editors' collection)*

indiscreet changes in the board by placing Blakesley, Rose, and Lowery instead of Dick, Thorp, and Shaws.

June 11. Oil City with Mumford relative to right of way and ground for station. Find it very difficult to locate track without expensive improvement on property occupied for wells and tanks and values at enormous prices.

June 18. With Church, Shryock, Kennard, and others left for Dayton to assist in driving the last spike for the Cincinnati connection.

June 20. Dayton. A large party of the officers of the several companies arrived here early A.M. and found all prepared for the interesting and memorable ceremony of laying the connecting rail of the A&GW with the broad gauge of the Cincinnati, Hamilton & Dayton RR—a day looked for through many years of hope and disappointment and change. More than twelve years, but at last accomplished.

The day was all that could have been desired. We were a joyous party, comprising a large representation of the A&GW, and L'Hommedieu, President, and A. McLaren, Superintendent of the CH&D. The last rail was laid and [Marvin] Kent, Kennard and I each drove our spikes after the others had been driven by the various officials.

June 21. L'Hommedieu gave a complimentary dinner to our party at the Phillips House, Dayton, as an appropriate finale of the interesting occasion of the union of the A&GW and the CH&D, and the afternoon and evening were spent in toasts, congratulations, amid *mutual admiration.* And thus terminated the ceremonial of the completed track of the Atlantic & Great Western Railway.

Sale of the Oil Creek Railroad

July 7. On the evening of this day Col. Thomas A. Scott of the PRR, Dean Richmond of the New York Central (NYC RR), and Streator of the OC RR met in the city of Erie. The two former companies purchased the stock or at least the controlling amount from Struthers and Streator of the OC RR.

This was the disastrous result of the shortsighted policy of Kennard and McHenry. For more than a year I had succeeded in preventing the

A&GW Locomotive built by Rogers Locomotive Company. According to the back of the photograph, the man in the uniform is James Henry Russell, with the engine he used on the first trip from Meadville to the 'far west.' *(Crawford County Historical Society Collection)*

transfer in the hope that it could be secured to the A&GW interest to which it was of such vital importance. Twice supposing all was certainly arranged, I went to New York with Streator to perfect, only to be met with some frivolous excuse for delay. I, after repeated warnings, abandoned further effort. The sale was at the time a great disaster, as the control would for a long time have given the oil traffic to the A&GW to the full extent of the capacity of the road.

Disappointment in Kennard

Among other causes preventing the purchase by the A&GW RR interest was the fact of the useless use of the money sent for the building of the road in the personal expenditures and extravagances and private speculations of Kennard. Fond of show and susceptible to flattery, he was easily led into many expenditures of company money for personal purposes and projects.

Large investment was made in coal banks; in the purchase of the Angier House in Cleveland, and refitting the same as the Kennard House; in the purchase of the Wilson Park for purposes of private residence (to be built); building a steam yacht at Cleveland; the purchase of house in New York; and of Burton's country home "Glencove," and most extravagant improvements of the property and conservatories, etc. Many of these investments in the end proved profitable but at the time were very disastrous to the interests of the railway by absorbing the money so much needed for its necessities.

With success were developed in full force some of the peculiar characteristics of Kennard, which were not so noticeable at the more adverse periods. He was vain and very susceptible to flattery, was very fond of show, and reckless of expenditure to accomplish his ends. Yet, he was kind and generous. With appearance of wealth he was soon beset with shrewd and designing persons who found no trouble in taking his measure, and adopting the sure methods of accomplishing their ends. He soon was enlisted in numbers of worthless schemes and his attention diverted from the true interests of the A&GW.

The prestige and success was soon in great measure lost by these indiscretions, and all connected with the road suffered. Intoxicated with flattery and adulation Kennard was desirous of exercising a control in every department of the company. For all connected with the management of the business of a company he was entirely unqualified, having neither steadiness of purpose nor of opinion, and being entirely devoid of discretion in conversation with interested parties.

It had been evident for some time past that the future success and prestige of the enterprise would be jeopardized unless he could be brought to reason, and his vagaries suppressed. This I endeavored to do in vain. He freely admitted the errors and promised that they should not be committed in future, but only to be forgotten at the first temptation. I appealed to McHenry to exert his influence, but he was so much embarrassed with his financial efforts, and was so compromised with Kennard's friends, that he did not dare to act.

My letters to McHenry will fully explain our great difficulties arising from these causes.

Feb. 11. "I do not assume the right to advise as to any of your plans not directly connected with the railway over which I have charge, and I yet do not wish it to be taken for granted that I esteem the various and numerous side operations as at this time in all respects judicious— involving as they will, a very large expenditure of means at a time when the financial world is much disturbed, and when the A&GW will of itself require a very large additional amount of expenditures for rolling stock for its business.

"I will now simply say that some of these schemes will, in my opinion, if carried out, prove very unprofitable if not worse. The enthusiastic temperament of Kennard causes him often to adopt opinions upon first impressions, and those impressions often derive from persons who have their own ends to attain in their representations.

"The A&GW is in itself an immense undertaking, and the absolutely necessary additional projects in connection therewith for the full development of its vast resources, will be sufficient for the ambition and enterprise of yourself and friends for the next two years; and these will call into requisition all the energy that can be given. . . . A report will be made as *soon as the accounts between yourself and the company can be settled.*

"I have used every effort in my power to have this brought about, and think it will be closed this week. The delay has resulted in great measure from the manner in which your accounts have been kept in the construction office. . . . I expect Kennard and Palmer here tomorrow . . . for settlement. That you may appreciate the impossibility of a report until some settlement [shall be] made, I will state some of the difficulties.

"We are operating the road under a central organization. This department, after payment of transportation expenses, makes divisions of earnings to each company, who pay their own expenses. This division must be made upon the local as well as through business, and according to mileage and use of cars. There has been no special designation of rolling stock in either Penna. or Ohio by Kennard," and the above mentioned division of earnings can only be approximate until this shall be done.

March 7. "Our road is all that was ever promised, or rather it will be—when it shall be completed and supplied with rolling stock. Until that time, you can only expect it to earn according to its capacity for business. Every day is extending its length, but its capacity does not increase in proportion to its extension.

"I regret to say that the *new* schemes which arise day by day to engross attention have not, in my opinion, a salutary influence, either upon our A&GW enterprise, or the *credit* of the same.

"Some of these projects are good in their time and place others will if carried out, in my opinion, result in loss; and *all* had better be postponed until you are in proper shape in the A&GW enterprise. I tremble for you when I see the vast schemes which loom up day by day in times as uncertain as the present."

March 30. "Under proposed arrangements with Kennard, the stock will be increased in the A&GW of Penna. to an additional amount of $1,000,000 being in the aggregate $3,000,000. This increase will be submitted for the approval of the stockholders . . . on April 7.

"I must say [again] that I am not satisfied with the manner in which things are done. I have thus far solely for the interests of yourself and others who have invested in the enterprise retained a position as head of the Central Department. Nothing but the consciousness that all interests would be imperiled by my withdrawal from that position has prevented me from doing so long since. I have remained at the insistence of friends of the road and to promote the best interests of the enterprise with which I have been so long identified. In doing so I have done injustice to myself by being placed in a false position, As the head I have borne the responsibility of the unauthorized acts of others over whom or whose acts I have no control and who represent you.

"I have concluded to retain the supervision of the general business of the companies until in better shape than at present. I shall then withdraw. . . . [Kennard] lacks the essential requisites of attention to detail, steadiness of purpose, and perseverance in the *completion* of a plan commenced before being carried away with new ideas. His disposition to work independently and without knowing or caring for the arrangements already made, make it dangerous to the business reputation of anyone to work with him. His system, or rather his *want* of system would throw the most carefully devised plans into chaotic confusion. . . .

"The credit of the A&GW is not enhanced on this side by the constantly presented *extravagant* schemes which day by day find their way into the newspapers for the personal aggrandizement of Kennard. With substantial influential businessmen, who look upon all schemes in their naked worth, the effect is not beneficial, but the reverse. With them these newspaper articles are accepted at their value as a cheap method of gratifying personal vanity, or to use an American expression 'Gas'."

April 4. "The report of statistics of the Ohio company is nearly prepared. . . . For this delay you must only blame the lack of business punctuality of your own agent Mr. T. W. Kennard. . . . I have become utterly discouraged in the effort to carry out the business arrangements of the companies in a perfect manner. . . . With Kennard's headlong and thoughtless policy pursued, the A&GW as a remunerative enterprise must be a *failure*.

"No such enterprise can be conducted with these spasmodic impulsive efforts which in most cases ruin the very object to be obtained. . . . The enterprise has been weakened in public estimation and has lost credit when it was most important it should have gained in reputation.

"Railway credit is not gained in this country by extravagant living and superb mansions. Nor do capitalists highly estimate those promises the fulfillment of which is, to say the least, very problematical. . . .

"I have hoped to have seen you here, and thus spare these comments. I have been identified with the road so long that I feel the strongest desire for its success, and especially for the profitable remuneration of those who have built it. I am free to confess that under ordinary circumstances I would have wished to retain my connection with it, but nothing would induce me to share the responsibility of the management of the enterprise with one whom I know to be unfitted for the work."[2]

April. "I know that all our business arrangements over which I have control are in good order, and in so far as we control will continue so. . . . Let me most earnestly assure you that disaster *must* result from the manner in which your business has been conducted, if the same course is persisted in. . . . You may think my letters *blue*. That may be. Could I have seen you, they would not have been written. Could you have seen for yourself, they need not have been written."[3]

May 23. "The Penna. company sent by last steamer a further sum of $500,000 of shares, on account of work yet to be done, not included in contracts as now made."

May 26. "You have no doubt before this received a list of the directors elected by *Kennard* in the New York company . . . [excluding] members who have been identified with the project from the very commencement, and who at all times have been your active and warm supporters. . . . It was a gratuitous insult to your warmest friends, upon whose good offices you may in some measure be yet dependent.

"It was as *foolish* as it was unnecessary. I feel safe in saying that henceforth the A&GW Company has not a friend upon its line in the state of New York; and with Kennard's persistence in his course, it will soon have no supporters or friends in Penna. or Ohio, other than those influenced by dollars and cents. . . . This last exhibition of his shortsightedness, while it has greatly mortified me, has not in any degree caused surprise. If he is to be clothed with your full power, I regret the *certain* result.[4]

"If long tried supporters of the enterprise like Gen. Dick and Thorp are to be thrust aside to make place for persons such as Kennard's private secretary and Rose who, however estimable they may be, have only the interest in the road as measured by their salary, you cannot expect that you will retain active and efficient friends.

"I am becoming thoroughly disgusted with the thousand past and never ceasing follies which tend to render the enterprise, so magnificent in itself, a subject of ridicule in its agents. *I must either be entrusted with power from you to protect the interests of the company from such re-*

sults, or I must in justice to myself withdraw from all further connection with it. May I request your answer by return mail."

July 9. "In my last I mentioned the sale of the controlling interest in the Oil Creek RR to the New York Central and Pennsylvania RR companies. The President of the OC RR Company informs me that the purchase was made by Dean Richmond (NYC RR) and Thomas Scott (PRR) as a private investment!!!

"I need not express to you the intense mortification I have felt from this result which I have long foreseen, and have used every effort to prevent. I have by my personal effort delayed this sale for more than a year, with the hope that I could awaken your agents to a reality of the danger of the control passing into other hands. My efforts were unavailing, as Kennard seemed infatuated with the belief that no other parties wished to purchase. I knew to the contrary. . . .

"This is *one* of the calamities your timely presence here would have averted. Others will follow unless you come without much further delay. . . .

"From the beginning I have considered the control of the OC RR essential to the interests of the A&GW, and obtained a promise from Streator that if the stock of the company should at any time be sold, that the first offer should be made to the A&GW upon as favorable terms as to any other parties.

"More than a year ago Streator informed me that overtures had been made by Scott to Streator who was disposed to sell. I, at that time, obtained a verbal offer of a controlling amount of the stock at par and requested Kennard to authorize me to negotiate the purchase and stated that I thought I could buy at less, possibly at 80. He most positively refused to consider the proposal. Some months since an offer was made by persons prominent in the PRR that they would give 150. It was then offered to me at the same rate. Kennard, relying upon the statements of Edgar Thomson . . . again refused. . . . Upon my solicitation, . . . having satisfied myself of the certainty that adverse interests were desirous to buy, I took occasion to again urge the matter upon Kennard and stated to him that it was my advice as the friend of yourself and as an officer looking to the interests of the road that the purchase should be made without delay. He then agreed that it should be done and I took Streator to New York upon the strength of that promise. Upon our arrival Kennard was engrossed with the Toledo stock arrangement and would not have anything to do with it than he would write and submit the matter to you. I again obtained a delay of six weeks, and in the meanwhile ascertained that Richmond had made some overtures. All of which I mentioned to Kennard, who said he did not wish to hear further about the matter.

"I have only to do as I have done, say: *Come with the least possible delay. Your most important interests are in jeopardy.* No settlements have been or are likely to be made without your presence. The financial condition of the country[5] renders it imperative that you should come."

July 27. "Having learned that you are expected in New York this week, and feeling that it is important to have a day or two with you."

McHenry's Visit

July 28. McHenry by letter announced his presence in New York, and on August 3rd, I left for New York, and on August 4th, met McHenry and Kennard. After a long interview in relation to affairs of the company, and the state of the accounts between the contracts, McHenry and the company, it became evident to me that the future was uncertain if not hopeless for a creditable administration of the affairs of the company.

The company had, by my estimates, paid McHenry almost if not the entire sum due him on completion of his engagements. Yet his work was by no means finished. Notwithstanding this, he was evidently greatly distressed for future means, and was very urgent for great additional issue of stock upon statements made by Palmer, his accountant, who had furnished a statement utterly inadmissible, without vouchers, and denying the company auditor access to the contractors' books for verification.

As the contracts with McHenry were plain, and the evidences of compliance by the company with all obligations equally [so], I could not allow the claims.

From left to right, Sir Samuel Morton Peto, Thomas W. Kennard, James A. McHenry, Samuel Wann, and S. S. L'Hommedieu. *(Reynolds Collection, Allegheny College)*

As the control of the following elections would rest entirely with McHenry, and all the discredit of future disaster or wrongful appropriations fall upon the officers of the company, my resolution was taken to withdraw from the enterprise while it could be done with credit to myself, and before new and interested boards of directors elected by the contractor should have power to manipulate the accounts of the company in his interests if necessity should drive him to the alternative.

I consequently gave a full and frank explanation of my views to McHenry, and stated my determination to withdraw on October 1.

Aug. 8. McHenry wrote from New York of his intention to go through to St. Louis, and wishing me to go with him and others. This trip was delayed for some days, but on the 22nd he wrote: "We leave on Wednesday and hope to take you up next day. Palmer has sent me account. I find due me $3,000,000 Penna. shares $1,000,000 New York, and I must have these to take with me to London. Please let there be no delay."

It may well be imagined that this preposterous demand only added to my satisfaction at the release from connection with the company.

Aug. 25. Left Meadville with Shryock, Gen. Dick, Thorp, and others for Salamanca, to meet McHenry. The train from New York was three hours late, and did not arrive at Salamanca until 6:30 [A.M.]. Lord Earley and Belmont accompanied McHenry, also Kennard and Wann. Arrived at Meadville 6:30 P.M. and left at 8 P.M.

Aug. 26. Arrived at Dayton. We found engine waiting, with McLean, Superintendent of CH&D RR, [and] were joined near Cincinnati by L'Hommedieu, and at Vincennes by the Superintendent of the Ohio & Mississippi (O&M RR).

Aug. 27. Arrived at St. Louis and went to Liddell House. After breakfast took a drive with McHenry and Kennard.

Aug. 28. McHenry, Kennard and Wann left in the morning for Chicago. I left at three P.M. on the O&M RR for home.

Aug. 29. Arrived at Cincinnati at 7 A.M. and at Weddell House, Cleveland, 4 P.M.

Aug 30. Left Cleveland 9:10 A.M., home 2 P.M.

From the *Crawford Democrat*, September 2, 1864

GRAND OVATION

James McHenry arrived in a special train from Cleveland at 3 P.M. The depot and the McHenry House were tastefully and gorgeously ornamented with wreaths of evergreen interspersed with countless numbers of miniature flags, while large ones graced the more prominent parts of the edifice.

On the top of the building were displayed the ensigns of Great Britain, Spain, and the United States, and on the south end displayed in large letters "Welcome McHenry."

At the appointed hour, 3 P.M., amid the firing of cannon, the sound of music, and the shouts of the people the train arrived at the depot.

Mr. McHenry was received at the cars by Mr. Reynolds, President of the

Drawing of the McHenry House and Meadville Depot as it was decorated to welcome James McHenry to Meadville, September 2, 1864. *(Crawford County Historical Society Collection)*

Central Board, and conducted to the south portico of the McHenry House, where he was met by the Burgess and Town Council. . . .

In the evening a dinner was given to Mr. McHenry in the Grand Dining Hall, many of our citizens partaking of the generous feast of welcome.

A fine display of fire works was exhibited on the beautiful grounds of the hotel during the evening.

Sept. 13. I left with General Dick, Shryock, and Church. At Jamestown we were joined by Bradshaw.

September 14–16 were spent in the City, and on the 17th at noon, a very large party was assembled on the *Alice Rosa* comprising many of the railway officials of other roads, and prominent citizens of New York. The day was beautiful, and the sail very enjoyable. Glencove with its bright paint and gold and numerous banners presented a charming sight. The grounds, flower gardens, shrubberies, fountains, statues,

This photograph of Thomas W. Kennard's house at Glencove, Long Island, was taken during a gathering of railway officials and prominent citizens of New York, September 17, 1864. *(Reynolds Collection, Allegheny College)*

and lawns were in perfect condition, and altogether presented a beautiful landscape. Mrs. Kennard received her guests on the piazza with the charming cordiality natural to her (alas for her future fate). Kennard was an excellent host, and until near the hour for dinner led his guests to points of beauty and interest.

A photographer was ready just as the company assembled on the veranda before dinner, and a picture of the numerous company was transferred to permanent remembrance.

The dinner was given in the gothic music room, and was as well served as money could command. The company broke up late and at the wharf. Black was near losing his life by stepping off the gang plank into the water. He was fortunately rescued with no greater misfortune than a thorough wetting.

I spent Sunday in Glencove with Kennard and McHenry very pleasantly; returned to New York and [then] home September 22nd.

On September 5th, McHenry sent me the resignation of Kennard as V.P., also Wann [as] director in New York and Penna. McHenry: "Commending all these important matters now in your good hands for early solution, and thanking you most heartily for your great kindness to me personally. Robb will accept office on October 1."

Resignation

Sept. 30. At a meeting of the directors of the A&GW RR Co. in New York, the A&GW RR Co. of Pa. and the Central Board, held in Meadville, Sept. 30, William Reynolds tendered his resignation as follows:

"TO the Atlantic & Great Western Railway Company of Penna., and The Atlantic & Great Western Railway Company in New York

"I herewith present to you my resignation of the office of president in your companies, which position I have occupied from the times of their organization in 1857 and 1859.

"To most of you this determination on my part will cause no surprise, as you are aware it has been some time in contemplation; and is now only hastened a few months by a combination of circumstances which have rendered the present a more favorable time for withdrawing from the companies than the future.

"The work contemplated in existing contracts has in great measure been completed, and it is in all respects advisable that any new arrangements or contracts should be made under the same supervision and direction by which they are to be completed.

"I have the great satisfaction in withdrawing from my connection with the companies, to congratulate you upon the success which has crowned your untiring efforts, not only in the completion of the enterprise to which you have devoted so many years, but also upon its present prosperity and future prospects.

"I need not assure you that the chief regret in the step I have taken will arise from the severing of the relations which have so long existed between us through the many eventful periods in the history of this enterprise.

"For the constant and ever confident support I have received from you under circumstances the most discouraging, you will accept my sincere acknowledgement."[6]

After acceptance of the resignation of Reynolds, the following proceeding of the several companies and Central Board were ordered to be entered on the records of the several companies and Central Board:

"At a meeting of the Board of Directors of the Atlantic & Great Western Railroad Company in New York held on the thirtieth day of September, A.D. 1864, in Meadville, Penna., a full quorum of the directors being present, viz: Wm. Reynolds, A. G. Allen, G. Church, C. E. E. Blakesley, J. J. Shryock, T. W. Kennard, and James Robb, the following preamble and resolutions were presented by J. J. Shryock and unanimously adopted.

"Whereas, William Reynolds Esq., has tendered his resignation as president of the board of directors of this company, it is but justice to a faithful and efficient officer that a suitable testimonial from the Directors be placed upon the minutes of the board, Therefore,

"Resolved, That in accepting the resignation of Mr. Reynolds as president, we do so with many regrets.

"To him we are indebted for his untiring energy and perseverance, being foremost in all that has led to the completion of the road of the company.

"Resolved, That it is with pride and satisfaction we look back upon the various actions of our board that have so firmly sustained him in the many trials and difficulties with which he has had to contend; his energy and zeal has enabled us to surmount all opposition from every quarter which threatened to crush the great enterprise that calls from the citizens of the counties, through which it passes, their unqualified and lasting obligation.

"Resolved: That our esteemed president may be assured that he carries with him the heartfelt desire of every member of this board for his future prosperity, and that we will long and fondly cherish a recollection of the official and personal intercourse from the organization of the company in 1859.

"A. Bradshaw, Secy."

At a meeting of the Board of Directors of the Atlantic & Great Western Railroad Company of Pennsylvania held on the September 30, at the office of the company in Meadville, Pa., a full quorum of the Directors being present, the following preamble and resolutions were unanimously adopted, viz:

Wm. Thorp, Secy.

"At a meeting of the Central Board of the Atlantic & Great Western Railway Companies held on the thirtieth day of September, A.D. 1864, in Meadville, a full quorum of the members being present, viz: Wm. Reynolds, A. F. Allen, J. Dick, J. J. Shryock, M. Kent, and T. W. Kennard,

"On motion of T. W. Kennard, Esq., the following was unanimously approved

"Resolved that the Chairman be authorized to procure a service of plate to be presented to Wm. Reynolds, Esq., our late Chairman, as a testimonial of high regard, and for services rendered by him to the Atlantic & Great Western Railway.

"J. M. Dick, Acting Secy."[7]

❧ Editors' Afterword

O ne of the purposes of this afterword is to tell something about William Reynolds and Marvin Kent in the decades following their separation from the A&GW RR. Another aim is to see what happened with this railroad once Reynolds and Kent had departed from it in 1864. Were their fears of the railroad's future justified?

Upon their resignations both men returned to their business and civic pursuits. In 1865 Kent succeeded his father as president of the Kent National Bank and retained this position for forty-three years. He did take time off in 1875 to serve as a Republican senator in the Ohio legislature. Afterwards he continued to be active in promoting business enterprises in his town.

Reynolds likewise dabbled a little in politics by becoming Meadville's first mayor in 1866, when it became a city of the third class. Most likely he viewed his stewardship as mayor more as a duty than as a stepping-stone to higher political office. Politics, like the law, held little charm for him. Shortly after leaving office, he and William Thorp, a longtime associate of his in the railroad business, established the Athens Mill in Meadville, a dealer in rough and dressed lumber. There were other business adventures.

Yet it was public service for which Reynolds is best remembered after his railroad years. Many charitable groups profited through his generosity. Giving something back to the community was a family tradition that he, his children, and his father cherished. He served as trustee or board member of a number of organizations, including Allegheny College and Park Avenue Church of Meadville. He helped organize the city's waterworks system that pumped water from the feeder canal to a reservoir high on a hill in the northeastern suburb of the city. Also to his credit was Island Park. Started in 1876, this twenty-five-acre park proved to be a popular attraction, with its walks and gardens.

The position he may have enjoyed the most was the presidency of the Meadville Library, Art, and Historical Association. As an amateur historian Reynolds took the lead in preserving his county's documentary heritage. It was through his efforts that prized collections like the papers of the A&GW RR and the complete run of the *Crawford Weekly Messenger* were saved. He also wrote numerous essays on the county's past in addition to two fine but unpublished histories of the bench and bar of the county and the story of the A&GW RR.

His contributions to the community seemed limitless. It is no wonder that on the day of his burial, January 13, 1911, the entire city of Meadville came to a standstill. In his honor, public offices, factories, and small shops closed for an hour as townspeople mourned the loss of their favorite neighbor.

Long before his death, Reynolds undoubtedly mourned the loss of the railroad he had helped build. He had good reason to, considering the amount of time and energy he had devoted to it. From late 1864 until its final demise in 1880, the story of the A&GW RR was agonizingly predictable. After Reynolds and Kent resigned from their respective boards, McHenry succeeded in having James Robb elected chief executive of all three companies, or divisions. He remained for only three months, however, from October 1 through December 31.

What prompted his departure after such a short tenure was Robb's claim that he had been deceived into accepting the office. He charged McHenry, Kennard, and others with having skillfully manipulated the company's books involving millions in pound sterling. The true condition of the railroad turned out to be quite different than what he had been told. Robb's utter disgust in having been misled and his shock to learn how the company was conducting itself probably contributed to a heart attack just prior to his resignation.

Before he left office Robb had urged, as Reynolds had before him, that both retrenchment and a better administrative system be adopted. He pointed to the decline of traffic on the A&GW RR. There was little sense in forecasting for 1865 a promising $200,000 per week in earnings that could alleviate some of the financial distress. It could never happen. He harped on the many bad policies the company insisted upon retaining. For example, he cautioned against offering shares in payment for new work, a practice that would erode the value of the shares already issued. Second, the company had also announced the issuance of 8 percent debentures to liquidate liabilities. This raised serious questions in light of the fact that collateral for the debentures were stocks and bonds which, in reality, were not available because a significant part of them had been hypothecated for loans.

But general trust in McHenry by European investors and overly optimistic publications and forecasts kept the truth of the company's financial health in the shadows. As inaccurate, and perhaps even illegal, as the accounting and publicity were proven to be, McHenry continued to lure investors to feed his ambitions for further expansion.

With railroad mania as robust as it was, some of the shady practices of the A&GW RR did not seem outrageous to many investors. They were willing to pay high prices for securities that promised huge returns. It is doubtful that price/earnings ratios ever entered their thinking. Besides, to the casual observer in 1864 the future of the A&GW RR indeed looked bright. The main line was complete—388 miles from Salamanca, New York, to Dayton, Ohio. In addition, there were another 113 miles of branch lines, giving a total of 501 miles of railway built in approximately thirty-eight months and during a major war. Not bad. There is nothing like success to fan the flames of capital investment.

With the new year, a number of administrative changes occurred. James Shryock of Meadville became president of the A&GW RR of Pennsylvania while S. S. L'Hommedieu was elected chief executive of the A&GW RR of Ohio and New York. He had been president of the

Cincinnati, Hamilton & Dayton Railroad. In late 1865, an agreement of merger and consolidation brought the three companies together in a new corporation known as the Atlantic & Great Western Railway Company. Stock of the merging companies was exchanged for shares in the new company. Authorized capitalization was 600,000 shares at $50 each and mortgage bonds of 60,000 at $500 each.

Despite these changes, differences over management practices continued. The English hold on executive offices tightened and McHenry's position was as strong as ever. Periodic announcements of the company's successes, some real and some imaginary, prompted further plans of expansion and increased capitalization. They also prompted the Americans to insist that their English partners were deliberately covering up the true health of the company. In one instance, they pointed to the fuzzy procedure of combining transportation and construction accounts in order to hide the employment of more than 1,000 workers. Why should there be so many workers, they asked, when company officials had already proudly proclaimed the railroad's completion? Second, why should the earnings of the Oil Creek RR be included among reports when the railroad was never a part of the A&GW RR?

There were other discrepancies to which the Americans alluded. Regular audits had not been possible because of London's failure to submit regular statements. Reynolds had argued the same point. At one time, McHenry asked what happened to $4 million he had remitted on the drafts of Kennard! Faulty bookkeeping and misinformation to stockholders and the public only delayed the inevitable. When the company defaulted on its interest payments, a number of creditors in 1867 initiated legal action.

By the order of the courts of Ohio, Pennsylvania, and New York, the railroad was placed in the hands of Robert B. Potter, receiver. Operating the company until December 1868, he found the properties of the road, especially the tracks and fences, to be in a deplorable state and urged immediate repairs. Furthermore, shops to perform maintenance on engines were generally inadequate; many of them were temporary structures. In short, the railroad needed a great deal of fixing at a time

James Shryock, Meadville businessman, director, and later president of the A&GW of PA. *(Crawford County Historical Society Collection)*

when it suffered from poor earnings and credit. Analysis revealed that a broad-gauge system was inherently more expensive to operate than a narrow-gauge line, somewhere between 5 and 20 percent. Use of the six-foot gauge increased costs in unloading and reloading freight to and from lines using the standard gauge. Subsequently agitation grew for a shift to the standard gauge of four feet, eight and one half inches.

More serious problems lay ahead for the railroad. McHenry used the financial reorganization of the company to take it out of receivership and move it toward a formal lease to the Erie RR. The architect of this plan proved to be Jay Gould, president of the Erie, whose ambition was to extend control over a number of railroads. The lease was for twelve years, but in less than one Gould preempted the role of receiver.

Suddenly McHenry realized that he was dealing with some strange bedfellows. During the notorious "Erie War" of 1868, Gould and his equally unscrupulous colleague Jim Fisk did battle with Cornelius Vanderbilt for control of the Erie RR. Both sides distributed lavish bribes to members of the New York legislature to support favorable measures. The market price of winning over a lawmaker was about $15,000 a head. In some cases politicians openly demanded bribes.

Gould had served only a year as receiver when angry investors started proceedings in the courts of Ohio, Pennsylvania, and New York for foreclosure of the company's mortgages. The courts responded by appointing Reuben Hitchcock as the new receiver. Under court authority he leased the company and its properties, including the branch lines, to the Erie RR, to begin January 1, 1870, and continue until foreclosure of the mortgages and the sale of the properties were effected. Meanwhile, a reorganization committee, selected by holders of securities, moved to acquire these properties in the three states. One of the committeemen was former Union general George B. McClellan.

In 1871 the committee finalized the sales. After acquiring the properties and franchises of the Atlantic & Great Western Railway Company, the committee arranged for a new company, to be known by its old name, the Atlantic & Great Western Railroad Company, with a capitalization of $50,000,000. The main office of the company was to be in New York City.

Hope and a brief period of limited expansion followed this reorganization. In 1872 the company leased the properties of the Niles & New Lisbon RR and the Liberty & Vienna RR. The former line ran from Niles to Lisbon, Ohio, and a short distance beyond; the latter line extended from a point near Mosier, Ohio, to the coal mines in Vienna township, Trumbull County. In the same year the two railroads merged with the Cleveland & Mahoning RR to form the Cleveland & Mahoning Valley Railway Company.

Neither reorganization nor expansion mattered much when the Panic of 1873 struck. It began with the failure of the investment banking firm, Jay Cooke and Company, which had invested heavily in postwar railroads. It swept across industrial America, setting off a serious depression that lasted for several years. During the first year the company failed to pay interest on its first-mortgage bonds. Estimated earnings of $10,000 per mile were needed to meet the company's interest payments. This feat lay beyond the capabilities of the A&GW RR, especially in a national slump.

To make matters worse, Gould and the Erie people convinced McHenry that the two railroads could improve their profits by acquiring a controlling interest in the Cleveland, Columbus, Cincinnati & Indianapolis RR. Hoping to prevent suspicion, Gould allegedly devised a scheme to have one person (Samuel Barlow) buy the stock of the CCCI RR with money from London, about $400,000. It is doubtful that he fooled anyone, but the purchase did enable two Erie nominees to be elected to the board of directors. The scheme failed. Earnings of the CCCI RR fell sharply and dividends were stopped. McHenry's credibility fell and so did confidence in the company.

Again, demanding that something be done, creditors appealed to the courts in the three states. And, again, the railroad went into receivership and foreclosure proceedings followed. The routine was both familiar and monotonous. This time the company's difficulties commanded unprecedented press coverage. The comments were not always gracious. Probably the kindest remark made referred to the cheapness with which the A&GW RR was worked. Its rates on freight, which made up the bulk of the business, were lower than those of the Erie RR and the New York Central. Yet it still could not compete favorably with bigger and more aggressive companies.

Other problems plagued the railroad. An orgy of civil suits further demoralized management. In one of them, the United States Rolling Stock Company sued to recover rent due on rolling stock and damages for violation of contract. In another, the Pennsylvania RR went to court to prevent the company from switching to the standard gauge instead of continuing to use the six-foot gauge as stipulated in its charter.

In late 1879 a decree of foreclosure and sale was entered in the court of common pleas of Summit Township, Ohio; similar decrees followed in the courts of Pennsylvania and New York. With legal authority granted to sell the railroad, such sale took place on January 6, 1880, in Akron, Ohio. John H. Devereux, receiver, sold the A&GW RR to the lone bidder who represented the reorganization trustees for $6,000,000—the minimum appraised valuation.

Creditors, bondholders, and stockholders gave the trustees the go-ahead to form a new company that was called the New York, Pennsylvania & Ohio Company. The agreement was filed in the offices of the secretaries of state of Ohio and Pennsylvania, but not in New York, although the company did operate a portion of the line in New York State. Devereux became president of the new railroad that was now a part of the Erie system; its name was shortened in 1896 to the NYPANO RR. The gauge was changed from the six foot to the standard four feet, eight and one-half inch.

James McHenry fought a long battle to recover money that he insisted had been misappropriated. Insufficient evidence makes it difficult to determine either the money he talked about or the losses he and his creditors sustained. Estimates run as high as $200 million. McHenry repudiated charges of personal bankruptcy; the Erie RR had a judgment against him for $2 million.

Thus, the story of the A&GW RR finally came to an end. It had begun with three struggling companies in Ohio, Pennsylvania, and New York, and emerged as an interstate system that stretched from New York City to the Mississippi Valley. Failure of the American public to finance the enterprise adequately resulted in dependency on European venture capital. Unfortunately, this led to increased domination of management by foreigners and troublesome relations between American and European partners.

Much to his credit, McHenry used whatever means were available to draw huge amounts of money from European investors. As long as they were willing to invest, he demanded more securities from America to accommodate them. Extension of branch lines into rich areas of coal and oil reserves, plus the leasing of other lines, caused an inflation of the railroad's capitalization. Watered stock became the order of the day, and retrenchment retreated as a likely option. A point was finally reached when reduced earnings fell below increased costs and debts. With delayed maintenance affecting efficiency, competition from bigger lines, and financial panics paralyzing the nation's economy, the A&GW RR moved closer and closer to its demise.

While Reynolds and Kent did what they could to achieve responsible management and prevent overcapitalization, their European colleagues pursued a policy of development that proved to be fatal. What the Americans demanded was to see every mile of track paid for before proceeding to the next. Not being able to meet payroll consistently was, in their opinion, a shoddy and disreputable way of conducting business. A constant lack of understanding and honest communication between European and American managers lay at the heart of the problem. Accurate accounting procedures, reliable reporting, and simple good faith were all missing in the work formula.

Once they had departed from the company, Reynolds and Kent could only watch it deteriorate. McHenry, Kennard, and Sir Morton Peto may have been shrewd investors and builders, but they lacked the know-how to deal with such unprincipled Americans as Gould. Even had they been clever enough to succeed on that front, they still would have found the problems harassing their railroad becoming acute and insurmountable. Competing with larger and more prosperous lines forced management to lower its rates to levels equal to or below the others. This simply resulted in less earnings, postponed maintenance, and more debt. Often overlooked was the fact that the A&GW RR and its branches ran through areas and towns sparsely populated. The problems went on and on.

It was a railroad born in a time when rail transportation was popular and then made necessary by the exigencies of the Civil War. There is no question that the A&GW RR benefitted from the situations created by the war and the oil boom. But its maturity was in a period of peace, national expansion, unfettered competition, and depression. For the railroads, it was a time that called for wise management, fiscal responsibility, and honest reporting to the public and holders of securities. Unfortunately, such responsible management was lacking with the A&GW RR.

❧ Biographies

James McHenry

Born in County Antrim, Ireland, in 1817, James McHenry was raised in Philadelphia, where his father engaged in mercantile pursuits. At an early age, James entered a commission house in Philadelphia and succeeded enough to become a partner. After the death of his father in 1845, James founded a company in Liverpool, England, for the sale of American farm products. He is generally given credit for originating this import trade which, at first, experienced much difficulty because of the English Corn Laws and protectionism. Still, the business flourished until trouble with his American partner forced McHenry into bankruptcy. New business adventures fared so well, however, that he was able to invite all his creditors to a banquet where he paid them in full their principal and interest.

After agreeing to furnish money and iron to the contractors of the Atlantic & Great Western RR, McHenry removed in 1861 to London, where he teamed with Sir Morton Peto. In time he became the principal stockholder of several railroad companies, but careless management of the funds of the A&GW led that company into receivership. He then entered into a business relationship with Jay Gould of the Erie RR, a move that proved to be unfortunate. Years of protracted and expensive litigation to protect his interests resulted only in financial disaster and failing health. McHenry died just as his claims were about to be decided by arbitration.

McHenry's railroad adventures brought him into close relations with Queen Christina and Don José de Salamanca of Spain. After the Spanish Revolution of 1868, when Queen Isabella (daughter of Christina) was dethroned, she and her son found refuge at McHenry's residence, Oak Lodge. A good deal of credit for restoring the royal family to the throne went to McHenry because of his influence with Spanish bankers and creditors. He was also a good friend of Napoleon III of France. And when the Empress Eugénie and her

Don José de Salamanca, Spanish
nobleman and railroad builder who
was a major backer of the A&GW.
Photo by Ancienne Maison Legray,
marked as 1861. *(Reynolds Collection,
Allegheny College)*

son fled to England after the collapse of the Empire in 1870, they too found
hospitality at Oak Lodge.

McHenry died in his seventy-fifth year. Reynolds said of him: "McHenry
was a man of courteous address and pleasing manner. He was earnest and per-
suasive in business negotiations, enthusiastic in all his enterprises. He was apt
to be led astray by his own over-wrought expectations. He had a host of warm
friends among prominent men of Europe and America."

Marvin Kent

Born at Ravenna, Portage County, Ohio, in 1816, Marvin Kent attended the
Tallmadge Academy. He pursued mercantile interests and then, in 1850, engaged in manufacturing at Franklin Mills (now Kent), Ohio. But it was the future of the railroad that fascinated him. He envisaged a rail network that would

link the Ohio and Mississippi Valleys with the eastern seaboard—a dream that became a reality with the A&GW. He became president of the Ohio division of this railroad and retired after its completion. Later in life he recorded his recollection of its construction. In 1875 he was elected to the state senate of Ohio. The city of Kent, Ohio, was named after him.

Horace Cullum

Born in New York City in 1811, Horace Cullum came to Meadville seven years later with his father, Arthur Cullum. He engaged in mercantile business until he began to operate a grist- and sawmill at Bemistown, a few miles north of Meadville. His reputation as a builder, however, soon exceeded his success as a businessman. He assisted in the construction of the feeder canal through Meadville and the aqueduct and dam at Bemistown. (Water for the feeder flowed from French Creek at Bemistown to Conneaut Lake.) Cullum was an early enthusiast of the railroad and became one of the contractors of the Meadville Branch. He enjoyed many credits in his building career. In one year (1868) it is recorded that he supervised the construction of thirty storerooms, two hotels, several houses, and one tenement building. The opera house in Meadville was also one of his accomplishments. He died in California at the age of eighty.

Christopher L. Ward

Raised in Susquehanna County, Pennsylvania, Christopher L. Ward was admitted to the bar of that county in 1837, having studied under the eminent lawyer William Jessup. The following year Ward moved to Towanda, Bradford County, where he established himself as both a lawyer and a banker. He became the president of the Towanda Bank. He also became active in politics, joining the Democratic Party, which was split between those who supported future president James Buchanan and those behind the local hero, Congressman David Wilmot, of Proviso fame. Ward rallied behind the anti-Wilmot forces by helping set up the *North Pennsylvanian* with Wien Forney at Towanda. It lasted less than a year, just long enough to help defeat Wilmot's bid for reelection in 1852. Ward was for a time chairman of the National Democratic Committee.

He was also a man of literary tastes. His library was said to have been the largest in northern Pennsylvania. The collection, comprising many books, prints, and coins, became the Ward Library of Towanda. Eventually the collection was donated to Lafayette College at Easton, Pennsylvania.

John Dick

Son of William and Anna (McGunnegle) Dick, who came from Pittsburgh to Meadville in the year of John's birth, 1794, John Dick became a successful merchant and a founder of the banking house of J. R. Dick and Co. His business interests and his concern for economic development moved him into politics. Elected to Congress in 1852, Dick served three successive terms. Two of his greater accomplishments were his participation in the building of the Eastern Plank Road and the A&GW RR.

Samuel Hallett

A native of Hornellsville, New York, Samuel Hallett became a banker in that town and later established the banking firm of Samuel Hallett & Company on Broad Street, New York City. He conducted the early negotiations for the contractors of the A&GW RR. Afterwards he was one of the leaders of a railroad building scheme called the Union Pacific Railway, Eastern Division, not affiliated with the Union Pacific Railroad, then under construction. He was murdered on July 27, 1864, by O. A. Tallcott, a business associate who was distressed by the shoddy work done on Hallett's "UP Eastern Division."

Sir Samuel Morton Peto

Born at Woking, Surrey County, England, in 1809, Sir Samuel Morton Peto was descended from an old Norman family. He served an apprenticeship of seven years with his uncle, Henry Peto, a builder of some reputation. Upon his uncle's death in 1830, young Samuel succeeded to a moiety of the large business with his cousin, Thomas Grissell. Afterwards he assisted in the construction of railways in England and Canada. Among his important works were the Norwegian Grand Trunk and Royal Danish line. Upon the opening of the latter he was honored by the King of Denmark.

From 1847 to 1854 Peto represented the City of Norwich in Parliament.

During the Crimean War (1854–56), when the allied armies were embedded in mud before Sebastopol, Peto and a group of engineers in twenty-one days built a railway and had trains carrying war supplies from Balaclava to Sebastopol. In honor of this service, for which he refused compensation, a baronetcy was conferred upon Peto.

He is generally given credit for introducing the Underground railway in London, the first four miles of which was finished during the American Civil War. At about the same time he was assisting McHenry with the A&GW RR. Contemporaries called him the world's greatest railway builder.

Gaylord Church

Gaylord Church was born in New York State in 1811, the son of William and Wealthy (Paler) Church, natives of Connecticut. They settled in Mercer County, Pennsylvania, when Gaylord was five years of age. He attended Mercer Academy and then studied law with John J. Pearson. Admitted to the bar in 1834, he moved the same year to Meadville. He was appointed Deputy Attorney-General (District Attorney) and in 1840 was elected to the legislature, serving two terms. In 1843 he was appointed President Judge of the Sixth Judicial District (Erie, Crawford, and Venango) and served for eight years. In 1858 Governor William Packer appointed Church Judge of the Commonwealth's Supreme Court. Church was recognized as an honest and indefatigable worker.

James J. Shryock

Born in Conneautville, Crawford County, in 1821, James J. Shryock was educated at the Meadville Academy. As a teenager he became active in merchandising and soon earned the reputation of being a smart businessman. It was the railroad, however, that fascinated him. He was a director of the Pittsburgh & Erie RR and in 1858 became an incorporator of the New York division of the A&GW RR. Seven years later he was elected President of the Pennsylvania division of the A&GW and also served as director of several other railroads.

Darwin Finney

Born in Vermont in 1814, Darwin Finney moved to Meadville when he was in his twenties. He graduated from Allegheny College, where he expressed interest in both the law and politics. He read law in the office of Hiram Richmond of Meadville, a leading attorney and Whig. It was probably the influence of Richmond, who went on to become a member of the national House of Representatives, that drew Finney to political issues. He served as Meadville's burgess in 1848 and then served in the state senate from 1856 to 1861. In 1866 he was elected to Congress. He had a reputation of being hotheaded in temperament, but generous to his friends.

Robert Thallon

Born in Scotland, Robert Thallon came to the United States in 1853, where he became a leading pioneer in the import-export business. He superintended the importation of all the iron used in the construction of the A&GW RR. In 1864, after accumulating a fortune, he retired from business and took his family to Europe, where he remained for ten years. Upon his return, he settled in Brooklyn, where he died in 1882 at the age of sixty-six.

Thomas W. Kennard

The son of Robert Kennard, a member of Parliament and a wealthy banker, Thomas attained a reputation as a brilliant engineer early in life. His accomplishments extended from India to Europe and America. In England he was known as the founder of the Monmouthshire Crumlin works as well as the primary designer and builder of the Crumlin Viaduct. Kennard owned the Falkirk ironworks where the iron castings for the viaduct were made. Four years after work had begun, the viaduct was opened to the public in 1857. It was 1,588 feet in length and 200 feet in height. The last passenger train passed over the viaduct in 1964.

In association with the railroad entrepreneur, the Marquis de Salamanca, Kennard also built a number of bridges and viaducts in Spain and Italy. Because of his professional reputation and European connections, he was selected to be the engineer-in-chief of the proposed Atlantic & Great Western Railway.

Kennard commissioned the famous English architect Jacob Wrey Mould to design "Glen Chalet"—a spacious wooden residence on Long Island, New York. After reputed financial difficulties, Kennard returned to England, where he died at Orchard-house, Sunbury, in 1893 at the age of sixty-eight.

Don José de Salamanca

One of the leading capitalists of Europe during the nineteenth century, Don José de Salamanca was educated at the University of Granada and worked as a journalist in Malaga, for the *Advisador Malagueno*. Later he joined the cabinet of Queen Christina of Spain as finance minister and helped resuscitate the country's economy. His personal investments in the railway industry brought him enormous wealth, prestige, and international fame. He became associated with lines in Spain, Portugal, and Italy. In America, his interests were with the A&GW RR and he helped finance its construction. Personable, he enjoyed a reputation of entertaining at his home leading citizens from every segment of society, including the government, business, and the arts.

George Francis Train

Born March 14, 1829, in Boston, Train went to Liverpool, England, as a young man to manage a family business. But he had too much wanderlust to remain in one place. In 1853 he emigrated with his wife to Melbourne, Australia, where he became a merchant and builder of port facilities. Returning to America, he described his travels in articles for the *Boston Post* and the *New York Herald*.

Next to travel, rail transportation fascinated Train. He helped promote the A&GW RR and then went back to England, where he promoted the building of street railways in Liverpool and London. Again returning to America in 1862, he began to work with the Union Pacific RR, where he is credited by some with suggesting the name for the notorious Crédit Mobilier. He made a little money by investing in real estate in Omaha, Nebraska, at least enough to pay for a home in the East.

Train also identified himself with some of the reform movements of the times, including those of women's suffrage and a free Ireland. When he visited Ireland, the British arrested him for carrying pro-Fenian literature. He also spent time in a French jail for associating with the Socialists. With reform a strong feature of the 1872 election in America, he returned and campaigned for president.

Always a traveler who loved to lecture and write on his travels, his forte was going around the world. He made the long journey a number of times, always attempting to break his own record. It is said that one such trip inspired the French writer Jules Verne to produce his captivating work, *Around the World in Eighty Days.*

⚜ Notes

Editors' Introduction

1. James A. Ward, *Railroads and the Character of America, 1820–1887* (Knoxville, Tenn.: University of Tennessee Press, 1986), 14–15. *Eds.*

2. Sarah H. Gordon, *Passage to Union: How the Railroads Transformed American Life, 1829–1929* (Chicago: Ivan R. Dee, 1996), 5–6. *Eds.*

3. Albro Martin, *Railroads Triumphant: The Growth, Rejection, and Rebirth of a Vital American Force* (New York: Oxford University Press, 1992), 15. *Eds.*

4. Sylvester K. Stevens, *Pennsylvania: Birthplace of a Nation* (New York: Random House, 1964), 155. *Eds.*

5. James D. Dilts, *The Great Road: The Building of the Baltimore and Ohio, the Nation's First Railroad, 1828–1853* (Stanford, Cal.: University of Stanford Press, 1993). *Eds.*

6. John Majewski, *A House Divided: Economic Development in Pennsylvania and Virginia before the Civil War* (New York: Cambridge University Press, 2000). *Eds.*

7. Donald Kent, "Erie War of the Gauges," *Pennsylvania History* 15 (Oct 1948): 253–75. *Eds.*

8. John Reynolds, "One Hundred Years Ago" (Unpublished essay, CCHS, 1869). *Eds.*

9. *The Diary of William Reynolds, 1841,* ed. Robert D. Ilisevich (Meadville, Penn.: CCHS, 1981), 16, 19. *Eds.*

Author's Preface

1. For the sake of clarity and consistency, the A&GW companies will be referred to as Railroad as opposed to Railway companies. Official company reports, documents, and correspondence use the terms interchangeably. *Eds.*

2. The Branch was the first incarnation of the railway from New York to Ohio through Meadville, Pennsylvania. It was legally justified by the branching rights given to the Pittsburg & Erie Railroad in its charter. *Eds.*

Chapter 1

1. Reynolds is referring to the New York & Erie Railroad, which later became the Erie Railroad. For clarity we will refer to the company as the Erie RR. *Eds.*

2. Father of William Reynolds. In a letter to John Reynolds from Kinsman, Ohio, Dr. D. Allen asked if Meadville leaders would support a railroad through their town from near Jamestown, New York, to Warren and Akron,

Ohio. Should they agree, Meadville would have to obtain a charter by a ruse, for Pennsylvania would not grant such a charter to New Yorkers. Allen claimed the plan was being discussed in Ohio and New York. Allen to John Reynolds, Feb. 17, 1851, Reynolds Collection, Allegheny College. *Eds.*

3. In 1843 a "snake" was used as a rider in Pennsylvania legislation reviving the Pittsburg & Connellsville RR. *Eds.*

4. The Mahoning Valley RR was represented by Jacob Perkins, President, of Warren, Ohio. The Clinton line by Prof. H. N. Day, President, and Mr. Clark. The Franklin & Warren RR afterwards A&GW, by Judge Kinsmen, Marvin Kent, and Dr. Earle, and Mr. Boyer, of Newton Falls. (These roads were at this time only commenced.) The Cleveland & Ashtabula RR by Judge Humphries, and the Erie & New York City RR by Judge B. Chamberlain of Randolph, New York, D. A. Finney and William Reynolds represented Meadville interests. The Pittsburg & Erie RR was represented by Dr. Wm. Gibson, David Garber, and E. Sankey.

5. George W. Howard of Meadville, Charles Howard, broker at Detroit, and S. Howard.

6. Cash $2,833.33, County bonds, $1,416.66, Stock $4,256.

7. This was the first of forty-three trips to New York City and two trips to Europe which Reynolds cites in his memoir. Considering the inconvenience of travel at that time, this was an incredible expenditure of time, patience, and energy on Reynolds's part. *Eds.*

8. Reynolds, Gibson, John A. Waugh and Sankey, Thomas I. Power, chairman ex officio.

9. For the railroads, times were difficult. This period is remembered as the era of Erie's Railroad War. The road from Ashtabula to Erie had been completed under the covert legislation of the Franklin Canal Company charter, making a line from Buffalo to Cleveland with the six-feet-gauge line of the E&NE RR. The effort of the companies to connect the lines without first going to the harbor, and the attempt to change the gauge of the E&NE RR, led to the riot and destruction. For newspaper coverage, see *Crawford Democrat* and *Crawford Journal* Nov.–Dec. 1853.

The selfish feeling of preventing railway connection was not limited to Erie, but extended to other places, and found sympathizers in Meadville who used every effort to thwart the railroad project. To counteract this effort, a public meeting was held at the Court House on November 15, 1853. I. Potter, President, Noah Town and W. Keplar, V.P. James Buchanan and Wm. McLaughlin Secretaries. Wm. H. Davis, H. L. Richmond, J. C. Hayes, H. B. Brooks, and Harper Michell were appointed a committee to draw resolutions condemnatory of the efforts of the enemies of the road and reports circulated. The meeting included John Reynolds, John Dick, Hon. Jas. Galbraith, Wm. H. Davis, and others.

10. After the abandonment of the contract with the Howards, a new contract was made with George Merriman and Horace Cullum for the line east of Meadville, on the condition of $60,000 of subscription first secured on that part of the line. This contract was never implemented.

11. William Kelley was a prominent citizen of Erie, Pennsylvania. *Eds.*

12. Committee consisted of E. Sankey, W. S. Lane, Wm. Kelley, Hon. Wilson Laird, and Wm. Reynolds.

13. Union Mills, Pennsylvania, is now called Union City. *Eds.*

14. Columbus, Pennsylvania, is just west of Union City. *Eds.*

15. David Sexton, chairman, Kennedy Davis and John M. Osborn, vice presidents, and James T. Chase and D. A. Finney, secretaries.

16. General C. L. Ward, of Towanda, Pennsylvania, in 1856 had been elected president of the A&GW RR (Ohio), and A. C. Morton of New York, formerly one of the engineers of the Grand Trunk RR under Mr. Brassey, had been appointed consulting engineer of the Ohio company. The contractor was Henry Doolittle.

17. The E&NY City RR was represented by Messrs Baker, President, and Wm. Holt., W. D. Shaw, and Daniel Williams. The A&GW of Ohio by Ward, President, Bierce, Bushnell, Coolman, Birchard, and Riblett. The P&E RR by Thomas J. Power, President., Church, and Reynolds. Ward was appointed Chairman, and Reynolds, secretary.

A committee consisting of Ward, Power, Shaw, Hall, and Reynolds, Morton, and Thomas Hazzard, engineer, was appointed to report the objects of the convention.

18. C. L. Ward, T. J. Power, and Henry Baker were appointed and reported Articles of Agreement which were signed by the members present.

19. Writing to a newspaper editor, Marvin Kent takes credit for conceptualizing a plan to link New York to St. Louis with a six-foot-gauge railroad. He proclaimed himself "the father and originator of the entire enterprise." *Meadville Morning Star,* Sept. 1, 1902. *Eds.*

20. This contract would have been of great value to the company. The modified arrangement afterwards made by the Meadville RR (A&GW) with a bonus of only 5 percent for eastward business for five years netted the company over $400,000.

21. On July 3 the charter was granted to Merriman, Mumford, Gill & Shryock, Church, Finney, McFarland, John Dick, Craighead, Reynolds, McFarland, James Dick, each with twenty shares except Craighead with ten, for a total of two hundred and ten shares.

22. October 25, 1858: Court ruled that the county subscription of $200,000 so far as unexecuted is vacated and annulled and set aside, and plaintiff totally discharged from any further performance thereof.

Reynolds: "It should be noted that the decree is based upon the fact that the P&E Co. at the time the county subscriptions were 'authorized by the legislature, was destitute of legal basis on account of the acts of the original subscribers in withdrawing their capital and subscriptions and passing the charter into the hands of thirteen men not one of whom appeared to have paid or subscribed or intended to become responsible for a single share of stock.' The decree in no way reflected on the acts or proceedings of the company as connected with the Branch, but was based exclusively on acts of the original subscribers long previous to the time our friends undertook to build the Branch under the P&E charter."

23. On July 21, 1857, the *Crawford Journal* editorialized that the Meadville Company is said to be bankrupt—"It has neither money, credit, nor property, that we know of." Reynolds was accused of deceiving the public into voting for subscription. A week later, the commissioners responded to Reynolds's charge that they had acted in a "silly" and "criminal" manner. They insisted that they favored a railroad, but one built upon honorable principles and, at the time, when the interests of trade and travel demand it, "with-

out involving innocent taxpayers in the toils of a souless [*sic*] corporation" (*Crawford Journal*, July 28, 1857). *Eds.*

24. The economic depression of 1857 that mainly affected the North resulted from several factors: the overextension of railroads, especially in the sparsely settled areas of the Northwest, that caused a drop in value of railroad securities; the liberal granting of credit by state banks to farmers, many of whom later defaulted on their mortgages; the glutting of European markets with surplus American grain and meat following the Crimean War, which brought a sudden drop in food prices. *Eds.*

25. John Dick, Horace Cullum, A. W. Mumford, John McFarland, James R. Dick, James J. Shryock, Geo. Merriman, and L. D. Williams were present.

Chapter 2

1. U.S. Consul at Liverpool. *Eds.*

2. Isaac S. Doane was a civil engineer from Crawford County, Pennsylvania. He did considerable survey work on railroads before becoming associated with the A&GW. Eventually he became city engineer for Meadville. *Eds.*

3. One of the leading Welsh ironworks. *Eds.*

4. Later named Salamanca, New York. *Eds.*

5. Among other early backers were the Bank of London, Hope, Dodgson & Co. of London, E. F. Satterthwaite of London, and Phillipp N. Schmidt of Frankfort.

6. The Power of Attorney set forth in its preamble: "Whereas, the company is desirous of appointing a financial agent or trustee in Europe for the more effectual promotion of the interests of the company, the purchasers and holders of the stock and bonds thereof, and of the contractors for the construction of the railroad of said company." All powers of the attorney were to be exercised in the name of the company as their attorney, agent, and trustee.

Furthermore by said company and their trustee and atty. that the mentioned "power is conferred upon him at his request and to enable him the better to perform and comply with the recited contract between him and Henry Doolittle, dated Aug. 11, 1858. All services performed in about the premises by virtue hereof or otherwise shall and are to be rendered gratuitously in so far as the Railway Company is concerned. Although this Power and authority is very general in its terms . . . It is executed and delivered to him with the express understanding and agreement on his part and in full confidence that he will at all times act under it in such way as will be best calculated to advance the prudent and economical construction and completion and furnishing the said railroad and according to instructions from time to time received by him from the president of the company and at the end of each month and whenever by said president required, render to the said R.R. Co. a correct report in writing," etc.

"All money, iron, or other materials, etc. which shall be received or obtained by him on behalf of the company shall be deposited with some firm of Bankers in London or Liverpool and letters of credit or bills of lading in New York in trust and for the use of said company and subject to the orders of the president thereof . . . are hereby specifically applied towards the payment of Doolittle and Streator upon their contract and in trust and to be used in the construction and furnishing of said railroad, and for no other purposes whatever. This power being only and intended to enable the company more effectually to comply with the provisions of the said contract."

7. Distance 92 miles at	$38,000	$3,496,000
5 Miles sidings at 28,000		140,000
Contract cost		$3,636,000

Stock	$317,600	
Cash	794,000	County bonds & subscription
Cash	2,064,400	Proceeds of mortgage bonds.
	$3,176,000	

The amount of mortgage bonds required to yield the above would be $2,752,333.

Making cost of contract to company exclusive of interest of $4,423,800

8. The contractors to receive 1st mortgage bonds at 75 cents, $400,000. They were to negotiate at their own cost the balance of interest mortgage $600,000 and receive the proceeds and the residue in stock shares at par, McHenry agreeing to make the negotiation of the bonds for money and iron for the same bonus from the contractors as paid by them on the Penna. contract.

Length of road 33 miles at	$33,000 per mile	$1,089,000
Three miles sidings at	28,000 per mile	84,000
		$1,173,000

| Bonds $1,000,000 | Stock | $333,000 |

9. The lack of public confidence in the efforts of the railroad's promoters was growing. One local newspaper believed the A&GW was another failure (*Venango Spectator*, Aug. 10, 1859). *Eds.*

Chapter 3

1. Messrs Allen, Hall, Shaw and Baker were of the party.

2. Brother of Marvin Kent, president of A&GW of Ohio. *Eds.*

3. Marvin's Mills, Pennsylvania, was just outside Cambridge Springs. *Eds.*

4. The Waldron Chair was a sleeve of boiler iron to take the place of fish joint. It was used for ten miles but, according to Reynolds, it proved worthless. *Eds.*

5. The money [was] appropriated, New York Co. $9,400, T. W. Kennard Ex. $1558.18 Pa. $13,200.

6. Secretary of the Erie & New York City RR. *Eds.*

7. A grampers car was a hand-pumped railcar. One assumes that the president of the company was not supplying the power. *Eds.*

8. S. L. M. Barlow was counsel to the A&GW RR and later the Erie RR, eventually involved in legal action against Jay Gould for wrongdoings as president of the Erie RR. *Eds.*

9. Steamburg, New York, is just west of Salamanca. *Eds.*

10. Stock subscription at time of organization	$45,000
Since increased to	$450,000
Paid by work of E&NY City Co.	$204,500
To be paid as work progressed by contract	$245,500

1st Mortgage $1,250,000, of which included in the mutual guaranty of $1,000,000.

First 32 miles nearly ready for the iron,

Track laid to near Randolph.

Right of way east of Jamestown and the greater part west of Jamestown.

11. Poland Center, New York, is just east of Jamestown. *Eds.*

12. Deposit, New York, is just north of the Pennsylvania border on the Erie Railroad. *Eds.*

13. Niblo's Garden was a well-known New York City nightclub. *Eds.*

14. President of the Pennsylvania Railroad. *Eds.*

15. Instructions from A&GW to McHenry with Power of Attorney dated March 26, 1859. *Eds.*

Chapter 4

1. Bemustown Dam of French Creek, two miles north of Meadville. *Eds.*

2. Unfortunately, Reynolds does not identify the "influential director." *Eds.*

3. Klecknerville is a village about eight miles north of Meadville. *Eds.*

4. Reynolds here refers to the Philadelphia & Erie Railroad (P&E RR) which was the successor to the Sunbury & Erie RR (S&E RR). We will continue to use the label S&E RR to avoid confusion with the Pittsburgh & Erie RR (P&E RR) which still retains an important place in the narrative. *Eds.*

5. In his letters, Reynolds shows little apparent interest in the oil trade until the Pennsylvania RR later moves into the oil region. Neither does Kennard display any early enthusiasm, although he does admit in his report of March 1861 that the discovery of oil must not be overlooked. He thinks the oil traffic may someday be profitable, but he believes that this should be "extra." He prefers to base the profitability of the railroad on what is "above" ground, not below. *Eds.*

6. This letter, important for its contents relative to the old traffic, is from Reynolds's manuscript, but cannot be verified by the original September 4th letter to McHenry because of damage to the letter. *Eds.*

7. Here Reynolds is referring to the Oil Creek RR, organized in September 1860. Investors and officers of the line were local men like Streator, who was said to be the real owner of the enterprise. Eventually adopting the six-foot gauge, the line connected directly with the A&GW at Corry, giving it an immediate route to the seaboard via Salamanca and the Erie RR. *Eds.*

8. Chancery is a high court of equity in England with common-law functions and jurisprudence. *Eds.*

9. A large carriage similar to a stagecoach. *Eds.*

10. James Mason and John Slidell were Confederate diplomats taken off the British steamer *Trent* by Americans and arrested. The incident created a crisis between the two countries. *Eds.*

11. Peto subscribed another £50,000 but withheld payment until he received a satisfactory report from his confidential agent J. H. R. Rose, who joined Kennard on the line in America. *Eds.*

Chapter 5

1. Information concerning oil passing through Meadville is confirmed by numerous newspaper accounts. For example, *Crawford Journal*, Jan. 7, 21, 1862. *Eds.*

2. Disbursements per Merrill estimate May $69,500, June $281,000, July $284,500, Aug. $184,150.

3. Glenroie McQueen, a resident of Crawford County, whose family furnished lumber to the A&GW for its construction records in his "My First Forty" his memories of the "500 wild Irishmen" and a "whole colony of raw Swedes" who built the line. McQueen's unpublished memoir is in the McQueen Papers, manuscript collection, Crawford County Historical Society. *Eds.*

4. French Creek Feeder Canal. *Eds.*

5. LeBeouf, Pennsylvania, is just south of Waterford along the S&E RR. *Eds.*

6. Auditor's statement of cost of New York division stock accounts and right of way payments.

Length of line	47.87 Miles
Amount of land	515.47 acres
Paid for real estate	$38,260.53
Capital stock actually paid in	$667,872
Kennard's statement of drafts on McHenry in June	£23,000

Kennard's estimate of cost to complete to Akron made June 1861, and the means subscribed to complete the same, viz:

Work	£155,000
Rolling stock	130,400
Rails	66,000
	£351,400
Subscriptions	
Duke of Rianzares	£100,000
Kennards	75,000
Barnards	75,000
Peto	50,000
Ebbw Vale & Bailey Bros.	66,000
	£366,000
Balance on sale	30,000
	£396,000

7. On November 1 the Board authorized the execution of a mortgage on the above extension of $528,000 payable December 1, 1882 at office of Duncan, Sherman & Co., said bonds not to be issued at more than the rate of $16,000 per mile.

8. McHenry comments that he is being pressured by "numerous American railway" representatives who are seeking his services but he says "I will have none of them." (McHenry to Reynolds, December 20, 1862) *Eds.*

Chapter 6

1. The creation of a Central Board did not end the problems between the Americans and their English colleagues. Serious conflicts over finances and construction still persisted. *Eds.*

2. The weight of rail is measured in pounds per yard. *Eds.*

3. Native Americans of the Seneca Nation through whose lands this railroad line still runs. *Eds.*

4. A strong indication that McHenry and Kennard are trying to "pack" the Board of Directors with their European friends. *Eds.*

5. This is extremely light rail, the norm being closer to 50. *Eds.*

6. By this time, Kennard was exercising powers that only the president of the company possessed. When the celebration of the opening of the road to Cleveland was being planned, Reynolds was shocked to receive an invitation to the affair as a guest of the railroad of which he was president! On the invitation itself the official positions of both Reynolds and Marvin Kent were omitted. *Eds.*

7. Earlier an editor wrote that the Oil Creek RR was one of the "marvels of the Age." Built in space of three months, according to the editor, it transported an amount of freight probably unmatched by any line in the country of equal length" (28 miles from Corry to Titusville). Erie *Gazette*, July 30, 1863. *Eds.*

8. This account of the celebration was published in *The Cleveland Daily Herald*, Nov. 19, 1863. *Eds.*

Chapter 7

1. Ohio Coal and Mining Company, organized Feb. 29, 1864. Counties rich with coal lay mostly on or near the line of the New Lisbon Railway. Coal and limestone could be shipped to Cleveland by way of the New Lisbon RR and the Cleveland & Mahoning RR and east-west by the Pittsburg, Fort Wayne & Chicago RR and the Atlantic & Great Western RR. *First Annual Report of the Ohio Coal and Mining Company*, Cleveland, OH: Fairbanks, Benedict & Co. 1865. *Eds.*

2. In his manuscript, Reynolds does not make specific reference to Kennard, suggesting that perhaps, later in life, he felt less hostility toward his former colleague. His manuscript makes reference to "those whom I know to be unfitted." *Eds.*

3. The first page of this letter is missing. It is filed between letters written April 4 and April 11. *Eds.*

4. Once again Reynolds does not criticize Kennard by name as he does in the original letter. *Eds.*

5. Reynolds may have meant company rather than country. *Eds.*

6. Marvin Kent resigned as president of the A&GW of Ohio at the same time. *Eds.*

7. Reynolds's final service to the A&GW came in December 1864 when he sold his own stock for $82,000, a sizable amount for that day. He retained stock in a number of other companies which he served as trustee, director, or president. By his own admission, he was president of ten companies. *Eds.*

❦ Bibliography

This bibliography lists in brief form some of the principal sources that are cited or were used in the preparation of this book. The Reynolds Collection is the primary documentary source. It is housed in two repositories: the Special Collections area of the Pelletier Library at Allegheny College and the Crawford County Historical Society (CCHS), both at Meadville, Pennsylvania. Letters and papers that deal mainly with members of the Reynolds family are located in the society's archives; letters and papers that pertain to the Atlantic & Great Western are at the college.

There is a paucity of published or unpublished works on the A&GW. Paul Felton's 1943 dissertation still remains the best general history of this railroad. As mentioned in the Editors' Preface, this work was used by Edward Hungerford's *Men of Erie, a Story of Human Effort*. Edward Mott's *Between the Ocean and the Lakes: The Story of Erie*, considered by many to be the earliest definitive history of the Erie Railroad, includes a brief history of the A&GW in the section on the NYPANO RR. During his research, Mott corresponded with Reynolds. A good account of the A&GW's struggle for the oil market is Rolland Harper Maybee's *Railroad Competition and the Oil Trade, 1855–1873*. Unfortunately, Maybee did not avail himself of the Reynolds Collection.

Manuscripts

Dick, John, and David Dick. Papers. CCHS.

Doolittle, Henry. Papers. Western Reserve Historical Society (WRHS), Cleveland.

Kent, Marvin. Papers. WRHS.

Reynolds Family. Papers. CCHS.

Reynolds, William. Collection. Allegheny College, Meadville, Penn. This collection consists of many thousands of unorganized items. It includes correspondence, journals, reports of the A&GW, photographs, maps, and newspaper clippings. The following manuscript materials are some of the elements of this collection and were used in the preparation of the memoir.

1. A&GW of PA. Extracts of minutes, Mar. 19, 1858. Reference to English contracts.
2. Doolittle, Henry. Contracts with the Franklin & Warren RR, 1853, the Meadville Railway Co., 1858, and with James McHenry, 1858.
3. McHenry, James. Power of attorney granted to, for the New York A&GW.
4. Reynolds, William. Original and typescript of his memoir; daily journals, 1860–61.
5. Reynolds, William, James McHenry, and the A&GW. Correspondence, 1852–1865. Consists of twelve-bound volumes, which are not numbered and generally not paginated. Most of the letters are arranged chronologically in each volume.

Reports

Annual Report of the President of the Atlantic and Great Western Railroad Company. Ohio Division, Marvin Kent, President. London, 1863.

First Annual Report of the Central Board of Management of the Atlantic and Great Western Railway Companies. Buffalo, 1864.

Kennard, Thomas. *First and Second Reports to the European Bondholders of the Atlantic and Great Western Railways of New York, Pennsylvania, and Ohio.* London, 1860.

———. *Report from T. W. Kennard.* London, 1861.

———. *Report of Kennard to the Directors in London of the Atlantic and Great Western Railway Company.* London, 1865.

Report in Regard to the Western Extension of the New York and Erie Railroad. New York, 1856.

Second Annual Report of the Atlantic and Great Western Railway Companies to the Stockholders and Bondholders for the Year Ending December 31, 1864. New York, 1865.

Newspapers

Cleveland: *Daily Herald*
Erie: *Gazette*
Observer
Franklin: *Venango Spectator*
Greenville: *West Greenville Times*
Meadville: *Crawford Democrat*
Crawford Journal
Crawford Whig Journal
Morning Star
New York: *New York Tribune*

Books, Articles, and Unpublished Works

Barnes, L. Diane. "Urban Rivalry in the Upper Ohio Valley: Wheeling and Pittsburgh in the Nineteenth Century." *Pa Maz Hist &Bio* 123 (July 1999): 201–26.

Burgess, George H., and Miles C. Kennedy. *Centennial History of the Pennsylvania Railroad Company.* Philadelphia: PRR, 1949.

Cleveland, Frederick A., and Fred W. Powell. *Railroad Promotion and Capitalization in the United States.* New York: Longmans, Green & Co., 1909.

Comstock, Henry B. *The Iron Horse.* New York: Thomas Y. Crowell, 1971.

Dilts, James D. *The Great Road; The Building of the Baltimore and Ohio, the Nation's First Railroad, 1828–1853.* Stanford, Calif.: Stanford University Press, 1993.

Felton, Paul Ellsworth. "A History of the Atlantic and Great Western Railroad," Ph.D. diss., University of Pittsburgh, 1943.

Giddens, Paul H. *The Birth of the Oil Industry.* New York: Macmillan, 1938.

———. *Early Days of Oil.* Princeton, N.J.: Princeton University Press, 1948.

Gilmore, Harlan W. *Transportation and the Growth of Cities.* Glencoe, Ill.: The Free Press, 1953.

Goodrich, Carter. *Government Promotion of American Canals and Railroads, 1800–1890.* New York: Columbia University Press, 1960.

Gordon, Sarah H. *Passage to Union: How the Railroads Transformed American Life, 1829–1929.* Chicago: Ivan R. Dee, 1996.

Hallett, Samuel. *My Commissions.* New York: N.p., 1860.

Hicks, Frederick C. *High Finance in the Sixties.* 1929. Reprint, Port Washington, N.Y.: Kennikat Press, 1966.

Hungerford, Edward. *Men of Erie, a Story of Human Effort.* New York: Random House, 1946.

Kent, Donald. "Erie War of the Gauges." *Pennsylvania History* 15 (Oct 1948): 253–75.

Kent, Marvin. *History of the Atlantic and Great Western Railroad.* N.p., 1899.

Klein, Maury. *Unfinished Business: The Railroad in American Life.* Hanover, N.H.: University Press of New England, 1944.

Lance, William. *Views on American Railways with Especial Reference to the Atlantic and Great Western Railway.* N.p., 1860.

Majewski, John. *A House Divided: Economic Development in Pennsylvania and Virginia before the Civil War.* New York: Cambridge University Press, 2000.

Martin, Albro. *Railroads Triumphant: The Growth, Rejection, and Rebirth of a Vital American Force.* New York: Oxford University Press, 1992.

Maybee, Rolland Harper. *Railroad Competition and the Oil Trade, 1855–1873.* Mount Pleasant, Mich.: Extension Press, 1940.

McQueen, Glenroie. "My First Forty." Unpublished essay, McQueen Collection. CCHS.

Mott, Edward H. *Between the Ocean and the Lakes: The Story of Erie.* New York: John C. Colling, 1900.

Mould, David H. *Dividing Lines: Canals, Railroads and Urban Rivalry in Ohio's Hocking Valley, 1825–1875.* Dayton, Ohio: Wright State University Press, 1994.

Peto, Sir Samuel Morton. *Resources and Prospects of America, Ascertained during a Visit to the States in the Autumn of 1865.* London: N.p., 1866.

Reiser, Catherine E. *Pittsburgh's Commercial Development.* Harrisburg: PHMC, 1951.

Reynolds, John. "One Hundred Years Ago." Unpublished essay, 1869, Reynolds Family Papers, CCHS.

Reynolds, John Earle. *In French Creek Valley.* Meadville, Penn.: CCHS, 1938.

Reynolds, William. *The Diary of William Reynolds, 1841.* Edited by Robert D. Ilisevich. Meadville, Penn.: CCHS, 1981.

Richardson, James D., ed. *A Compilation of the Messages and Papers of the Presidents.* 20 vols. New York: Bureau of National Literature, 1899–1917.

Ripley, William Z. *Railroads, Finance and Organization.* New York: Longmans, Green & Co., 1923.

Rosenberger, Homer T. *The Philadelphia and Erie Railroad.* Potomac, Md: Fox Hills Press, 1975.

Shaw, Ronald E. *Canals for a Nation: The Canal Era in the United States, 1790–1860.* Lexington: University of Kentucky Press, 1990.

Stevens, Sylvester K. *Pennsylvania: Birthplace of a Nation.* New York: Random House, 1964.

Stover, John F. *American Railroads.* Chicago: University of Chicago Press, 1961.

——. *History of the Baltimore & Ohio Railroad.* West Lafayette, Ind.: Purdue University Press, 1987.

Taylor, George Rogers, and Irene D. Neu. *The American Railroad Network, 1861–1890.* New York: Arno Press, 1981.

Vance, James E., Jr. *The North American Railroad.* Baltimore, Md.: John Hopkins University Press, 1995.

Ward, James A. *Railroads and the Character of America, 1820–1887.* Knoxville, Tenn.: University of Tennessee Press, 1986.

Wilkins, Mira. *The History of Foreign Investment in the United States to 1914.* Cambridge: Harvard University Press, 1989.

❧ Index

Note: Page numbers in italics indicate an illustration.

Series on Ohio History and Culture

John H. White and Robert J. White, Sr.,
The Island Queen: Cincinnati's Excursion Steamer

H. Roger Grant,
Ohio's Railway Age in Postcards

Frances McGovern,
Written on the Hills: The Making of the Akron Landscape

Keith McClellan,
The Sunday Game: At the Dawn of Professional Football

Steve Love and David Giffels,
Wheels of Fortune: The Story of Rubber in Akron

Alfred Winslow Jones,
*Life, Liberty, and Property: A Story of Conflict and a
Measurement of Conflicting Rights*

David Brendan Hopes,
A Childhood in the Milky Way: Becoming a Poet in Ohio

John Keim,
*Legends by the Lake: The Cleveland Browns at
Municipal Stadium*

Richard B. Schwartz,
The Biggest City in America: A Fifties Boyhood in Ohio

Tom Rumer,
Unearthing the Land: The Story of Ohio's Scioto Marsh

Ian Adams, Barney Taxel, and Steve Love,
Stan Hywet Hall and Gardens

William F. Romain,
*Mysteries of the Hopewell: Astronomers, Geometers,
and Magicians of the Eastern Woodlands*

Dale Topping, edited by Eric Brothers,
*When Giants Roamed the Sky: Karl Arnstein and the Rise of Airships
from Zeppelin to Goodyear*

Millard F. Rogers Jr.,
Rich in Good Works: Mary M. Emery of Cincinnati

Frances McGovern,
Fun, Cheap, and Easy: My Life in Ohio Politics, 1949–1964

Larry L. Nelson, editor,
A History of Jonathan Alder: His Captivity and Life with the Indians

Ian Adams and Steve Love,
Holden Arboretum

Bruce Meyer,
*The Once and Future Union: The Rise and Fall of the
United Rubber Workers, 1935–1995*

William Reynolds, edited by Peter K. Gifford and Robert D. Ilisevich,
*European Capital, British Iron, and an American Dream:
The Story of the Atlantic & Great Western Railroad*

About the Editors

Peter K. Gifford graduated from Muhlenberg College, in Allentown, PA, in 1977 with a BS in Mathematics and Computer Science. He has spent the last 25 years at Allegheny College in Administrative Computing Services, currently Systems Manager. For the last 6 years he has taught in Creating Landscapes summer arts enrichment program.

Robert D. Ilisevich is a retired professor of American history, having taught at Alliance College in Cambridge Springs, PA, for thirty-four years. He attended the University of Pittsburgh and Case Western Reserve University. His publications include several books and numerous articles and book reviews.

About the Book

European Capital, British Iron, and an American Dream: The Story of the Atlantic & Great Western Railroad was designed and typeset by Kachergis Book Design of Pittsboro, North Carolina. The display type is Birch and the text type is Monotype Bulmer. Bulmer was originally designed by William Martin in 1790 and redesigned in 1994 by Ron Carpenter.

European Capital, British Iron, and an American Dream: The Story of the Atlantic & Great Western Railroad was printed on 60-pound Sebago Eggshell paper and bound by The Maple-Vail Book Manufacturing Group of York, Pennsylvania.